Breakthrough Dreaming

Breakthrough Dreaming

How to Tap the Power of Your 24-Hour Mind

DR. GAYLE DELANEY

BANTAM BOOKS

NEW YORK

TORONTO

LONDON

SYDNEY

AUCKLAND

BREAKTHROUGH DREAMING
A BANTAM BOOK / MAY 1991

Library of Congress Cataloging-in-Publication Data

Delaney, Gayle M. V.
Breakthrough dreaming : how to tap the power of
your 24-hour mind / Gayle Delaney.
p.   cm.
Includes bibliographical references and index.
ISBN 0-553-35281-4
1. Dreams.   2. Problem solving.   I. Title.
BF1091.D378   1991
154.6'34—dc20   90-20587
CIP

Published simultaneously in the United States and Canada

Bantam Books are published by Bantam Books, a division of Bantam
Doubleday Dell Publishing Group, Inc. Its trademark, consisting of the
words "Bantam Books" and the portrayal of a rooster, is Registered in
U.S. Patent and Trademark Office and in other countries. Marca Regis-
trada. Bantam Books, 666 Fifth Avenue, New York, New York 10103.

PRINTED IN THE UNITED STATES OF AMERICA

OPM   0 9 8 7 6 5 4 3

DEDICATION

To Loma Kaye Flowers whose love, wisdom, humor, and honesty make her the best dream partner, colleague, and friend one could ever hope to have.

ACKNOWLEDGMENTS

First I must thank my clients who, over the last fifteen years, have offered their dreams and all the attention we have lavished upon them for use in this book so that you, our reader, might more readily learn how to tap the resources of your own dreaming mind. Many of my clients have enthusiastically responded to my phone calls asking about specific dreams and their long-term effects, sometimes many years after our working sessions. Some had to rummage through old dream journals, others through dusty tape recordings of the relevant consultation or group sessions. Some were good enough to transcribe their sessions and add current commentaries on their dream work. As you will soon see, a book such as this could not be written without the unusual luxury of access to the detailed dream and dream work accounts of hundreds of highly motivated and generous dream clients.

My thanks to Dr. Loma Flowers, psychiatrist extraordinaire and director of the Delaney & Flowers Center for the Study of Dreams with whom I have worked closely for over a decade, for her exhortations to make more explicit and structured the instructions on the dream interview method which we teach at the Center and which forms the core of this book. The love and support of my husband, Dr. Steve Walsh, my psychiatrist in residence, has given me the freedom and joy to write for months on end. The friendship and encouragement of our dear friend and colleague, Dr. Erik Craig, Director of the Center for Existential Studies in Worcester, Mass. and the president of the Association for the Study of Dreams, has made the experience of being a dream psychologist great fun.

Thanks to Dr. Milton Kramer, Director of the Sleep Disorders Center at Bethesda Oak Hospital in Cincinnati, for his work in sleep and dreams and for his thoughtful reading and critique of several chapters. I also appreciate the careful consideration Dr. J. Allan Hobson, Director of the Laboratory of Neurophysiology at the Massachusetts Mental Health Center in Boston, gave to the manuscript and thank him for his readiness to engage in fruitful argument. My gratitude to Gardner Stout, professor of English at the University of California at Berkeley, for being my first reader, to Gene and Linda Mihaly for the gift of time and calm, to Coreen Hawkins and Ray Mattoon for their careful and helpful critiques on the first draft, and to Karen Rice for her cheerful and kind assistance on my deadline date.

Annette Boyer and Beryl Shaw patiently and doggedly contended with the raw manuscript and my temperamental computer. Their good cheer was a great boon. Virginia and Bill Delaney have just kept on being enthusiastic parents, and their gift of a portable computer allowed me to spend a month working on the final manuscript revision and ice skating in Sun Valley, Idaho this summer, where I was the pampered houseguest of Virginia Allison, artist, Sand Tray therapist, and fellow dream worker.

San Francisco, September, 1990

CONTENTS

FOREWORD

OF SYMBOLS, METAPHORS, DREAMING,
AND THE BRAIN: A SCIENTIFIC VIEW
by J. Allan Hobson, M.D.

Professor of Psychiatry, Harvard Medical School
Director, Laboratory of Neurophysiology
Massachusetts Mental Health Center

Several surprising discoveries made by sleep neurophysiologists clearly echo the dream psychology articulated by Gayle Delaney in *Breakthrough Dreaming*.

The first surprise is that the brain never stops working. Even in the deepest stages of sleep—when our conscious minds may slow down, or even appear to stop functioning altogether—brain activity is only slightly decreased compared to the most alert waking. And when we enter the rapid eye movement (REM) stage of sleep—and we dream—brain activity is as high as when we are startled during waking. Thus Gayle Delaney is correct in assuming that the mind is continuously active and that some sort of information processing may well be going on in our brains twenty-four hours a day. This leads to a new view of the unconscious that is quite different from Freud's and a new view of dream symbols and metaphors that is correspondingly distinct and novel. Instead of assuming that unconscious ideas are actively *concealed* by dream symbols as did Freud, Delaney asserts that the dream is trying, in its own special language, to *reveal* them. The special language of the dream, according to Delaney, is metaphor.

Bearing upon Delaney's metaphor hypothesis, a second surprise is that the organization of brain activity changes dramatically in sleep and in dreaming. While waking and dreaming are both equally active states, they are quite different, if not distinct, *modes* of information processing. In particular, the mode of processing during dreaming appears to be much less constrained by the external rules of space and time than is the case in waking; thoughts are less ordered by linear logic; hence, in dreaming, the mind is operating more analogically. Delaney may therefore be justified in assuming that dreaming is a more metaphorical mode of information processing than is waking.

Of course, Gayle Delaney is not the first to emphasize this aspect of dreaming. Many eighteenth- and nineteenth-century European psychologists such as David Hartley and Wilhelm Wundt were struck by the enhanced capacity of the dreaming brain to combine, condense, and otherwise integrate the disparate data of dream content. And the symbol-rich quality of dreaming has attracted the attention of prophets and seers from Joseph of the Bible to Sigmund Freud of Vienna. The problem with these interpretive traditions is that they have never been put to any scientific test. Thus dream interpretation has stood apart from the mainstream of science and consequently its credibility has suffered. This is particularly true of psychoanalysis, whose modern adherents advocate an approach to dream interpretation called hermeneutics, which is decidedly unscientific—and even openly antiscientific. So one question is, can Delaney's approach help to overcome this problem?

My answer is a qualified yes, as Delaney proposes nothing about dreaming that is not compatible with the neurophysiology of sleep. Her theory is to be preferred to all those—

including classical psychoanalysis—that are visibly out of step with modern science. Better yet, some scientific tests of Delaney's ideas are imaginable. For example, it is now conceivable that artificial intelligence models of dreaming could be developed to generate artificial dreams from a biographical data base. These artificial dreams could be compared with artificial wake-state narratives for their metaphorical content.

But such an approach would only confirm the weak form of Delaney's hypothesis, namely that dreams are metaphorical in nature. The stronger form of the hypothesis, that they are uniquely so—and hence uniquely valuable tools of self-understanding—may be much more difficult to establish. Indeed, since both Delaney and we scientists share the assumption that waking and dreaming are not *qualitatively* different states of brain and mind, it is logical for us to conclude that the same *kind* of revelations could be achieved in either state. But here, I suppose, Delaney and her followers might be satisfied even if dreaming were only a quicker way to obtain the data. As a scientist, I can't resist pointing out that a comparison of dreams with her patients' waking fantasies might help to answer this question right away.

On what scientific evidence does my encouraging view of Delaney's approach to dreaming rest?

We know that dreams in general—and especially those exotic and elaborate dream scenarios that cry out most loudly for interpretation—are associated with a distinctive brain physiology. The electrical activation—or energy level—of the system is very high; this could support the very rapid and extensive information processing that might be involved in memory search for the most appropriate image, metaphor, or symbol to interpret the disparate (and/or emotionally conflicted) elements that the mind is trying to combine in a coherent dream plot.

Another neurophysiological fact favoring Delaney's approach is that this high-speed system is "off line" (as is a computer that is working on data in its memory but not accepting any new inputs). Both sensory input and motor output are actively blocked by specific brain mechanisms. Thus there is no need—(and indeed there is no possibility)—for the system to be "realistic" in the way that it must be to function effectively in waking. Even in our most exotic waking fantasies (and even in the freest associative modes achievable on the analyst's couch), the mind is constrained by moment-to-moment input-output realities. Not so in dreaming: In dreams the system is operating on its own. Thus the dreaming mind is not only "off line," but "out of this world."

A high-speed information processing system operating off line need not produce metaphors, however. It might simply count, perform mathematical calculations, or read out memories in a time-ordered way. But it does none of these things. Instead, it reads out scenarios that are usually dramatic, often ludicrous, and sometimes quite poetic. With respect to this creative aspect of dreaming, another possibly significant neurophysiological fact is that the brain produces its own pseudosensory stimuli during REM sleep. In other words, the brain sends itself intrinsically chaotic and cryptic messages. And this internally generated information is strongly visual in nature, so that the dreaming brain is prompted to see, or to "scenarize" in the filmic sense. We have no idea how these internal pseudosensory stimuli are synthesized into the surrealistic visual imagery of our dreams, but it does seem reasonable to assume that there is an active, instantaneous, and ongoing collaboration between the brain's highly activated and self-stimulated visual centers and the language area that identifies the imagery, names, and organizes it—as best it can—into a narrative. Indeed, it is the immense strain of this synthetic task that may make both symbol generation and metaphor elaboration inevitable during dreaming.

For me, symbols and metaphors are both the linguistic vehicles of multiple meanings and the carriers of data from multiple sources: perceptual, cognitive, and emotional. To appreciate this idea, consider the task of creating a high-order experience (the dream) from low-order electrical stimuli (eye movement directional signals). The only way it could be done would be to make huge inferential leaps. Such leaps are likely to reveal our psychological biases, our fears, and our hopes, which might, in the interest of efficiency, be best represented in a symbolic or metaphorical way. Supporting this speculative hypothesis is the fact that patients whose visual and language centers are disconnected by strokes stop dreaming (although they don't stop seeing and talking).

My own dream theory, called the activation-synthesis hypothesis, has come under attack because of my emphasis on this random nature of the internally generated dream stimuli arising in the lower centers of the brain. But it is precisely this chaotic quality that is needed to drive the networks of the upper brain in such a way as to produce the elaborate and creative dream syntheses that Delaney calls metaphors. These mental products are often bizarre, and I myself consider their interpretation as risky as any other organically determined cognitive anomaly. That the mind is straining to achieve cognitive integration of the internally generated data seems all but certain. Thus an open-ended approach such as Delaney's discussion of this material with her clients seems scientifically responsible even if its interpretive conclusions may not be scientifically demonstrable.

If we dream two hours per night, why is it so hard for us to remember even five minutes of dreaming? Freud said we needed not only to disguise our dream thoughts but to repress our dreams; dream forgetting, for a Freudian, is thus every bit as defensive as is symbol formation. But for the modern sleep scientist the answer is quite different: dream amnesia is organically determined. In REM sleep the brain cells that secrete the chemicals needed for memory to endure are shut off!

For dream psychologists such as Delaney, this change in

brain chemistry may also be related to such important cognitive features of dreaming as: 1) the loss of self-reflective awareness; 2) the loss of critical judgment; and 3) the loss of linear logic. The cognitive gains corresponding to these losses are: 1) total self-involvement in the dream; 2) acceptance of even the wildest dream events as real; and 3) the increase in analogical thinking, including metaphor and symbol production. Thus it seems scientifically justifiable to regard the dreaming brain as bio-chemically biased toward a metaphorical mode of information processing.

Having sketched a neurobiological picture of REM sleep that is compatible with the idea that the dreaming brain may well be a metaphor machine, it is important for the scientist to demand a price from the psychologist who wishes to take comfort from this formulation.

For starters, we need more rigorous definitions of such terms as metaphor and symbol, and we need quantitative measurements of them if the psychological hypotheses used by Delaney are ever to be accorded scientific status. That the problem is a serious and important one can be easily demonstrated by the following thought experiment. According to the *Oxford English Dictionary,* a symbol is "something that stands for or denotes something else, not by exact resemblance, but by vague suggestion," while a metaphor is "the transfer of a name or descriptive term to some object to which it is not properly applicable." Freudian symbols are thus easily identified according to his principles: "all weapons or tools are used as symbols for the male organ" and "landscapes in dreams, especially any containing bridges or wooded hills, may be recognized as descriptions of the genitals."

But now let us consider the more subtle but common dream feature of mistaken personal identity (my sister Harriet vaguely resembles my friend Maud). Freud would have called this a condensation and assumed disguise, say, of an incestuous wish. Is Maud a metaphor (or a symbol) for Harriet (or vice versa)? Or is the mistaken personal identity simply a symptom of the neurocognitive state of the dreaming brain? The latter view implies that the condensation of two characters' features into one is neither symbolic nor metaphorical, but simply representational. Thus dreaming may only intensify a mental function that is present all the time, namely the associative and representational nature of information processing.

Perhaps it is enough to assume that the two (or more) memory elements that contribute to a dream symbol, or the more elaborate dream constructions that Delaney calls metaphors (such as a broken plant that is for Delaney the symbol of a failed marriage), are derived from the activation of formally adjacent or formally congruent representations of waking reality in the neuronal nets of the brain. Thus the activation of brain cell net A (containing representation a) would prime the activation of net B (containing representation b). As in plane geometry, nets A and B (and representations a and b) are formally congruent. Maud and Harriet are formally congruent in at least one way—they are both females. They may share other properties (e.g., they are both sisters) that gives their congruence greater psychological significance and salience. But whether it is helpful or accurate to call such dream elements symbols or metaphors is debatable.

Most of us who work on the cognitive neuroscience of dreaming assume that the increase in associative processing is to be expected in REM sleep, when the brain is autoactivated and autostimulated, and processing the data in the absence of certain chemical constraints. Again, and finally, the problem is to know what dream product is signal and what noise. This uncertainty limits the assumption of Freud—partially shared by Delaney—that all dream content is hypermeaningful and interpretable.

Hopefully, Delaney's interview method will be a goad to scientifically inclined psychologists who would like to put these bold clinical assertions to the test. The objective definition and measurement of symbols and metaphors would indeed be a breakthrough in the study of dreaming.

THE 24-HOUR MIND

Dreams tell us the way we really think and feel, not the way we pretend we think and feel. We can blind ourselves and fool ourselves while we are awake, *but not while we sleep*. Through our dreams we have access to vast stores of memory, amazing depths of insight, and common sense as well as to resources of creative thinking, which offer us a richer and more productive life.

To some, dreams seem to be merely bizarre and senseless illusions. Yet almost everyone has, at least once, had the rewarding experience of sleeping on a problem and awakening in the morning with the problem solved. You can develop this natural problem-solving function of the sleeping mind and make use of it every night by learning to recall your dreams and by learning to direct your dreaming mind to work on specific problems you pose to yourself just before sleep. Many of my clients have used their dreams to solve problems and generate new ideas related to their careers in law, business, mathematics, architecture, writing, and the arts. *Living Your Dreams,* my first book on the use of dreams for practical problem solving, has been required reading at the Stanford School of Business and has brought a number of creative businesspeople into my practice where we work with dreams that deal with program designs, management innovations, interpersonal conflicts at work, and product development.

Many of us do not remember enough dreams to take advantage of the more literal, straightforward dreams that help us organize a lecture we are soon to give or a project we are working on. Most of us remember only our more metaphorical dreams that don't seem to make sense or relate to our daily life because we simply do not understand the picture language we think in at night. However, once we learn the language of metaphor, the practical function of even our bizarre dreams becomes evident. Because we are less defensive and more honest in our dreams, we can see our daily life situations more clearly, more objectively, and above all more creatively. Every night we take a sort of CAT scan of our psyches and examine the dynamics of the problems and challenges we face while awake. We speak to ourselves honestly and sometimes urgently while dreaming, and it is only our lack of education in this metaphorical language that keeps us from being able to make full use of the insights and creative ideas dreams present us every single night. Our brains work around the clock, and dreams offer us our most direct access to the night side of our twenty-four-hour minds.

If we fail to learn the language of our dreams, we cut ourselves off from a good part of our mind's potential and sometimes walk into unfortunate situations that we might have avoided. A new client who dreamt that Marilyn Monroe was picking his pockets while she was kissing him thought his dream was sheer nonsense. That is, until he described Marilyn in terms that reminded him of his sexy, but demanding fiancée. Then he began to recall a number of half-forgotten incidents that, when faced directly, made him seriously question the quality of her love for him. Later dreams continued to emphasize this theme and helped the dreamer to explore the issue directly with his fiancée. He believed his dreams had succeeded, where his family and friends had failed, in making him see that he was about to make a big mistake.

Most of us grew up believing that dreams were unimportant, if not irrelevant, to our lives and that people who were interested in dreams were, well, perhaps a little strange. Much of the public image of dreaming today is still shaped by fears and superstitions rather than by informed study of the modern developments in the field. It is time to take dreams out of the clutches of the superstitious and the superficial.

It is also time to retrieve dream interpretation from the confines of psychotherapeutic dogma and teach ourselves how to read our own nightly consultations. Everyone, even those who swear they never dream, dreams at least four or five times a night. This has been proven countless times in sleep laboratories where researchers have monitored sleepers' brain waves. When subjects are awakened after each episode of rapid eye movement (REM) sleep, they are asked if they were dreaming, and the accounts are tape-recorded. In the morning, even people who deny that they have ever dreamt and who do not recall having dreamt in the laboratory are treated to the sound of their own voices telling their dreams!

Because healthy, well-functioning, and highly productive people all dream, we cannot consider dreams simply as tools for the diagnosis and treatment of the mentally ill. Each of us has a built-in consultant on emotional and practical problem solving in the form of our dreaming mind, and we might as well learn to recall and understand our dreams and take advantage of the productive work we accomplish in our sleep. Even without recalling and understanding our dreams, we benefit from them. Students in an intensive language class were studied in a sleep laboratory and it was found that the students who showed more REM, or dream sleep, were those who learned the fastest. The students whose REM sleep remained at normal levels did not do as well in the class.[1] This and other studies suggest that dreaming plays an important role in processing new information even when we recall no dreams. Although our forgotten dreams probably give us new ideas and insights far more frequently than we suspect, bringing our dreams into our conscious awareness will greatly enhance their usefulness.

As countless well-documented cases of artistic, scientific, and personal breakthroughs made in or triggered by dreams attest, many dreams reflect a form of sophisticated thinking, problem assessment, and problem solving. In 1619 René Descartes was a young man struggling with the need to decide what career to pursue. In one night he had three dreams that he described as revealing to him the basis of a new philosophy to which he devoted his life; we now know this school of philosophy as Cartesianism.[2] John Milton, second only to William Shakespeare among British poets, wrote in *Paradise Lost* that his verse was regularly inspired, even dictated to him, in his sleep.[3] The philosopher Gottfried Leibniz held that thought continued in sleep and that it continues out of our awareness while waking as well as while sleeping. By carefully observing his own marginal states of consciousness, he noted the solution of problems in sleep and dreams and wrote, "For not to mention the wonders of dreams in which we invent, without effort but also without will, things which we should have to think a long time to discover when awake."[4]

The British poet and artist William Blake credited the discovery of his method of illuminated engraving to a dream and wrote that he received specific instruction in painting in his dreams. Eight years after Richard Bach had written and shelved the first half of his best seller *Jonathan Livingston Seagull,* he quite unexpectedly had a dream in which he finished the rest of the story. The dream picked up exactly where he had left off so long ago. In film, dreams have played important roles as both subject matter and inspiration for the artists. Federico Fellini's dream journal, *Le Journal des rêves,* includes the report of his 1961 dream of the airport director that not only influenced the airport sequence in *Toby Dammit,* but also illuminated the figure of Guido in *8½.* Later in the film Fellini "traces the artistic process by which a filmmaker converts his memories and immediate sensory experience into dreams and fantasies, which he uses to create his new movie." In fact, Fellini "claims that his films always begin with 'fantasy characters'—faces that have appeared to him in dreams or memories."[5] Ingmar Bergman's *Sawdust and Tinsel* portrays a scene from one of his dreams, and *Cries and Whispers* was inspired by another dream that haunted him for more than a year. Robert Altman's *Three Women* was also based on a dream. And Claude Lelouch has said that "people don't realize that dreams are the most determinant elements in our lives. I dream a film before I make it. Someone had to dream the plane or TV before they were invented."[6]

The field of organic chemistry was launched by Friedrich August Kekulé who discovered in half-sleeps both the process of the formation of carbon chains and the circular structure of the benzene ring. In 1890, Kekulé addressed his fellow chemists who had gathered to honor him at a "Benzolfest" celebration organized by the German Chemical Society with these words: "Perhaps it will interest you if I let you know, through highly indiscreet disclosures from my inner life, how I arrived at some of my ideas." After describing how his ideas came to him while dozing, Kekulé closed his address saying, "Let us learn to dream, gentlemen and perhaps we will then find the truth . . . but let us also beware of publishing our dreams before they have been examined by the waking mind."[7]

Many other scientists have made important breakthroughs and overcome creative blocks by recalling and taking advantage of their dreams. Dmitry Mendeleyev reportedly told a close friend, who was a geologist, that in a dream he saw the periodic tables with which he had been struggling. In the dream "all the elements are placed as they should be. I woke up and immediately wrote it all down on a piece of paper. Eventually there was only one place which needed to be corrected."[8] Walter B. Cannon, a famous physiologist, wrote that some of his best ideas, including his formulation of the body's fight or flight mechanism, came to him when he awakened in the middle of the night.[9] Otto Loewi awoke with a dream that described the design of an experiment he had long sought, which would prove the chemical nature of the transmission of nervous impulses. He wrote down the dream and went back to sleep. But in the morning he could neither remember his dream nor decipher his notes! The next night he dreamt the same dream, and this time he was careful to write out the dream experiment clearly. In 1936 he won the Nobel Prize in medicine and physiology for his successful experiment, which has been called one of the most elegant in the history of science. Elias Howe invented the lockstich sewing machine and beat Isaac Singer to the patent, thanks to his recalling a frightening dream that gave him the right idea about where to place the eye of the needle. And in an unexpected dream, D. B. Parkinson came up with the idea that Bell Laboratories and the Defense Department developed into the first all-electric gun director, the M-9, which was so successfully used against the German buzz bombs in August 1944.

Because our defenses are less rigid while we dream, we are better able to see problems and challenges more objectively, and we are much freer to take risks and try out new approaches and new ideas. As writer/producer Ingmar Bergman has noted, "When you have dreamt, [the dream] can start your intellect. . . . It can give you new thoughts. It can give you a new way of thinking, of feeling. . . . It can give you new light for your inner landscape. And it can give you suddenly a little bit of a new way of handling your life."[10]

In spite of the fact that the arts and sciences have been enriched by pioneers who used their dreams creatively, and in spite of the fact that skilled dream analysts have helped people to understand themselves better through understanding their dreams, charlatans and shallow dabblers have often drowned out well-informed voices of people like Alfred Maury, Karl Scherner, Friedrich Nietzsche, Sigmund Freud, Carl Jung, and the many serious students of the dream who followed them. With their predictive and superstitious pronouncements, the charlatans made dreams the laughingstock of many educated and reasonable people by pandering to the common desire for easy, authoritative answers. At the turn of the twentieth century Freud insisted that the dream stage not be left to these pretenders but that it be occupied by those who would seriously study the phenomena of dreams as expressions of meaningful self-communication.

As the contradictory dream theories of Alfred Adler, Jung, Fritz Perls, Medard Boss, and others multiplied after Freud, the literate classes had a new reason to refuse to become literate in the language of dreams. They argued that if you give five different experts one dream you will get five different interpretations. This was often true when the experts based their interpretations on a generic theory of how the human psyche works and not on a methodical interview of the particular dreamer, who would then be able to provide his or her own interpretation.

This book presents a detailed method of interpretation, called *dream interviewing,* which dispenses with the external, authoritative interpreter and emphasizes the dreamer's unique history and ability to learn the language of dreaming in which each day's emotional and practical concerns are analyzed and reconsidered. While Freud, Jung, and Boss each exhorted the dream interpreter not to give prefabricated interpretations, but to find out from the dreamer what any given dream image meant to him or her, they rarely followed their own advice. They succumbed to their faith in their own authority and wisdom, and they frequently presumed to interpret other people's dreams according to their own beliefs in the proper meaning of dream symbols and images.

In this book I will try to show you the advantages of becoming a dream interviewer rather than an interpreter. You will learn how to conduct a self-interview or to assign the role of interviewer—not interpreter—to a friend, colleague, or therapist. The interviewer asks for definitions and descriptions of the dream images from the point of view of a visitor from another planet who must work with the dreamer's version of life on earth and put aside his or her own personal and theoretical preconceptions. When the dreamer plays the role of self-interviewer, this approach encourages a more careful exploration of the actual dream imagery and discourages formulaic, premature, and often incorrect interpretations.

For example, suppose that two people report dreams of German shepherd dogs. We could hypothesize about the possible meanings of dogs in myths, about things German, about the historical or archetypal traditions regarding shepherds, and so on. However, until we discover *each dreamer's* version of what these dogs are like, we are left to muck about with our own associations that, no matter how erudite, are not necessarily those that went into creating the dreams. Nor are they necessarily helpful or relevant when interpreting the significance of these dogs *for these dreamers*. Suppose that when asked to describe what German shepherds are like on planet earth one dreamer tells us that they are strong, loyal, intelligent, playful, and brave and that a German shepherd had, in fact, once saved her child's life. Now suppose that the other dreamer responds to the same question as one of my clients did: "These dogs are vicious, not to be trusted. They will attack the minute your back is turned. One almost killed me last year."

Clearly, there can be no theoretical formula, archetypal interpretation, or dream dictionary translation for the meaning of dogs in general, or for German shepherds in particular that can do justice to both these dreamers. The dreamer's own descriptions and associations must be elicited and held as the most relevant and important clues to the meaning of the dream if the interpretation is to be accurate, specific, and meaningful to the dreamer.

This method also dispenses with any specific formulation regarding the nature of the unconscious or the natures of the male or female psyches. Such formulations cannot be created with any certainty, and it seems to me that they are unnecessary and limiting. By mining the rich and meaningful metaphorical nature of dream imagery and plot construction, dreams make sense without recourse to a complex metapsychology.

Dream interviewers cross the boundaries of the various theoretical schools of dream analysis because they begin by carefully exploring the actual dream images through the dreamer's focused definitions and descriptions of those images. Pretending to come from another planet helps the interviewer to keep his or her theoretical biases out of the way. The "alien's" questions give the dreamer the chance to recognize in his or her descriptions an illuminating metaphorical reflection of a problem or situation in waking life, before placing the dream images or the dreamer's associations in the context of a psychotheoretical framework.

My own theoretical leanings are a minimalist blend of psychoanalytic, Jungian, and phenomenological perspectives, with an emphasis on practical applications of the revelatory, integrative, and innovative aspects of dream analysis. While dreams sometimes show us repressed feelings, they also help us recognize unrealized potentials and bring to our attention creative solutions to daily problems. Based on my experience of working with thousands of dreamers, I believe that when looked at as metaphors, dreams lead the dreamer to see meaningful connections to waking life that are conducive to greater insight and creativity. Where dreams come from and exactly why we dream are questions I leave to others to discuss. My interest is in seeing how the dream can benefit the dreamer in his or her practical, emotional, and aesthetic life.

I first became interested in dreams while I was a Russian studies major focusing on the economics and politics of the Soviet Union. At that time I had no interest in dreaming, which I thought to be a meaningless jumble of a mind debilitated by the loss of waking conscious thought processes. Economics and politics were my means of focusing on the real world, until I experienced a series of horrible nightmares that seemed to come from nowhere. For a month these bad dreams continued, and I began to wonder if they could carry any meaning. I was chagrined to realize that I knew nothing about how or why my mind worked in sleep. I read a number of good (and some awful) books on the subject, and one day I realized that my nightmares reflected my self-torture in the wake of a broken engagement. With this realization came the recognition that my nightmares hardly came out of the blue, but that they were closely related to my inner life, of which I allowed myself to know very little. My nightmares portrayed another reality, that of feelings, hopes, and fears, which greatly affected my waking "real" life. By understanding my bad dreams I was able to reassess my situation, and I decided that life wasn't so bad. I was twenty, living in Paris, loving school, and there were other fish in the sea. My nightmares ended and my study of dreams commenced.

While I attended graduate school in psychology, I discovered how seldom dreams were used by psychologists and psychiatrists; they had little training in the area and they often were unwilling to adopt what they did know of orthodox Freudian or Jungian belief systems. I was also struck by the lack of dialogue among psychologists in different schools of thought that considered dreams to be of great importance. In 1982 I began to work with a few colleagues and students to form the Association for the Study of Dreams, which would provide a forum in which professionals and nonprofessionals could discuss different perspectives, inform themselves and each other, and promote a greater public and professional interest in dreaming.

In my private dream-consultation practice and at the Delaney & Flowers Center for the Study of Dreams, which my colleague Dr. Loma Flowers and I have directed since 1980, we train mental health professionals and laypeople who come from a variety of theoretical backgrounds. We teach individuals, couples, and groups the basics of eliciting from the dreamer the most relevant associations and connections in the most efficient way possible. We are especially interested in promoting a greater appreciation for the practical applications of dream work that focuses first on the relatively straightforward metaphorical quality of the dream. While we believe that most schools of psychology have made important contributions to the understanding of human beings, we think that psychodynamic formulations are most helpful after, not during, the dream interview. For both professionals and nonprofessionals our dream center provides short-term training as well as one- and two-year diploma programs based on the techniques presented in this book.

In the pages that follow you will find a step-by-step method for conducting dream interviews for yourself and for other dreamers. As you read examples of actual dream interviews (all names, of course, have been changed) you will get a feel for the method and for the importance of following the dreamer by asking questions rather than making interpretations.

After an initial reading, this book can be used for reference and as a workbook. The major elements of a dream—its setting, people, animals, objects, feelings, and plots—are explored in separate chapters. When working with a particular dream element, you can look up the appropriate chapter to find relevant questions that will help you discover the meaning of a specific image. In addition, each of these chapters contains special "help key" questions and strategies for use when you get stuck in spite of having asked the questions that normally unlock the dream's meaning.

The chapters on intermediate and advanced strategies and techniques in interviewing will help you develop your skills, efficiency, and speed in conducting the interview for yourself or another dreamer. Most important, they will give you tools for coping with the various ways we unknowingly avoid recognizing important aspects of our personalities and relationships that dreams reveal. By reducing our defensiveness and resistance, we have a chance to clear away obstacles that can sabotage good dream work as well as good living.

To help you develop and practice your skills in understanding dreams and using them to solve problems and generate new ideas, you will find a chapter on how you can form a dream study group. I have been conducting such groups since 1974 in private, educational, business, and mental health settings and have yet to find a more fascinating or productive format for the study of dreams. Whether you choose to explore dreams on your own, with a friend, a professional, or in a group, the directory of resources will give you suggestions for further reading, video instruction, and training centers where you can continue your study of this endlessly fascinating subject.

□

**CHAPTER
ONE**

GETTING READY

The first step in understanding your dreams is, of course, learning to recall them frequently and vividly. Even if you have never remembered your dreams before, if you follow the suggestions in this chapter you should be able to remember a dream almost every morning with just two weeks of practice.

RECALLING YOUR DREAMS

Even though we all dream at least four or five times every night, many of us wake with only confused and broken tales, and some of us with nothing at all to tell. If you would like to develop your dream skills and tap your sleeping resources of creativity, insight, and dramatic entertainment, then the first step is to learn how to recall your dreams. Luckily, once we have decided to make the effort, it is an easy step for most of us, even for those who never recall having dreamed before. All you need to do is keep a dream notebook by your bed, record the date before going to sleep, and write *whatever* is on your mind when you awake. If you do not recall even a fragment of a dream, write down whatever thoughts enter your mind as you wake up. This discipline will soon convince the part of you that might feel lazy in the morning to remember a dream, because you will have to write a few lines no matter what. Form the habit of thinking backward as you wake so that you say to yourself, "What was just going on in my mind?" rather than, "What must I do today?" It is of the utmost importance that you write down even brief fragments of dreams because they help you to improve your recall, are often surprisingly informative, and may well develop into longer dream accounts as you begin to write them out.[1]

Sometimes simply concentrating on the feeling you have on awakening will lead you back to the dream. Lie still for a moment as you do this and, if nothing comes, move slowly into your favorite sleep position. This may trigger your memory of a dream or two. Waking up to talk radio or even gentle music will be distracting and will usually make recall more difficult. A gentle alarm ring is least disruptive, although waking without an alarm is best. Of course, if you are not allowing yourself to get enough sleep, you will be fighting an uphill battle. Take as much sleep as you need to awaken refreshed before your alarm sounds. If you need caffeine to wake up in the morning, ask yourself if you are cheating yourself out of one of life's great luxuries—plenty of sleep. Some of us were brought up with a puritan disdain for the pleasure and restorative rest of sleep. If you suffer from a prejudice against sleep and think of it as idle wasted time, read about the dreamers in this book and ask yourself if you still believe this myth.

Don't let your unpleasant dreams discourage you from recalling your nocturnal adventures. As you remember more and more dreams, you will probably find in them an exhilarating and fascinating variety of experiences that you may never know in your waking life. The excitement, the suspense, the wonder, the beauty, and the breadth and depth of emotion available in dreams surpass the limits of most waking lives. Joseph Heller wrote, "I want to keep my dreams, even bad ones, because without them, I might have nothing all night long."[2]

You may have heard of any number of tricks, magic potions, or vitamins that will help you to recall your dreams. For example, some people believe that eating pineapple or chocolate will help you remember your dreams. To the extent that you may eat so much of anything to give you indigestion severe enough to wake you up in the night, this might be indirectly true. If you awake more than usual or for longer than usual periods in the

night, you will have more opportunities to engrave your fleeting dream memories into the more efficient memory system of
the waking brain. But you can achieve the same results just as
pleasantly by setting your alarm to go off in the middle of the
night or by drinking lots of water before sleep . . . and whenever
you awaken! Vitamin B$_6$ is reported to increase dream recall, but
in doses greater than fifty milligrams per day it can be toxic and
long-term use of lower doses might someday be found to be
harmful. Abundant dream recall does not require draconian
measures. If you are relaxed, patient, and above all persistent in
using your dream journal you should recall plenty of dreams
in one or two weeks.

In times of heightened emotional stress or work overload
many people's reservoir of dreams seems to dry up. While the
amount of dreaming probably remains constant, the ability to
recall dreams is sometimes greatly reduced. Again, the key is to
persist in a steady, relaxed manner by writing *something* in your
journal each morning.

Taking a nap in the afternoon helps some people to remember very vivid dreams, so keep your notebook with you whenever you have the luxury to sleep midday. Some people never
recall dreams from their nap periods, but say that their morning
recall is much clearer and more copious when they nap regularly.

RECORDING YOUR DREAMS

The difficulty in recalling dreams for most of those who follow
these simple instructions for a week or two is not in recalling
too few dreams, but in remembering too many. If this happens
to you, decide how many dreams you care to record per week
and let the rest go. One dream a day is usually enough to satisfy
most people, and one dream a week is enough to keep you busy
if you study it closely.

Recording your dreams can be a pleasure, and if you include the information suggested below, your dream journal will assist you in understanding your dreams. In my private office and at our dream center, students all use the following format.

DATE. Be sure to remember to record the date of each entry.

DAY NOTES. At night before going to sleep, record three or four lines describing what you did and felt that day, and put a large bracket around your notes. Emphasize the emotional highlights of the day.

TITLE OF DREAM. Leave a blank line between your day notes and the dream you record in the morning. After you have recorded your dream give it a simple title that will help you to remember the dream at a glance when you review your journal. Dream titles will be a great help to you when you study your dreams in a series and look for recurring themes.

★ **INCUBATION QUESTION.** If you are incubating a dream to help resolve an issue in your waking life, write down the short, focused question you will repeat to yourself as you fall asleep in order to target a helpful dream.

✓ **THE DREAM.** Write down every detail and feeling you can recall in the time you have to record your dream.

▽ **COMMENTARY.** Use this space to record any thoughts or feelings you have in the last moment of the dream or immediately on awakening. Also write down any feelings or impressions you have about the dream as you awake. Later you can use this space and additional pages to make notes about your interview of

yourself or with a dream partner. Include any comparisons you might like to draw with other dreams or with
waking-life experiences.

The ✓ placed in the margin beside each dream entry, the ★
placed next to your incubation question, and the ∇ placed beside your commentary will help to organize your journal and
make it easier to locate specific sections as you review your
dreams. Here is an example of a page from the journal of
Bertrand, a cabinetmaker who would like to be a writer as well.

July 5, 1990

> Long day in the shop. How can I change my circum-
> stances so I can write rather than make cabinets all day
> long. I feel paralyzed and frustrated. Had fun playing
> with my children, Ian and Natalie, this evening. What is
> preventing me from creating the life I want?

BOSS ON MY BACK

✓ I'm carrying my boss on my back, piggy-back style.
We are in a visually stunning scene of meadow and ra-
vine surrounded by rolling hills and mountains. I'm
going downhill with my boss on my back. I'm at-
tempting to run, but he is too heavy for me. I'm trying
to be careful and strong. My boss says, "That's why I
liked using those five Green Bay Packers." As he says
that, implying that I am not as strong as they, I stumble
and fall to the ground on my belly slightly. As I get
back up I ask, "When did you use the Packers?"

∇ It felt awful to have my boss put me down. In our
group session interview, I realized how much like my
dad this critical and very demanding boss is. So I'm still
carrying my critical self-judgments learned from my

father on my back. Small wonder I lose my confidence if I compare myself to FIVE Green Bay Packers! The beautiful scene reminds me of the beauty of creative writing, and of how I stumble when I lose my confidence.

If you use a new, dated page for each dream you recall, you will have plenty of space to write your commentary at the time you recall the dream, after an interview, or during a monthly or yearly review of your dream journal. Brief but careful day notes will be a great aid to recalling the specific waking context that led to a particular dream. Frequently, the issues you outline in your day notes are the very ones you will dream about that night.

If you are beginning your dream journal, you might like to start by recording the dreams you remember from childhood as well as any particularly vivid or recurring dreams and nightmares you recall from your youth and adult life. These will give you a variety of important dreams to reflect on as you read the following pages.

TARGETING YOUR DREAMS TO SOLVE PROBLEMS AND GENERATE NEW IDEAS

Since the beginning of recorded history, and probably well before that, humans have slept in sacred places and prayed to their gods for dreams that would heal their maladies, direct them in choosing a role in their community, and answer their questions and appeals for help in making decisions. These sacred practices of what is known as dream incubation—performed in ancient Mesopotamia, Egypt, Greece, Rome, and elsewhere—were often organized and attended by priests who prescribed preparatory cleansing and sacrificial rituals and who sometimes interpreted obscure dreams.

We cannot know if the successes claimed for these incubations actually occurred, but we do know that most serious thinkers throughout history have noted that we tend to dream about the things that occupy our minds and hearts during the day.

In 1920 *The Intellectual Life,* a book by the French Catholic priest A. D. Sertillanges, was published and had a great success among intellectuals for the following thirty years. In the 1960s it was translated into English. Sertillanges wrote the book as a practical guide to a life of study and to the development of the mind through joyful, disciplined work. He devoted a section of his book to "the work of night" and wrote,

> Sleep itself is a worker, a partner of the daily toil; we can make its forces serve us, utilize its laws, profit by that filtering process, that clarification which takes place during the self-surrender of the night.
>
> A bit of brain-work begun, an idea just started, an idea that some interior or exterior happening had prevented from fully shaping itself or finding its natural place, is developed during the night and links up with others; do not miss this opportunity to gain something; fix, before it vanishes again into the night of the mind, this light which may help you.
>
> How will you set about it? Sometimes no particular ingenuity is required. When you wake, you find the collaboration of sleep all performed and recorded. The work of the previous day appears to you in a clearer light; a new path, a virgin region lies before you; some relationship of ideas, of facts, of expressions, some happy comparison or illuminating image, a whole passage perhaps or a plan ready to be realized, will have surged into your consciousness. The whole is there,

clear and distinct; you will only need at the right moment to utilize what Hypnos has condescended to do
for you.³

Sertillanges commented that one must make the effort to re-
cover the treasures of the night more often. He suggested that a
man of study keep a notebook by his bed and write down any
ideas or insights immediately without waking up too fully or
turning on the light. He says that every thinker has these moments of morning lucidity: some slight, some almost miracu-
lous. Sertillanges noted that "night collaborates royally with the
inventor and the thinker and presents insights in one morning
that might have taken days or weeks for the waking mind to
hammer out." But these gifts, he reminded the reader, come
only to prepared minds; sleep can work only on the findings of
experience and the labor of the day.

Many artists and scientists have reported dreams that have
inspired them and helped them to solve problems, but only a
few have reported that they took an active role in requesting
such dreams. Robert Louis Stevenson went to sleep expecting or
asking his dreams to help him create or revise a story. Cannon,
one of the greatest and most creative American physiologists,
asked for dreams to help him solve his childhood algebra problems, and later he sought help with difficulties he had in preparing lectures on his work. Cannon commented that "this process
has been so common and so reliable for me that I have supposed
that it was at the service of everyone. But evidence indicates that
it is not."⁴ Since the publication of my work with dream incubation in 1977,⁵ I have received many letters from scientists, and
especially from mathematicians, who express the same surprise
at discovering that most people don't know they can solve
problems while dreaming.

Giorgio, a young architect whose career was beginning to
take off, had just landed his biggest job, designing a huge and
elegant home that would cost $3 million. He was anxious about

the organization of the project and about his ability to work well with the rather demanding owners, the Milnes. Giorgio decided to incubate a dream asking, "What is the secret to keeping the Milnes project together this year?" That night he dreamt:

> **I am George Bush's architect.** I dropped by his house for a brief (token) visit to measure something (the piano?). While at the house I see several pretentious designer types mingling around. I know I already have the job and am wearing my pajamas. Mrs. Milnes is also in pajamas. (Now it seems that the Milnes, not the Bushes, are my clients.)
>
> I make friendly small talk with Mr. Milnes who looks like Jonathan Hunter.
>
> Next, I am in a church. A young man is in charge of gently helping the children present to recite a blessing which begins with, "I thank God for. . . ." It seems that these blessings involve or relate to Bush.
>
> (GEORGE BUSH'S ARCHITECT)

Giorgio described Bush as a man of great power and influence who was not turning out to be as bad and selfish a president as he had feared. He resented Bush's privilege much as he did the privilege of the wealthy Milnes. He found that he had recently suspended his negative judgments and opened up to both Bush and the Milnes. Giorgio said that there were many things he did not like about his new clients and that he had acted like the pretentious designers when he was with them, putting on airs to enhance his sense of his own importance. But recently he had begun to relax around them (putting on pajamas rather than airs) and found that they relaxed too. The Milnes were looking more like regular people than an intimidating presidential couple.

Giorgio described Jonathan Hunter as a former major client

with whom he had managed to get on well only after he had opened up and dropped his pretentious designer act. Finally, Giorgio said that learning to count his blessings in getting such big contracts would help him drop the pretentious architect style that was sure to sabotage his relationship with these people whom he would be working very closely with for the next year. He used this dream to remind himself to develop an open, non-defensive, relaxed style with his new clients.

The phrase focusing method of incubation,[6] described below, is designed to be used at home on those nights when you don't have time to go to the temple, to fast, or to make offerings, as the ancient petitioners did. If you would like to try incubating a dream to gain insight about a personal or professional problem that is of immediate concern, here is what you do.

1.   *In your journal, under your day notes, write five or ten lines about the issue you would like your dreams to help you better understand and resolve.* Use this step, the "incubation discussion," to focus and amplify your feelings about the issue. The more motivated you are to resolve the issue, or to make a creative breakthrough, the better your chances of success on the first try.

2.   *On a separate line, write out a one-line phrase or question that clearly states what it is you want to know.* Many people are tempted to ask two or three questions a night, are unable to decide which problem to incubate, or are unsure how to phrase their question. By making yourself choose one specific question, you will clear away distracting concerns, and have a clearer focus.

3.   *Go to sleep repeating to yourself your incubation phrase, and if your mind wanders, just bring it back to the repetition of the phrase.* As you repeat your question or request, try to feel within yourself the fullness of your desire to learn something new that will help you out of your rut. Because dream responses usually point out an unexpected cause or solution to a problem, cultivating an

attitude of openness to surprising results will increase your
chances of recalling the dream.

Once you learn to focus on your incubation phrase, you will
find that your problems no longer keep you awake at night.
They will put you to sleep because repetition is calming and
sleep inducing. When you awaken, write down whatever is in
your mind, even if it seems to have no relation to your incubation question. You may awake with a dream, a fragment, or just
the good idea you were asking for. A number of my clients have
awakened from an incubation with a song in mind, the title or
lyrics of which turn out to be important clues to the problem.

You can successfully incubate dreams on almost any topic if
it is important to you and if you are open to learning something
new about it. If you are a good dream recaller, but recall no
dream the night after an incubation, see if you are less open than
you thought and try again, perhaps phrasing the question in
another way. Be sure not to jump to conclusions about the relevance or irrelevance of your dream response. Conduct a careful
interview with yourself or ask a friend to help. Then see if the
dream sheds light on your problem.

A few years ago, I was training a married couple in dream
work. The husband, Gregory, was having a difficult time recalling his dreams. He was an engineer whose wife had initiated the
dream sessions hoping to help him develop a greater awareness
of his inner life and emotions. Gregory was apparently willing
to study his dreams but guessed he was more reticent than he
had thought. In an effort to trigger a dream, he incubated the
request "I want to remember a dream to bring to Gayle tomor-
row." He triumphantly brought in the following dream in
which he pictured me in the role of a midwife:

> **We were pregnant.** Preparations for the birth were in
> progress. Gayle was going to be our midwife. The time

drew near. We did breathing exercises. We called Gayle to say that it was going to be time for her to come over. "Did your water break yet?" she asked me. "My water?" I looked down and sure enough, I was the pregnant one! Not my wife, Shoko, but me! I had a pregnant belly and a hairy perineum. We decided to shave it. I was getting nervous. "Breathe! breathe!" everybody said.

We decided to have me give birth outside. I thought that would be nice with all the animals and such; they would form an understanding audience. "Let's go to the park," Gayle said. I worried that there would be too many people and that it would not be very private. My water broke. We went to the park. Gayle said it would be especially nice because they had picnic tables there. I lay down on the only picnic table in sight. "Are you dilated yet?" Gayle asked. I looked and felt and I wasn't. Perhaps some massage would help. Chickens walked around the table, ducks quacked in the pond. There were people everywhere, but nobody seemed to pay particular attention, except for my small circle of friends.

I still had a pajama top on and I wondered if I should be totally nude for the occasion but felt I did not really want to be, because of the public. My friends were good to have around; they were all in a very festive mood. I was sweating profusely. Shoko was at my side, reminding me lovingly to keep breathing. Gayle said I could give birth to anything I liked: chickens, cats, birds, even ideas or books. She suggested we do a printing test first. I pushed hard and sheets of printing paper came forth with test patterns on them.

Everyone was standing around my picnic table, cheering me on. The great moment was about to come. I could clearly see that I was dilating. What did I go through all this trouble for? WHAT WAS I GIVING BIRTH TO? **(WE ARE PREGNANT)**

I woke up and realized that it was a DREAM I wanted to give birth to! So I got up and typed this up right away before this dream escaped me like all the others had.

Gregory was delighted with his dream. During his interview, he saw that his nervousness about producing dreams was related to his anxiety about sharing personal dream material with other people, "in public" as the dream put it. As is usually the case with dreams of being naked, or awkwardly exposed in public, Gregory noted that the people around him were not at all disturbed by his exposure. He was encouraged to think that his engineering career was not the only thing he could do well, and that perhaps he *could* give birth to ideas and books as well.

Alvaro was a graduate student of mine who had become addicted to coffee while in the Spanish army and who now wanted to liberate himself from this substance that kept him on edge most of the time and robbed him of his tranquillity. He incubated a dream with the phrase "I want a dream that will help me quit my coffee habit without suffering from withdrawal headaches." That night he dreamt:

I'm back in the army reserve where I always used to be hung over, stressed, and rushed. But now I feel fine. In fact, I feel great. We are in the mess hall. I ask someone, "What are you doing?" He says, "We are waiting in line to get coffee." I look and see that I have a cup of coffee in each hand and say, "You can have one of these, I have quit." The people in line are SHOCKED! They say, "You can't *live* without coffee!" Sigourney Weaver is standing there, I give her the other cup and feel liberated. **(ARMY RESERVE COFFEE)**

Alvaro said he had no desire for coffee for the next five days, then had one special cup on the sixth, but then stopped for the next two days before our class. Alvaro told us that he had not experienced the headaches so common when one stops drinking coffee. It has been a few years since I've seen Alvaro, and I wonder if he has stayed coffee free. Often dreamers who use dreams to break a habit relapse if they don't keep working on the problem while awake as well as while asleep.

If you like to draw, paint, sculpt, or write, a good way to start incubating dreams is to ask for an idea for your art from your dreams. School teachers at all levels from kindergarten to the Stanford School of Business have suggested this to their students and have been delighted with their responses. Bernard Walt who teaches at the Corcoran School of Art in Washington, D.C., wrote to say that at the end of a semester-long class on dreaming, his art students displayed and discussed the art derived from their dreams.

One of my clients has the job of deciding what will go on the cover of the magazine she works for. Whenever she gets stuck and is unsure what story and picture to choose, she targets her dreams on the question and reports that she almost always comes up with a decision in her dream. Another client, a lawyer, uses his dreams to generate ideas on how to rewrite contracts when the two concerned parties are unable to come to an agreement. And there are famous examples of artists who use their dreams for inspiration like Richard Wagner who credited his dreams with much of *Tristan und Isolde* and with the overture to *The Ring, Das Rheingold*. So whether you have a term paper to write, a masterpiece to complete, or some finger painting to do, you can probably get some inspiration from your sleeping mind.

As you read the dreams contained in the following chapters, you will see many different examples of how you can use incubation to explore problems in forming and maintaining romantic relationships, in getting along with your children and parents, in understanding why you have trouble relating to certain kinds of people, in being as creative and as productive as you would like, and so on. For now, why not incubate a dream on any topic you like and use the resulting dream to practice the interpretation method described in the following chapters?

■

UNLOCKING THE SECRETS OF YOUR DREAMS

The dream interview method of interpretation was born of my frustration with dogmatic applications of psychotherapeutic dream theory and of my conviction that so universal an activity as dreaming should not require a psychotherapist to interpret it. Like reading or speaking a foreign language, dream skills can be taught to anyone who has the motivation and discipline to study and practice seriously enough to become proficient.

Because the dream interview concentrates more on method than on theory, it can be used by therapists of different theoretical persuasions. But just as important, it can be taught as a practical skill in educational and professional settings where problem solving and creativity are highly valued. Once dreams are freed from their long captivity in cult followings and psychotherapeutic doctrine, their practical value in helping us to deal with daily challenges will become more evident.

The dream interview helps dreamers speak for themselves as they discover more about what they think and feel about their own imagery, rather than have their dreams interpreted in an authoritative manner by a therapist, priest, guru, or well-meaning friend. It is tempting to act the role of the wise one who has specialized knowledge and impressive erudition in a true theory of psychology or in mythological or religious truths. What could be simpler than to consult the writings of your favorite patriarch to find out what snakes or circles mean? Of course, this modern version of the dictionary approach leads to some embarrassing moments if your dreamer asks someone with another patriarchal preference to give a second opinion. As long as a dream is interpreted according to a given psychological doctrine, there will be almost as many interpretations as there are different schools of thought.

If, instead, we explore a dream following the dreamer's lead rather than the theory of a would-be sage, and if we resist preconceived notions regarding the nature and dynamics of the male or female psyche, we will have a far better chance of hearing what the dream is really saying.

By learning to ask the dreamer (or yourself, if you are conducting a self-interview) questions that explore dream images and reveal their metaphorical similarities to people and situations in the dreamer's life, you can avoid forcing the dreamer into preconceived, ill-fitting interpretations. Even in cases in which interpreters have an accurate understanding of dreamers' dreams, asking questions rather than making interpretations allows the dreamers to discover the meanings on their own. As we all know from our teen years, parents can warn, teachers can inform, but most of us have to learn life's lessons for ourselves. When someone gives me a sound interpretation without helping me to discover it myself, I can much more easily deny its uncomfortable accuracy by saying, "Well, that's one person's opinion." Or, just as unfortunately, I could accept an entirely or largely inaccurate interpretation on the authority of the interpreter and thereby forfeit the opportunity to discover for myself the genuine insight the dream offers.

Still, having said all this, wouldn't it be wonderful to find someone who could just tell us what our dreams mean? Our human desire for easy answers and for an authority who can direct our lives leads us as individuals and as world citizens to be dangerously gullible and malleable. In abandoning our responsibility and authority to others, we renounce the most important tools we have to discover the truth about ourselves and our world. The way we work with our inner images in dreams often reflects the way we see ourselves as citizens in relation to our peers and in relation to the authorities in our society. Our hierarchical, authoritarian tendencies will tempt us to ask for, accept, and give authoritative interpretations. The non-authoritarian democrat in us will be more willing to question authority, ask the dreamers what they have to say for themselves, and finally take more responsibility for personal action or inaction either as dreamer or interviewer. As we work on developing interviewing skills, it will help to keep an eye on the struggle between our authoritarian and democratic tendencies.

To give the dreamer an effective forum in which to speak for herself, my method involves setting up a dream interview in which the dreamer is questioned by a friend, colleague, or dream analyst who pretends to come from another planet. The would-be interpreter becomes an interviewer who will be curious to discover what life is like seen through the eyes of the dreamer. Thus the interviewer tries to set aside or bracket any personal knowledge, beliefs, opinions, and associations regarding the images in the dream. The interviewer then asks the dreamer to define and describe the images as if she were describing them to someone who has never heard of them before. For example, someone who dreamt of George Bush would be asked, "Who is George, and what is he like?" The dreamer is asked for a concise, frank, and opinionated description, not for a long and often overwhelming list of associations to the man. Meanwhile, the interviewer resists expressing her own opinions and hypotheses.

Next, the initial descriptions are fed back or "recapitulated" to the dreamer, who is then asked if a given description reminds her of anyone or any situation in her life. In this way, the dreamer is asked to "bridge" or make the connection between her dreaming and her waking experience. If the dreamer hears that she described George as a trustworthy and solid, if undramatic, man who is uncommonly well prepared for his job, she might say that her description reminds her of an applicant for the job of supervisor in her company. She may then see that the competent George in her dream highlights important qualities in the applicant that she had failed to appreciate fully in waking life. On the other hand, if she described George as one of the "old boys" who utterly fails to understand or meaningfully improve the lot of women in the country, she might say that her description highlights the most troublesome trait of her father, or her husband, or her boss. Until the dreamer takes the time to describe the dream image and then review that description, she will usually be unable to appreciate what feelings and ideas the image carries for her.

After the dreamer has given a concise but feeling-rich *description* of each major element in the dream (the setting, the people, the objects, the feelings, and the principal actions), listened to a *recapitulation* of these descriptions, and looked to see if these descriptions remind her of anything in her waking life *(bridge)*, the interviewer asks her to connect all the images and their descriptions and bridges in the context of the dramatic structure of the dream *(summary)*. The dreamer can, of course, act as her own interviewer. However, especially as one is learning the method, it is much more effective (and more fun!) to assign that role to a dream partner, be that a friend, dream specialist, or psychotherapist. While there are more steps in a complete dream interview, these four—description, recapitulation, bridge, and summary— are the core ones that require attention to recognize and practice to master. Soon we shall discuss each of these steps in detail, but first, let's see how they operate in a specimen dream interview.

Diana, a beautiful thirty-year-old psychotherapist, brought this surprising and pivotal dream to her first session in one of my long-term dream study groups. As you read it, see what interpretations come to mind. Later you will be able to compare your interpretations with Diana's.

> **I am going to seek some advice.** I am somewhat scattered, not certain where or to whom to turn. Who is expert enough? The matter I am pondering is how to handle my house in the middle of this financial breakup with my husband, Jeff, so I don't lose my house in pay-

ing off his and our debts. I feel panic, wondering which way to turn to make substantial money if there is not a man in my life to help with the finances. . . .

I find myself at the impressive office of Edward, a client of mine who has a big real estate firm. There are huge old-fashioned desks and a pulpitlike loft where there is much hustle and bustle of work among the stacks of what look like law books. As I walk in, an attractive gentleman, who looks as if he were Edward, is sitting behind a desk with Edward's name on it. Rising to greet me, he introduces himself as Edward and begins to tell me about the office and how it works. As if he were taking me into his confidence, he tells me that they work on the properties in the Marina district of San Francisco. He says that since those old-timers down there hang on to their land, the agents wine and dine them and apply plenty of coaxing and pressure. This also requires that the firm have elaborate offices with a dining room. They must spend long hours convincing and wooing for a sale.

As he talks, I become concerned. What if my client is not who he claims to be? I tell this supposed Edward person that I have recently seen a client who claimed he was Edward and I am checking out the validity of his story. When I tell him this, he appears a bit crestfallen and admits to misrepresenting himself. He does not do this overtly, that would be an admission of guilt. Rather, he excuses himself, saying it was just the plaque on his desk with Edward's name on it that must have misled me (indicating that I am just dumb). He says he simply sits there to meet customers when Edward isn't there. I sense his deep disappointment in not being able to pull off the impersonation. He then points out the real Edward, who is just coming into work and is taking off a deep maroon tweed wool coat.

I tell the newly arrived Edward that I am seeking some real estate advice. He asks me to follow him back to his private office. It is down a dark hallway past a bedroom with a large, wooden, old-fashioned, Italian four-poster bed. As I'm walking behind, I realize I can't tell him the whole story, which includes the question of how I will finance my house when I no longer want to do the kind of work I've been doing. That would put an end to his wish to remain my client. Without that part of the picture, getting his advice would be a waste of time. Also, seeing the bed, I realize he often sleeps there and I wonder if he has affairs, simply using women for his pleasure. Swiftly through my mind flits the question of what he'd be like to have an affair with. . . . This I quickly put out of my head.

I feel I have made a worthless trip. I can't get the informed advice I need here. I have wasted precious time.   (EDWARD/EDWARD)

If you found yourself making interpretations or forming interpretive hypotheses about this dream you could jot them down and note what, if anything, leads you to modify, change, or refine them as we proceed.

Diana, at the time of the dream, is a psychotherapist who is not sure she wants to stay in private practice. She has just received a phone call from an unknown woman (and former wife of Jeff's) who told her that Jeff, Diana's husband of five months, is not the secret government agent he claims to be, but a liar with many undivorced wives, all of whom he has taken for various amounts of money. At this point it dawns on Diana that Jeff's financial promises are not being kept. Jeff had convinced her to borrow a great deal of money with Diana's house as collateral. Part of the money was used (at Jeff's instigation) to set up elaborate professional offices for Diana, to buy advertising, a white Cadillac and a Great Dane. Jeff had assured Diana that as soon as a big real estate deal came through involving the sale of some of Jeff's considerable property, he would not only be able to reimburse her but also to finance a luxurious lifestyle for both of them. His top-secret position with the government complicated and slowed down his financial dealings, but paid him very well. While she didn't want to believe what the woman on the phone had told her, Diana's creditors were growing impatient and she was becoming anxious about her responsibility for their joint debts.

Just before the dream, Diana confronted Jeff with her information. Confessing to some of her accusations and asking for forgiveness, he promised to reform and entered psychotherapy as proof of his good intentions. Diana said that she had irresistible urges to forgive and care for "the hurt, abandoned, condemned, little boy" in Jeff.

Does any of this information lead you to modify your earlier hypotheses? Now let's look at what happened in the dream interview we conducted with Diana.

Having told us all this, Diana, like most dreamers, could not understand the dream beyond assuming that it had something to do with her financial worries, which were clearly stated in the first scene. She wondered why she was dreaming about her client Edward. While this well-focused background information offered many clues to possible meanings of the dream, the interviewers in our training group knew better than to offer interpretive hypotheses that might be threatening to Diana and that might also be quite inaccurate, being based on the interviewer's and not the dreamer's associations. Far better to give her the opportunity to arrive at her own interpretation after a careful consideration of the dream. Here are the highlights of our dream interview:

INTERVIEWER. What are the major feelings in the dream, Diana?

DIANA. Confusion. I am anxious, wanting help with

my financial problem. I am suspicious, then disappointed. That pretty well describes how I've been feeling lately.

I. Describe the setting of the dream. [Eliciting a description.]

D. It is Edward's office, which I've never seen in waking life. In the dream it is big, impressive, and it has a pulpit that gives it an air of power and seriousness. The law books enhance that air. It gives the impression that there is power, efficiency, and wealth there. [Description.]

I. Who is Edward in waking life, and what is his personality like? [Eliciting a description.]

D. He's a client I have in therapy who is very wealthy and successful in real estate. He is an overworker. [Description.]

I. What is the first Edward in the dream like? [Eliciting a description.]

D. He seems like an attractive and helpful gentleman at first. Then as he takes me into his confidence he reveals himself to be a maneuverer and manipulator who has set up an office policy that has no ethics regarding his clients' needs or desires. He has no intention of working on his clients' behalf and his methods are to beguile, wine, dine, promise, and fool them out of their land and money. [Description.]

I. He works in the Marina district. What kinds of people would he have for clients there? [Eliciting a description.]

D. Older Italians who usually want to hold on to their property, but who would be vulnerable to Edward's methods. [Description.]

I. Does Edward, the manipulator, who wines and dines and beguiles his clients and has no ethics, remind you of anything? [Recapitulation and invitation to bridge.]

D. Well, this closely resembles, or rather duplicates, Jeff's pattern with me and with the woman who called me. [Bridge.]

I. How does Edward respond when you let him know you suspect he is not the real Edward? [Eliciting a description.]

D. He is crestfallen. [Description.]

I. That's an unusual word. Crestfallen? [Eliciting additional description.]

D. But it fits Jeff exactly. He is crestfallen now that he is found out. He is disappointed that he could not keep up the scam better. And he certainly did misrepresent himself. [Bridge.]

I. You said that as the real Edward enters, he takes off a deep maroon wool tweed coat. Can you describe it further? [Eliciting a description.]

D. I don't know. It was fashionable. [Description.]

I. What sort of people would wear such a coat? [Eliciting additional description.]

D. Mafia types. [Description.]

I. Pretend I come from another planet. What are Mafia types like? [Eliciting a description.]

D. They will do anything to get what they want. Lie, cheat, steal, kill. [Description.]

I. So the Edward you first see is not the helpful gentleman he at first seemed to be. The real Edward is a Mafia type who would do anything, lie, cheat, steal, or kill to get what he wants. Do these Edwards remind you of anything? [Recapitulation, summary, and invitation to bridge.]

D. Well . . . Jeff, if what I have been told is true—and it must be. He has lied to and manipulated me and at least one other woman. In fact, the law books make me think how he has manipulated the law just as the Mafia does. [Bridge.]

I. So in the dream you are looking to Edward, who reminds you of Jeff, for financial help. Remind you of anything? [Summary and invitation to bridge.]

D. Jeff came on real strong when I met him. He wanted to set me up in these fancy offices, buy me a car, and generally take very good care of me. [Bridge.]

I. Are you still looking to Jeff for help?

D. Well, I have to maintain the relationship or I'll lose any hope of his helping to pay off this debt. And he has offered to repair the roof of my house.

I. Do you think Jeff might come through and pay off his debt to you?

D. He might.

I. In the dream, Edward's specialty is wining and dining the Marina matrons to get them to sell . . . [Recapitulation.]

D. Well, Jeff may have many wives and I'm sure he has wined and dined us all. [Bridge.] But Jeff is so alone now and he may break out of this pattern if he is in therapy . . . [The waking Diana is still in the grips of denial. It would be unwise to challenge her while her defenses are up. Better to return to the dream and let her move at her own pace.]

I. Tell me about the Italian bed. [Eliciting a description.]

D. It's huge, a four-poster—a good Mafia man's bed. I wonder if he uses it just to crash after a long day's work or if he uses it to avoid dealing with his wife or if he uses it to exploit women. [Description.]

I. Then what happens?

D. I think of having an affair with him but realize he's too dangerous a man to deal with.

I. Like anyone else in your life? [Invitation to bridge.]

D. You mean Jeff . . . ? He *has* been two sided, fraudu-
lent, and self-serving. Just like a mobster. He set up
my elaborate offices and his attitude toward clients
was uncaring and exploitative. Mafia men are heart-
less, evil, criminal, and very dangerous. [Bridge.] Yet
Jeff has gone into therapy. He cries, wants me to help
and forgive him, and he promises to give back the
forty thousand dollars.

At this point, the group session was about to end and we
encouraged Diana to write out her dream, her recollection of
the interview, and any commentary or summary she cared to
make. Here is a part of that summary written a few days after
the interview:

Reactions as I type this dream. It makes me sick. I can
hardly sit still. I am angry at myself. I keep forgiving
him and taking care of him. He is coming over today to
set up a repayment plan and help me tar the leaking
roof. I am getting sucked back in. He will presently
offer to do anything to be with me. Money is a consideration in calling a roofer, but in all honesty I could
probably get instructions from the hardware store man.
I haven't talked with any of the other wives. I don't
want to believe he is still doing this.

I remember being numb as the group interviewed
me. The connections are blatant. No one could miss
them. My unconscious speaks loudly. Why am I so resistant to recognizing the obvious? Am I rescuing
Daddy? My mother sacrificed herself for my alcoholic
father then forever felt guilty for leaving him. She
always felt sorry for him. Edward the Mafioso is too
dangerous to feel sorry for. Funny how I see so much of
the hurt, abandoned boy in Jeff. I don't want to sacrifice
my life for him, but I don't hold him accountable for

adult responsibility for his lying maneuvers. I must break out of this delusion.

Several scenes come to mind as the nausea rises. It is the night I confronted him and told him to leave. He managed to coax me to forgive him. I didn't fix him dinner that night, we went out to dinner. I try to mollify myself as I work on this dream when I remember I PAID FOR DINNER! He had a strange smile on his face. He had got me again. This process is painfully self-revealing, but awfully important. Thank you, dream interviewers.

Diana learned a great deal by commenting on and summarizing her interview. Even if our preinterview hypotheses about the meaning of Diana's dream had been accurate, can you imagine that as interpretations they would have been accepted by a dreamer who was fighting hard to deny the obvious regarding her relationship with her husband? The dream interview allowed Diana to explore and recognize her own very private web of feelings and associations without being pushed. Because of the threatening nature of the dream message, we did not ask Diana to summarize the dream interview in class, but to do it in writing at home. This gave her time and privacy, which were helpful in reducing her defenses.

Now let's take a look at how the four phases of *description, recapitulation, bridging,* and *summary* fit into a complete interview.

THE TEN STEPS OF A DREAM INTERVIEW

STEP 1.   *Creating an atmosphere conducive to good dream work.*

There are several factors to consider when creating an environment for dream work. These range from a feeling of safety to the implementation of tactful humor. Let's examine some of the important elements.

Confidentiality and a Nonjudgmental Attitude

The interviewer must create an atmosphere of comfort and safety for the dreamer. Almost everyone feels surprisingly vulnerable when working on a dream, but most novice interviewers underestimate how very sensitive dreamers are to any comments, looks, or gestures that could possibly be interpreted as being critical or judgmental. A dreamer will feel safer if you assure complete confidentiality and maintain a nonjudgmental attitude toward whatever the dreamer reveals. Creating a good ambience for dream work is much harder than it seems and requires careful attention to the factors discussed here.

Curiosity

Keep a conversational tone as you ask questions; don't turn the interview into an inquisition. Let your curiosity show as you ask your dreamer for her unique description of Texas, spinach, tigers, or blue suede shoes. Dreamers often silently worry that they are boring their interviewers with their prosaic descriptions. In fact, interviewers are usually fascinated to see how each person's descriptions vary and how they fit into the dramatic structure of the dream. Reassure your dreamer of your interest and pleasure in the challenge of working with the dream. It is helpful (although not necessary) to have a copy of the dream account in front of you. You can ask the dreamer for a copy of the relevant page from her dream journal, handwritten, typed, or photocopied, or you can write the dream down as you hear it. In any case, try not to fall into the habit of looking at the dream account more than at the dreamer. Eye contact is very important to reassure and encourage the dreamer and to alert you to unexpected responses in the form of facial expressions and body language that may be worth pursuing. Remember that if your face expresses confusion, anxiety, distraction, or impatience, this may distract or discourage the dreamer.

Humility and Tact

Humility and tact are both essential in dealing with dreamers and with the surprising and often disconcerting insights triggered by dream work. Unlike some interpreters, the interviewer recognizes that she has no hot line to the truth of another person's dream. And she understands that the most direct way to discover how another person sees and feels the world within and without is to *ask,* not tell, that person. Experienced interviewers often tell us that the most difficult part of their early training at our dream center was not finding the right questions to ask, but restraining themselves from blurting out their interpretations. Again and again, Dr. Flowers and I hear a familiar saying, "I kept finding myself just wanting to *tell* my dreamers what their images or whole dreams meant!" Often, later interview questions revealed that these stifled interpretations were incorrect. Sometimes they were accurate but would have robbed the dreamer of the pleasure and useful exercise of discovering the meaning step-by-step. And often they were inadequate and would have lacked the impact and exquisite specificity of an understanding based on the dreamer's exploration of her own images.

Humility will reduce the interviewer's anxiety that comes from wanting to do a good job for the dreamer. If you don't hold yourself out as a sage, your dreamer's as well as your own expectations will not be so intimidating. Interviewers who are just learning this method often fall into the trap of nodding their heads with a sage "Aha," or "Hmmm," meant to tell the dreamer, "I understand something you do not." Is there anything more insufferable? If you try to keep a curious and open countenance and eschew any know-it-all tendencies, you will have a more comfortable dreamer spared the distraction of wondering anxiously what you know or *think* you know that she does not. For a while, you will have to fight to overcome the natural tendency to demonstrate to your dreamer your skill, insight, and knowledge. This struggle is more like a battle—especially in the beginning—but winning it will set you free to explore the dreamer's experience with unfettered curiosity.

Courage

Asking questions from the point of view of someone from another planet will establish the principle that the interviewer is not an authority, but a very curious and accepting visitor to a world known intimately only to the dreamer. Freud asked for his patients' associations because he wanted to know what was in *their* minds, not just his. This was an extraordinary break with all the dream work that had occurred before his. Jung reminded his students to be naive as they considered a patient's dream. Yet both felt that the interpreter needed a great deal of special knowledge about the Freudian or Jungian version of the psyche to put the associations gathered from the dreamer into their proper perspectives before arriving at an interpretation.

An interviewer, in contrast, refrains from relying on specialized knowledge of this sort and tries to limit her assumptions to the most minimal ones involving the belief that dream images are metaphorical expressions that meaningfully relate to the dreamer's life. In this way she can maintain an open curiosity and naïveté. If you have an opinion about how the human psyche works or about how the dreamer should be acting or thinking try to put it aside while you are working with the dream. Let the dream teach *you* about the nature of this particular human psyche. It takes a great deal of courage to try to understand a dream without the comforting security blanket of preconceived formulas. Many of our students, especially those who are psychotherapists, find this difficult and say things like, "I hate not knowing how to do something!" and "It is very uncomfortable not having the answers." The interviewer can learn to accept that she doesn't have the answers, but only has the questions, by recognizing that formulaic interpretations frustrate productive interviewing.

A good interviewer wants to uncover the dreamer's story, not selectively gather points that will bolster the interviewer's pet hypotheses. Therefore, it is helpful if you invite the dreamer to help you do your job by correcting you whenever you mis-represent a description and by interrupting you whenever she has the feeling that you are going off course with your questions. This will also remind the dreamer that she is not asked to play a passive role, waiting for you to ask the right questions, but that she has a certain responsibility in making the interview work. Encouraging the dreamer to attend to and express any strong associations that arise during the interview, even if they seem logically irrelevant, will give needed permission to reticent dreamers.

Empathy and Enthusiasm

While it may be obvious that an interviewer should empathize with the dreamer, it is important to stress that dreamers are ex-traordinarily sensitive. They need clear yet subtle signs of em-pathy. Brief, simple statements like "Oh my" or "Well, well" let the dreamer know you are involved without putting words in her mouth. If you say things like "I'll bet that felt very scary," the dreamer has to accept or correct your estimation of her feel-ings. Better to ask the dreamer to find her own descriptive words for her feelings. The effort to describe and name her feelings will help her experience them more vividly and more clearly.

Enjoy your job as interviewer. Let your curiosity and your pleasure in the search for clues to the meaning of the dream show. Your facial expressions and tone of voice can communicate your enthusiasm, which can motivate your dreamer to carry on even when the going gets tough.

Humor

Tactfully expressed, humor can help the dreamer overcome resistance to vividly reexperiencing her dream. For example, when a dreamer feels frustrated or embarrassed that her dream seems bizarre or nonsensical, you can note how funny dreams are, pick one of the dream images, and say something like "Where else but in a dream would you find a giraffe with a camel's hump?" Humor can relieve the dreamer's anxiety regarding a particularly embarrassing revelation. You can always say something along the lines of "You too? Welcome to the human race." If the interview becomes laborious, a bit of humor can liven it up and put the dreamer in a better mood, more conducive to seeing puns and metaphors. The basic rules we follow are to be careful to laugh *with,* not *at,* the dreamer and not to laugh at a humorous dream punch line before the dreamer has the first laugh. Used sensitively, humor can help the dreamer feel safe about looking silly or feeling confused and perplexed.

STEP 2. *Inviting the dreamer to tell the dream and listening to it.*

When you ask the dreamer to tell you her dream, it is often useful to ask for a little background information. For example, ask her when she had the dream. The dream invariably will be about something that was going on in her internal or external life at that time. If she has been keeping a journal, she will be able to tell you the activities and emotional highlights of the day preceding the dream. If this information was recorded before going to sleep on the night of the dream, it will often be relevant to the issues dealt with in the dream. If it was written the morning after the dream, it will be of much less help because at that time the dreamer usually notes only the preceding day's events that appear in the manifest dream account. These events are usually used in the dream as a metaphor for a waking situation and do not explain the meaning. For example, Diana may well have seen the movie *Al Capone* the evening before she dreamt of Edward the Mafioso in a maroon coat. But to say that she had the dream because she saw that movie would be to miss the point. She was better able to recognize the ruthless, dangerous qualities of her husband thanks to the dream's use of the vivid image of a Mafia-like Edward. Her day notes written before the dream discussed her current distress about her husband and were central to the concerns dealt with in the dream. Of course the dreamer may well fail to note in the day journal the concerns she dreams about that night, so you can never assume that the day notes are reliable clues. However, if you keep them in mind without counting on them, they will usually be rich resources for nonleading questions.

If the dream is a recurring one, ask, "How long and how often have you had this dream?" Asking "Between what dates approximately?" will help the dreamer to be more precise. The problem the dream refers to will have been part of the dreamer's life for at least as long as the dream has recurred.

Even if the dreamer wants to tell you more than one dream, it is best to work on only one at a time to avoid confusion. Sometimes the dreamer will overload the interviewer and thereby disable her from getting a close look at anything. Certain dreamers who like to control their interpersonal interactions closely, who are uncomfortable with feelings and thoughts that they cannot immediately understand and fit into a logical picture, or who are mental health professionals who think they have mastered the psychological arts present a particular problem. These dreamers will at first enter the interview less to explore the dream than to figure it out. They often feel they should be able to skip exploring the description and immediately bridge from the initial description to some aspect of waking life. Instead of first discovering the specific dimensions of the dream image from a vantage point within the image to see if anything in waking life springs to mind, they stand outside the image, hunting around in waking life for something that matches the dream's superficial appearance.

Trying to figure out a dream before you discover what you actually feel and think in words about the images in the dream is like estimating the temperature of a pool of water without ever putting your toe in it. Even therapists who are more careful with their patients' dreams try to take shortcuts with the discovery process when it comes to their own dreams. When dealing with dreamers who jump to premature interpretations, invite them to withhold their interpretive efforts and just sit back and enjoy the interview's exploratory phase. If the dreamer cannot do this, her descriptions will be flat and of almost no help. If the dreamer cannot give up the role of interpreter, the chances of her ever recognizing the new insights the dream has to offer are practically nonexistent.

Finally, invite the dreamer to tell you the dream with feeling, as if she were telling it to an alien who loves to hear dream tales. Don't interrupt this narrative unless you absolutely must to clarify the story. Enjoy the story. Don't try to figure it out yet. Listen for the basic action or the structure of the dream and for the feelings the dreamer expresses or fails to express. It will be easier to listen attentively if you already have a photocopy of the dream in front of you. If not, you'll have to try to jot down the dream at the same time. When the dreamer arrives at the end of her tale she will want some response from you. You could congratulate her on recalling however much she did; empathize with the joy, anger, or fear she expressed in the dream; or simply say, "That is quite a dream." Remember, dreamers are vulnerable and require tender loving care, whether they admit it or not. It is important to them that you appreciate the realness of their dream experiences and not just focus on the symbolic. Rushing to interpretive work before first acknowledging the vivid reality of the dream experience can abruptly rob the dreamer of something that feels precious.

STEP 3.   *Diagraming and outlining the dream.*

My colleague Loma Flowers was the mother of two young boys when we started our dream center in 1980. In helping her sons learn to diagram sentences, she came up with the idea of teaching the students at our center how to diagram their dreams. Her idea was to help the dreamers and interviewers identify the basic categories of dream images about which they needed to ask questions. Diagraming gave the novice interviewers a helpful navigational map to follow during the interview.

Here is how to do it:

- Place a rectangle around each setting in the dream.
- Circle each person.
- Underline each animal and major object.
- Circle each feeling with a wavy cloud.
- Underline with an arrow the major actions.[1]

Let's look at the diagram of a short dream of a New Yorker named Cesare.

I am with Renata Tibaldi, the legendary opera singer. We are at the top of the Statue of Liberty. She is beautiful, an exquisite talent. She asks me to go to Paris with her. I am profoundly tempted and want to go but she is crossing the Atlantic in a forty-foot boat that

seems to me entirely inadequate for the dangerous voyage. I tell her we would be at great risk of drowning.
She understands that I am afraid, smiles, and gives
me the *Sunday New York Times* then leaves. I am sad,
but accepting. I let her go.

As you can see, the point in diagraming is not to split hairs,
but to highlight the major elements of the dream about which
the interviewer will ask specific questions and elicit relevant descriptions and associations, as discussed in the next chapter.

Although my purpose here is to demonstrate diagraming,
not interpretation, I imagine that you, like me, may be curious to
know how Cesare understood his dream. He described Renata
as a thrilling, exhilarating woman of great passion and adventure. He immediately recognized a parallel to his fiancée, who
was a famous ballerina. He also saw that her lifestyle was just
too adventurous for him, even though he longed to share it with
her. He didn't want to admit it, but being at home Sunday
mornings in bed with the *Times* was more his style. He was
strongly attracted to her freedom (liberty) but it made him very
anxious.

Another way to map a dream is to outline it. List the major
actions in your dream and write them on one side of a piece of
paper, or blackboard, divided into two wide columns. Then for
each major action ask yourself what feeling was associated with
it and write it down next to the action. Either the dreamer or the
interviewer can summarize by simply repeating the major
actions and linking them with their associated feelings. This
procedure helps the dreamer and interviewer keep in mind the
dramatic thrust or structure of the dream and sometimes en-
ables the dreamer to recognize parallel situations and feelings in
waking life. If we were to outline Cesare's dream we would list
the following actions:

1. Renata asks me to go to Paris with her in a small boat.
2. I tell her it would be dangerous to cross the Atlantic in that boat.
3. She understands my fear.
4. She gives me the *Sunday New York Times*.
5. She leaves.

Now we would ask Cesare to describe the major feeling associated with each action. Here's what we would record for each action:

1. I'm excited, but afraid.
2. I'm anxious and hope to dissuade her from the trip.
3. I'm grateful that she doesn't criticize my reluctance.
4. I'm surprised.
5. I'm sad, but I accept that she must go without me.

As you outline your dreams remember that your purpose is to highlight the main actions and feelings. To do this you must omit all the enticing details, which you will be able to explore when you begin the interview. The more concise you are at the outlining stage, the better sense you will have of the structure of the dream—especially when working with long, complex dreams.

Diagraming and outlining are optional, but they are especially useful in learning the method and in working with long dreams.

STEP 4. *Highlighting the feelings in the dream.*

By encouraging the dreamer to describe briefly the major feelings and moods in the dream, you will be underlining the importance of feelings and reminding her to attend to them. It may or may not be appropriate to ask the dreamer to bridge these feelings by asking if they remind her of any feelings in waking life. Sometimes the feelings in the dream are so unfamiliar or surprising to the dreamer that it is far better to wait until each feeling can be explored in depth in the context of the dream as the interview proceeds image by image. This step may not be necessary if you have incorporated it in a dream outline.

STEP 5.   *Eliciting a good description.*

The interviewer from another planet asks the dreamer to define and describe each of the major elements in the dream. These elements fall into five categories: settings, people, objects, feelings, and action. We have found certain specific and carefully phrased questions to be especially effective in eliciting rich, yet economical, descriptions for each dream element.

Some of these interview questions were used in Diana's interview, and in the next chapter you will find a list of the most commonly used questions that our students use as a guide in their early training. In the six chapters devoted to the specific dream elements, you will find more questions to use as you develop your interviewing skills.

In most cases it is better not to try to help the dreamer find words to describe her images. An impatient or overly eager interviewer who suggests words to describe the dreamer's images risks aborting the important process of discovery, which requires the dreamer to reflect on and recognize certain thoughts and feelings in order to find the words to describe them. Finding the right words to describe a dream image or feeling gives the dreamer the opportunity to acknowledge, clarify, and express attitudes, opinions, thoughts, and feelings that she might not have been quite aware of before. The dramatically powerful effects of using waking language to describe dream language is often underestimated by those who suggest that dream imagery is distorted by verbal descriptions and that the feelings and images of dreams should not be reduced to words. Yet it is in looking for the right descriptive words that the dreamer forces herself to ask, "Just how *do* I feel and think about this?" In searching for the right words she must closely examine what she is trying to describe. This discovery process is exciting to most dreamers and it has taught more than a few how to think, feel, and express themselves more clearly. So beneficial is this discovery process, precipitated by seeking descriptions for someone from another planet, that many of our students who are psychotherapists use it in their general nondream-related therapy work.

By using these questions—asking the dreamer to describe, and in some cases define, the image as it appears in the dream and as the dreamer knows it in waking life—the interviewer avoids encouraging an avalanche of overwhelming, and often tangential, free associations. The dreamer is reminded that she need not worry about being accurate or fair in her descriptions of the thing as it exists in waking life, only that she give a concrete description that portrays how she *thinks* and *feels* about it. For example, if the dreamer tells of a dream in which she is shot in her gallbladder, she would be asked to define and describe the functions of that organ. She should be reassured that she need not give an accurate medical-school description, just a summary of what she happens to know about gallbladders.

When a dreamer is asked to describe her waking and dreaming images of people of a particular nationality, race, or profession, she is encouraged to give frank rather than polite descriptions. In fact, a description must be considered inadequate until the dreamer reveals how she judges or values the place, person, object, feeling, or action she is describing. This approach to eliciting good descriptions is somewhat different for each dream element.

Settings

A good description of the dream setting usually leads the dreamer to a bridge that reveals the metaphor showing the area of the dreamer's life the dream explores.

In Diana's dream, the first setting is vague. It is somewhere en route in her effort to seek advice. She feels panic and does not know where to turn. The emotional identity of the metaphoric bridge is self-evident: The dream is exploring her current panic about her financial needs. The second setting of the impressive office with its rich appointments, pulpit, and law books turns out to be very descriptive of Jeff and signals the importance of her seeing Jeff more clearly if she is to deal effectively with her financial and security concerns. If your dreamer tells you of a dream set in Paris, you won't learn much if you assume you share the same impressions of the place. If, however, you ask her what Paris is like and what sorts of people live there, you will both gain informative material for a bridge. This will show how the setting relates to the dreamer's life.

People

The dreamer describes each person in the dream as if to someone who comes from another planet and has never heard of the person before. Ask the basic "Who is X, and what is he like?" question even and especially if the character has appeared in a recent dream, is a famous public figure, or is the interviewer of the dreamer. Elicit a fresh, personal description that takes into account the feelings aroused by the context of the current dream and by the dreamer's current life situation. The particular words used by the dreamer are the best keys to the dream's meaning.

Diana's description of the first Edward helped her recognize the manipulative qualities of her husband, which she was underestimating and pretending would disappear in therapy. Her description of Mafia types helped her to face how dangerous a man her husband really was. By asking Diana simply to describe what Mafia types are *like* rather than asking her what Mafia men *mean* to her, we obtained a nondefensive, frank description that she could then look at and bridge. Had we asked what Mafia types mean to her, we would have been asking for an interpretation before she could appreciate what she thinks and feels about them and before she had found the descriptive words that would identify her own metaphor. We did want to know what Mafia men meant to her, but we knew from experience that phrasing the question that way would greatly reduce our chances of finding out.

Objects

Ask the dreamer to define and/or describe each object generically as well as to describe it specifically as it appears in the context of the dream. Again, avoid getting bogged down in voluminous associative material by keeping the dreamer focused on the thing itself. Postpone statements like "This reminds me of X, Y, or Z" until the bridging phrase, because after the dreamer has found a good description, she is much better able to be discriminating and specific in her associative bridging.

In describing the real Edward's maroon tweed coat, Diana said it was the sort worn by Mafia types. That description, which could be seen as a highly focused association, led quickly to one of the most important discoveries in the interview.

Feelings

Ask the dreamer to describe what she feels at various moments in the dream action. Invite her to say how she feels as she discusses the dream in the present interview.

In our interview with Diana, we did not ask these questions directly, because she was already so clearly distressed by her feelings about her waking situation and about the qualities of the Edwards in her dream that we decided to leave her feelings implicit rather than asking her to make them explicit. This unusual strategy worked, as we can see from her commentary on the interview.

Action

Ask the dreamer to describe and judge the major action in the dream. When Diana described the first Edward telling her of the unethical office policy he had set up, she saw more clearly some things about her husband and herself, who together had set up a similar office policy.

Eliciting good descriptions of the various elements in a dream takes discipline and practice. It is useful to remind yourself that you are here not to show what you know, but to find out what the dreamer knows. I am reminded of my favorite quote from the late existentialist psychologist Paul Stern: "What is needed more than anything else to understand the gesturing of the dream is an almost childlike, incorruptible simplicity which is not taken in by contrived complexities and is able to see, in the midst of them—the obvious. Such simplemindedness is, among clinicians, a very rare commodity."[2]

STEP 6. *Recapitulating the description.*

After eliciting a good description of one or more images, repeat verbatim, or in a condensed form, the description the dreamer has just provided. You may have to edit the description; you should include the relevant and emotionally charged definitions, descriptions, and associations but omit words that are redundant and less forceful or that seem to distract from the thrust of the overall description. With experience, you will learn to edit out repetitive, superfluous, or tangential detail skillfully, without impoverishing or distorting the description. It is important to use the dreamer's exact words in the recapitulation to take advantage of custom-tailored appropriateness of these words as potential triggers. This practice will also help you avoid putting your own words into the dreamer's mouth; protecting the dreamer from your own projections is one of your most important duties.

If the dreamer has just described a person she despises, and you suspect that the dream image may reflect an aspect of the dreamer's own personality or of that of someone she loves, you might consider omitting the most potentially offensive descriptive words in your first recapitulation. Let the dreamer get used to the idea. Be gentle. If the dreamer has downplayed the emotional charge in her description, sometimes it helps to recapitulate using her words, but adding emphasis with your voice that will amplify the emotion. The risk in adding your own emphasis rather than simply mirroring the dreamer's emphasis is, of course, that you may insinuate your own prejudice or projection, which might be inappropriate and distract the dreamer. If you recognize when you are amplifying or emphasizing certain aspects of the description, you will be able to watch your dreamer carefully for signs that you are intruding rather than assisting. When in doubt, ask the dreamer if the recapitulation feels accurate in spirit.

You may want to recapitulate after each description, or you may find it more effective to string together several descriptions depending on their nature, the openness of the dreamer, and your sense of timing. For example, we asked Diana for five descriptions before our first recapitulation and bridge because the possible bridge from Edward the manipulator to her husband would probably be an uncomfortable one for her. It was important to gather plenty of supporting information before challenging her to make a potentially upsetting connection.

STEP 7. *Bridging to waking life.*

Only after the dreamer has given a good description of the dream feeling or image and has listened to a recapitulation of that description is she ready to be asked or to ask herself what it reminds her of in her waking life. As with recapitulation, the timing of a potentially difficult or threatening bridge question can make the difference between hastening or retarding a connection. Asking the dreamer to bridge her dream experience to some parallel waking experience is, in fact, asking her to identify the dream metaphor and note what new light it sheds on the relevant waking situation or attitude. The last bridge we asked Diana to make concerned her client Edward in the role of the real Edward whom she described as Mafia-like, who may exploit women and who "is too dangerous a man to deal with." When asked the bridging question, "Like anyone else in your life?" she reluctantly had to admit that her husband was "just like a mobster."

If a dreamer says that a dream image reminds her of X, ask the dreamer to tell you how the dream situation resembles one in waking life, if she does not spontaneously offer this information. We call this procedure, "unpacking the suitcase one carries over a bridge," or "unpacking" for short. It can be initiated by the simple question "How so?" Unpacking gives both parties to the interview the chance to see if the image really fits the waking situation in all its important characteristic features. Unpacking is a check against premature, inaccurate bridges that may be offered out of impatience, a need to please the interviewer, a need to be a bright dreamer quick at getting insight, or out of the dreamer's desire to assign the dream image to an old, not-very-challenging formulation of what is going on.

Now and again, an invitation to bridge is met by a blank stare. The dreamer will look disoriented and may be overwhelmed by too complex a bridge. Remember that the dreamer is usually reexperiencing the dream images as real things, not as metaphors. The dreamer is thinking concretely, thanks to your descriptive work, and now you are asking her to make a huge leap to metaphorical thinking. In these cases, step down the complexity of the bridge by being sure you are asking for only one bridge at a time, or back off entirely and come back to the bridge after further descriptions of this or other images. Courage! Frequently a dreamer will not be able to make any bridges until the eleventh hour, after most or all of the images have been described and recapitulated. Patience and a disciplined for-bearance from inserting your own interpretive bridges will maximize your dreamer's chances of arriving at an accurate understanding of the dream.

STEP 8.   *Summarizing the exploration.*

The summary is an important step in obtaining a true under-standing of the dream and its significance to waking life. There are two types of summary: full and partial.

Full Summaries

After all, or as many as possible, of the dream's images have been explored (described, recapitulated, and when possible, bridged), either the interviewer or the dreamer retells the dream, linking each image to its description and bridge (if one was made). The dreamer is then asked to say how she under-stands the dream so far and to indicate what parts remain un-clear. This allows both parties to see if the interpretive hypotheses created by the bridging are consistent with the dra-matic structure of the dream as a whole. If there is a part that doesn't fit, either the main hypothesis is inaccurate or the part needs further exploration.

In the real world of practical dream work, time is often short and the dreamer's defenses are sometimes very powerful. So it is frequently best to let the dreamer go home with her uncertain-ties in the hope that further reflection will clarify things. One can almost always work with the dream again at a later date rather than force it to fit together neatly. Because Diana's bridges seemed to be consistent, because she needed more time than we had to summarize them, and because she was dealing with a sensitive issue, we suggested that she write out her sum-mary at home.

Partial Summaries

Partial summaries, executed by either the interviewer or the dreamer partway through the interview, are extremely useful. After a series of descriptions, recapitulations, and bridges in one scene, you can say, "Let me (or why don't you) summarize the dream up to this point." To avoid a dulling repetitiveness and to keep up a lively tempo, partial summaries must be careful condensations of the salient features of the previous descriptions and bridges. As the pieces of the dream fall into place, later summaries can be more and more condensed.

Partial summaries are especially effective in leading up to a sensitive or difficult bridge because they help to reconfirm the descriptive facts and reanimate the feeling and action context of the dream that makes the bridging easier. I call this use of summary "priming the pump." In Diana's interview, I was using this technique when I said, "So the Edward you first see is not the helpful gentleman he at first seemed to be. The real Edward is a Mafia type who would do anything, lie, cheat, steal, or kill to get what he wants. Do these Edwards remind you of anything?" A partial summary after a difficult bridge has been accomplished helps to verify and reinforce the new insight.

Good summaries, full or partial, reinvolve the dreamer in the drama and assist in the correction and incorporation of new associations and insights. They give the dreamer time to digest the fruit of her varied explorations. Both the interviewer and the dreamer can use the summary to review the descriptions and connections made so far and to bring the dreamer up to speed for the next scene. Summaries also allow time to listen and make further connections; recall previously forgotten images, associations, and feelings; and to devise new questions.

If, while a dreamer is making her own summary, she strays

off track by drawing conclusions or bridges that reveal a high level of denial (such as offering esoteric, hackneyed, or irrelevant bridges and conclusions), you can gently interrupt and ask, "What led you to that conclusion?" or "How do you see that?" By doing this you call for an unpacking and can look together at the process behind the summary.

STEP 9. *Reflecting on the dream and the dream interview.*

The most important work the dreamer will do with a dream is in the week following a successful interpretation. Insights flow copiously from this sort of dream work, but as most therapists know, insights are soon overwhelmed by old habits of thought and feeling unless they are deepened and reinforced by reflection and review. I encourage my students to reread their dreams at least twice in the week following our interview. If the dreamer has tape-recorded the interview, I suggest listening to it once and, if possible, transcribing it. These exercises give the dreamer the opportunity to correct and modify inaccurate bridges and interpretive hypotheses, to complete and elaborate incomplete bridges, and to appreciate more fully and enlarge the significance of accurate bridges and interpretations.

For dreamers receptive to additional homework, we discuss which dream images would be the best to hold in mind during the days following the interview. We often choose the most positive and the most troublesome images. For example, if the heroine in the dream were the dreamer's friend Edith—whom the dreamer described as an especially courageous, cheerful, and uncomplaining woman who survived adversity without growing bitter—I would say, "During the week, in private moments, or in interactions with others, pretend that you are Edith. See how it feels; imagine how she would react to your life." In Diana's dream, the most dangerous figure was the real Edward, the Mafia type. For several weeks we encouraged Diana to keep in mind how she felt in the dream and to consider that image of her husband, Jeff, daily—especially when she started thinking about Jeff as a sweet, abandoned boy who could change his con-man ways with some psychotherapy and a lot of tender loving care from her.

By imagining (where appropriate, pretending) to be a dream character whom the dreamer has bridged to an aspect of herself, the dreamer has an opportunity to become familiar with these characteristics, to recognize the possibilities for developing the character's desirable qualities, and to recognize and modify the destructive traits and behaviors portrayed by the figure.

In cases where the images targeted for reflection were bridged not to the dreamer, but to someone in her current life, as in Diana's case, the dreamer is encouraged to keep in mind the dream's view of that person and check to see if it is an accurate (even if incomplete) one that describes qualities she would do well not to ignore.

Another example is a target image of a frightened rabbit that reminded the dreamer of a habit of thought learned from a parent. She bridged this image to her mother's fearful world view. This dreamer was encouraged to try for one week to keep a lookout for every time she hears herself thinking or saying things that remind her of her mom's fearful attitudes. If she notes these occasions in her dream journal, she will see more quickly just how much of her mother's fearful world view she has internalized and made her own. This exercise of invoking dream images is the single most effective means I have found to ensure that dream work will make a meaningful and tangible difference in the dreamer's life.

Most people discover more richness and depth in reviewing their dream work and are much more likely to be able to incorporate insights into their waking lives as well as to consolidate their gains after serious and active dream reflection.

STEP 10. *Considering options for action.*

Many insights gained in a dream interview are too new, too threatening, or too general to call for a specific action or decision to be made. For these insights, review and reflection are the most appropriate and fruitful responses. However, there are often strong and clear insights reinforced by other dream work, by the dreamer's life experience, or by material the dreamer may be working with in other growth settings, such as therapy or special interest support groups. These insights call for action. At our dream center, in my private office, and in academic settings, I teach interviewers never to tell a dreamer what to do about a particular situation. But I do discourage the hoarding of insights for storage purposes. Some dreamers, in and out of therapy, use their dream insights the way Scrooge used money before his dream of the spirits of Christmas. They store their insights, proud of their good work, but their lives are never enriched because the insights are never applied. Their lives remain constricted, and their dream insights continue to repeat themselves because the dreamers stay in the same old ruts.

Therefore, when a dreamer's insights seem sound and ready for application, the interviewer may ask her if she would like to do something about the insight, and if so, what, how, and when. The dreamer is encouraged to take small rather than large steps at first so that the change will be easier to accomplish and so that if her decision is not an appropriate one, it can be corrected. Testing insights gives the dreamer reassurance that she is doing well and gives her the confidence to carry on.

THE THEORETICAL MODEL OF THE METHOD

Now that you have seen how the dream interview method works in practice and are familiar with its basic procedures, we can take a brief look at its theoretical underpinnings. As in learning how to serve a tennis ball, it usually works best to see a demonstration and hear a description of the basic technique before you study the physics behind the action.

In developing the dream interview method, I have tried to keep my theoretical assumptions to a minimum. In my opinion there is not yet sufficient evidence nor are there sufficiently convincing arguments to answer the following questions:

- ▣ Where do dreams come from?
- ▣ Why do we dream?
- ▣ Why don't we dream in plain English?
- ▣ What part does the mind play and what part the brain in creating the dreams we remember? How much of dreaming is psychological and how much is physiological?

For enlightening discussions on the best research and arguments regarding these issues, I refer you to the works of Ramon Greenberg and Chester Pearlman, J. Allan Hobson, Harry Fiss, Milton Kramer, Rosalind Cartwright, and others that you will find listed in the resources. Strictly speaking, we have yet to develop scientific procedures sensitive enough to issues of meaning and feeling that are capable of proving or disproving that a dream has a message, that it intends to mean something, or even if the metaphor in a dream is inherent to it or projected into it. We still don't know why or how dreams are made into picture stories, and we don't know exactly where (the unconscious? God? nervous discharges?) the images come from. What most practitioners *do* say is that when the dreamer sees and grasps a metaphor in a dream, she usually understands more clearly a basic truth about herself or her relationships or about a problem she has been trying to solve. I will not enter what would be a lengthy review of the arguments here because I want to make a point: One does not need to decide these matters to take advantage of the insights and creative ideas provided by a careful exploration of a dream, however that dream is created and for however many purposes. My focus is neither to find the cause of a dream nor to decide its purpose. Rather, I ask my dreamers, "To what uses can you put the insights you have gained by noting the metaphors between your dream and your waking life?"

An assumption can open up possibilities for good work, or it can close them off. I have abandoned a number of assumptions (which are often presented as facts) because they close more doors than they open and because they have not been validated in my seventeen years of working with the dreams of healthy people. I have rejected the following assumptions:

▣ *Most dreams are nonsense.* There is significant research that demonstrates that dreams reflect our waking concerns and are helpful in coping with conflict, solving problems, and in generating new ideas. Almost anyone who works at understanding dreams as metaphors for even a few weeks will not fail to recognize the meaningfulness of at least some dreams.

▣ *Most dreams are the expressions of unconscious wishes.* Dreams show us in metaphorical form the dynamics of our important relationships, how we honestly feel and think about things, and about ourselves. They help us see our hopes, fears, talents, weaknesses, and heaven knows what else. While some dreams express wishes of which we are mostly unaware while awake, others express very conscious wishes as when a hungry dieter dreams of dining at a sumptuous banquet.

▣ *Dreams speak in a language meant to camouflage the truth.* Dreams certainly don't speak our waking language, but to say that their natural language of visual imagery is a camouflage is like saying the Chinese speak Chinese to keep secrets from the rest of us. If we want to understand what the Chinese are saying, we have to learn their language. Individuals seem to dream more direct or transparent dreams at times of emotional openness or in times of emotional emergency and to dream more obscure dreams when they are generally more defensive or when dealing with issues that are new or unfamiliar to them. I would rather describe this as a readiness for or resistance to straightforward dreaming, rather than suggest that the language of the dream is a disguise.

☐ *The male and female psyches are fundamentally different; therefore, the dreams of men and women must be interpreted differently.* Throughout history, the differences between men and women have been vastly exaggerated and often fabricated. It will be many generations, if ever, before we can separate the effects of our social training from any inherent psychological differences between men and women. In the meantime why not leave each person free from premature categorization? Too many dreams are inadequately explored and badly interpreted because the interpreter jumps to conclusions about certain images. These conclusions are often based on severely biased opinions about the natures of the male and female psyches.

☐ *Intuition plays a large part in good interpretation.* If you have carefully elicited the relevant information from the dreamer, you should be able to point to the very responses that led you to form a given interpretive hypothesis or that led you to ask the question that unlocked the meaning of the dream. What analysts Erika Fromm and Thomas French call an "act of intuitive imagination" in their interpretive work is usually a guess based on theoretical presuppositions, common sense, and experience.[3] *Intuition* is a word often misused as a long, dark cloak to hide a multitude of sins. The sins usually have to do with the interpreter's imposing her own preconceptions, associations, and personal projections. Beware the interpreter who depends on her "intuition"! A well-trained dream interviewer explores and assesses the elements of the dream with the dreamer's associations and bridges, then makes certain deductions from this information, which she uses to formulate further questions and hypotheses. The questions are based on theoretical hypotheses concerning the nature of dreaming (which we shall discuss presently), on the facts or information from the dream interview, and on an appreciation of the dramatic structure of the dream. It is through acts of critical judgment, not intuition, that the interviewer chooses her questions and forms interpretive hypotheses. It is impossible for an interviewer to have no presuppositions but it is important for the interviewer to recognize exactly what presuppositions she does have.

□ *There can be many good, divergent interpretations of the same dream.* When the interviewer accepts that many conflicting interpretations are true, or that interpretations that depart from each other in confusing ways are all true, she has usually failed to explore the dream adequately and to verify that the interpretations are consistent with the dramatic structure of the dream. There may be many levels of meaning in a dream and many ramifications of an interpretation, but they all will follow the general thrust and dramatic structure of the dream.

I have found the following theoretical hypotheses or assumptions to be helpful in conducting dream interviews that yield insights and creative ideas.

□ *Most dreams easily yield metaphorical expressions of feelings, thoughts, and ideas that, when understood, can help the dreamer to adapt to changes in life and to recognize, assess, and solve personal and professional problems.* It seems that, at least to some degree, some dreams have these effects without being understood or even recalled. However, in most cases, the dreamer must arrive at a conscious understanding of the meaning of the dream, of how it relates to waking life if it is to have any significant impact. Researchers Louis Breger, Ian Hunter, and Ron Lane studied the impact of dream work with people in highly stressful circumstances, and wrote,

Without work directed at integrating the dreams—at breaking down the dissociations that are present both in the dreaming and the reporting—the subjects do not learn anything about themselves. Just as one must work hard in the real world to transform a creative inspiration into a poem, a painting, or a piece of music or literature, so one must work hard at making individual sense of one's dreams if they are to be more than fleeting, uninformative glimpses of what is within.[4]

☐ *Dreams seem to have a point, and metaphorical reflections on dreams offer new or unappreciated pieces of information that can be grasped and used for the benefit of the dreamer.* Dreams rarely seem to present old news. We consider an interview incomplete if it has not uncovered new information or a new understanding of familiar issues.[5] Carl Jung takes this position,[6] but Medard Boss and others do not, saying that we cannot prove any intent on the part of the dream or on the part of the dreaming person. I would suggest that a careful reading of the dream yields to the waking dreamer metaphors that shed new light on her life concerns. Whether or not the dream intends this is of secondary importance.

While Boss describes the dreaming mode of existence as more dimmed and restricted than waking, which is more open and capable of abstraction and conceptualization, I consider dreaming a highly focused state of awareness. The intense focus of dreaming allows the dreamer to experience things vividly and often with intense feelings that are usually warded off while she is awake. Dream focusing carries with it a narrowing of attention, but not, in my opinion, a dimming or impoverishment of experience relative to waking. The ability to take a close look at something in a dream can be a highly enriching experience in itself. If the waking dreamer then employs her conceptual powers of abstraction to make bridges or metaphors from dreaming to waking, the concrete world of the dream becomes a valuable resource for insight and creativity.

◨ *The dreamer, on awaking, has all the information she needs to understand the dream although some may be out of her immediate awareness.* If the dreamer lacks the skills to tap this information, she will need to learn them or ask the assistance of an interviewer. Freud, Jung, Mary Ann Mattoon, and other contemporary dream workers not only make interpretations based on systems of thought external to the dream, but feel justified in explaining the whole or parts of the dream to the dreamer. Freud insisted that symbolic substitution was a necessary, if auxiliary, method to be used with free association.

Jung and many of his followers claim that the interpreter must be well versed in mythology, the history of religion, and alchemy among other things to properly amplify certain dream images and help the dreamer see her deeper meanings. This can easily lead to the analyst's usurping the private experience of the dream and its meaning all in the name of broadening its scope to the universal, archetypal level. All too often, such hijackings of the dreamer's attention by references to mythological, religious, or psychological systems of belief render impossible the recognition of the dream itself and its highly personal, highly relevant connection to the individual dreamer.

Minilectures to the dreamer about myths, or about how the male or female psyches work can mislead the dreamer and usually distract her from an immediate experience of her unique dream. More importantly, as Boss points out, a dependence on external explanations often seduces the dreamer to "take refuge from the personal and the concrete, in something distant and alien which does not oblige the patient in any way to become more responsible for the concrete ways of living his day-to-day life."[7] The interpreter, feeling pressure to solve the dream puzzle, is often tempted

to take refuge from her own anxiety in a prefabricated formulation of the dreamer's experience. I do not believe that
adding to the dreamer's associations the truths of explana-
tory systems contributes anything to the immediacy or
depth of the dreamer's appreciation of the dream. Quite the
contrary. Erik Erikson, in warning his fellow psychoanalysts against too hurriedly dismissing the manifest dream in
favor of attending to what they thought might be hidden
behind it, said, "So many in . . . [this] field mistake attention
to surface for superficiality, a concern with form for lack of
depth."[8]

If one learns to ask effective questions rather than give
interpretations,

> both the nature of the dream and its therapeutic mes-
> sage will emerge, contrary to the Jungian viewpoint,
> without any support from mythology or folklore,
> without any knowledge of primitive psychology or
> comparative religion, without any aid at all from psy-
> chology. In fact, no doctrine of the psyche is required.[9]

References to archetypal situations, and to mythological
character types can indeed be skillfully employed by therapists
in their work with patients, and it is always fascinating reading
for academics and laypeople. I would simply ask that these references be kept out of the interview while one is trying to help a
dreamer understand her own dream.

While the dream interviewer cannot work without any assumptions, the ones she does work from, as outlined here, seem
to me rather reasonable and modest. They require much smaller
leaps of faith than do the assumptions of some other schools of
dream interpretation.

■

**CHAPTER
THREE**

KNOWING WHAT
TO ASK AND
WHEN TO ASK IT

The most important thing to remember when you are playing the role of interviewer is to pretend that you come from another planet and ask the dreamer questions from that perspective. Since the early 1970s I have been experimenting with various ways of phrasing a number of basic questions that are effective in eliciting from the dreamer the information necessary to understand a dream. Through the years I have revised a list of these questions several times.[1] We call this list a *cue card* because students use it as a guide to asking their interview questions. Obviously, it is impossible to list all the questions you will need to explore every dream image, but this cue card will supply you with enough questions to give you a good start as an interviewer. Using these questions exactly as they are worded will give you a feel for ways to formulate your own follow-up questions when you need them. In later chapters you will find more questions aimed at specific images and situations that will add to your interviewing skills once you have mastered the basic cue-card questions.

THE DREAM INTERVIEWER'S CUE CARD

1. *Would you tell us your dream now?*

Highlight Feelings

2. *What are the feelings you are most aware of in the dream?*

3.   *Have you felt this way* (recapitulate the feelings) *in your past or your current life?* Sometimes, especially when interviewing people who are too quick to interpret their dreams before having carefully explored the images, it is better to omit these last two questions and wait to explore the feelings as they arise in the unfolding of the dream. All we need at this point is a highlighting of the dream feelings and an indication of whether the dreamer is aware of having experienced these exact feelings in waking life. Even if the dreamer is unable to recognize any parallel at this early stage, the questions will signal him to keep a look out as he proceeds. If the dreamer says that the dream feelings are familiar, ask him:

4.   *When? or When was the first or most recent time you felt this way?* If the dreamer does not volunteer this information spontaneously, asking him to be specific will serve at least four functions. You will both be able to see if the remembered occasion really fits the description of the dream feeling. The dreamer will become more familiar with the feeling and better able to recognize the times it has recurred in his life. You will both be better able to spot the patterns of situations that give rise to the feeling. And the dreamer will grow more comfortable discussing his feelings with you.

Settings: Descriptions and Bridges

5.   *Describe the opening (or next) setting of the dream.* What sort of place is Chicago, a ballroom, a school playground, a basement, your Aunt Tillie's house, etc?

6.   *What is this place like in waking life?*

7.   *What is this place like in your dream?* The way a dream modifies a setting provides clues to the particular qualities of the setting that are highlighted in the dream. For example, if the dreamer says, "I was in a prison, but now that you ask, it didn't look like a normal prison, it looked like my Uncle Willy's house," you need to get a description that blends both places. The dream prison then might be described as "a place that holds you captive in punishment for wrongdoing that looks like Uncle Willy's place where I was dumped by my parents every summer."

This description would perhaps lead the dreamer to consider if his feelings of being dumped included a sense of being put into prison for his wrongdoing. You could explore such possibilities by asking the following questions.

8.   *How does it feel to be in this setting? or How do you feel as you stand (or sit) there?* Questions like these will elicit the feeling or value judgment side of a description. You could also ask, "Do you like such places?" or "How would you like to be in such a place in waking life and why?"

9.   *Does this* (recapitulate the description) *remind you of anything in your waking life?* See where the dreamer goes with this question, then if appropriate you can ask whether it reminds him of anything in his past or current life. Be careful throughout the interview not to focus too much on the past. This can devour all your time and energy. Use past examples sparingly to warm up to looking at the present manifestation of the issue and considering its possible genesis. Remember to use only the dreamer's words in the recapitulation. Get a good description and a bridge (if possible) for each setting as it appears in the dream.

People and Animals: Descriptions and Bridges

10.   *Who is X?* Ask the dreamer to tell you who each character in the dream is as he makes his appearance. Remind the dreamer that you come from another planet and have never heard of John Wayne, Maya Angelou, Walt Whitman, the dreamer's sister, or little green men before. If you say, "Tell me about X," the dreamer who is not accustomed to this method may go on and on with unfocused and redundant anecdotes. If you ask, "What does X mean to you?" you will likely get a puzzled look from the dreamer and perhaps a premature and inaccurate interpretation. How can the dreamer really know what X means to him before he looks at what he feels and thinks about X as portrayed in the dream? Keep this response brief and move quickly to the next question.

11.   *What is X like in waking life (or in general)?* This question usually elicits the heart of the description in which the dreamer tells you how he thinks and feels about X. Other ways to phrase this question are "What kind of person is X?" and "What kind of personality does X have?" The dreamer will usually supply a few associations automatically as a part of the description. Encourage the dreamer to give you his impressions of X's personality in waking life and not to worry about being accurate or fair and objective. Ask questions that pull for the dreamer's gut feelings and opinions about X, such as "How do you really feel about X?" "Do you like him, dislike him?" "What are his most salient characteristics?" and "How do you feel about these?" In eliciting descriptions of animals, you will find that most of the questions one asks about people will do the job well. Asking the dreamer "What is the personality of an elephant (or cat or crocodile or cocker spaniel)?" yields terse, extremely useful, and often amusing descriptions.

Some dreamers will describe X in terms of what he does, times they've had together, and with statements like "He's the sort of guy who . . ." Descriptions of X's behavior, history, and physical appearance can be helpful in reconnecting the dreamer with his image of X. However, they can quickly reach the point of diminishing returns and eat up precious time while they threaten to overload both of you and distract you from the dramatic thrust of the dream.

It is extremely important to help the dreamer distill these descriptions into descriptive *adjectives,* which are much easier to handle and often bring more clarity. Asking the dreamer to give you three adjectives that describe a person who does such things, has such a history, or looks the way X does in the dream can help you get to the point and elicit a description that will more likely trigger a successful bridge later.

12.   *What is X like in your dream? What is X doing in your dream?* By moving from the general to the particular, you can find out what specific aspects of X are emphasized in a given dream scene. If X is a major figure in the dreamer's life, such as his mother or father, the qualities of X highlighted in the dream can be used to narrow the focus of what could become an interminable description, i.e., "Tell me about the part of your mom that is like the part of her portrayed in the dream." If X is a person or type of person unknown to the dreamer, ask, "What kind of a person would you imagine X might be like, given how he looks and acts in the dream?"

13.   *Does X, whom you describe as* (recapitulate the description) *remind you of anything in your waking life?* By recapitulating the dreamer's description using the same adjectives and tone, you will often elicit a bridge that links the description to someone, to a force in his life, or to an aspect of himself. By asking the dreamer if X reminds him of any*thing,* you leave him free to relate the image to some part of himself (the subjective level of interpretation) or to someone or something in his life (the objective level). Allowing the dreamer to choose the interpretive level diminishes the interviewer's possible distorting influence. If the dreamer seems to be avoiding a probable subjective interpretation by rushing to the objective level, you can always ask more pointed questions later. If X does not remind the dreamer of anything at this point, you can move on to the next image or you can ask the more direct question that follows.

14.   *Does X, who is* (recapitulate the description), *remind you of anyone in your life, or is there some part of you that is like X?* By moving from asking if X reminds the dreamer of any*thing* to asking if X reminds him of any*one* or of any part of himself, you are being more direct and challenging. You may encounter strong resistance with this bridging question, especially if the dreamer has just described someone he dislikes strongly. While you may see some of X's characteristics in the dreamer, or in someone close to the dreamer, don't volunteer this. Continue to help the dreamer further describe and bridge until he can see the connection for himself. Timing is all-important. An offended dreamer won't talk much. You can always return to this (or any other) question later when the time seems right.

15. *How so?* When a dreamer bridges an image and says something like "Now that I hear you feed back that description, X reminds me of my first wife (or my boss, or of the way I act when . . .)," it is important to ask the dreamer to "unpack" or explain his connection. Some dreamers need to take a moment to clarify and deepen the new perception, while others—on closer inspection—find that the similarities don't really match. Perhaps they were trying too hard to make something fit that just was not right. The dreamer's need to please can sometimes mislead both himself and the interviewer. In many instances, unpacking leads to more questions. For example, "You say X reminds you of your boss. Does X remind you of anyone else who is also (recapitulate the description once more)?" Not uncommonly, the dreamer for the first time sees similarities not only with his boss but also with his father and older brother. This question highlights important emotional and behavioral patterns.

Objects: Descriptions and Bridges

16. *What is a Y?* Ask the dreamer to define and describe each of the major objects in the dream and tell you what it is used for and how it works. Remind him that you come from another planet and have never even heard of a Y. Reassure the dreamer that you are interested not in scientific accuracy but in his ideas or understanding of what a Y is and how it functions. Again, if you ask, "What does a Y *mean* to you?" you usually get a premature interpretation—try to get a definition and a description first. Ask questions that elicit whatever value judgments the dreamer has about a Y: "Do you like Y's?" "Do you own, eat, wear, enjoy, or hate Y's?" "Why or why not?" "What kinds of people tend to own, eat, wear, etc. a Y?"

17. *What is the Y in your dream like?* This question moves from the general, or generic, to the specific. When the dreamer describes his dream objects he may also add some associations that you may want to explore further. With experience you will get a feeling for which trains of association are likely to be productive and which are likely to distract from the dream action and take up time. If the dream Y is oddly different from the generic Y, ask questions that clarify the differences then ask questions like, "How would a Y like the one in your dream look or function differently from a normal Y?" For example, if someone dreamt of a short basketball player with four hands, you would ask "How would a short, four-handed basketball player be different from a normal one?" Your dreamer might then surprise himself by saying, "Well, he would be at an obvious height disadvantage, but he might be able to make up for it with the extra hands. Which makes me think that I often put myself down for being short, but my girlfriend says that I am attractive to her especially because of the way I use my hands when we make love!"

Be sure to find out how the dreamer really feels about Y's in general and about the Y in the dream. If the dreamer is not forthcoming, coax him with questions like "Do you like or dislike Y's?" "Do you think Y's are wonderful, silly, necessary, or creepy?" As soon as possible, cease suggesting words and use those the dreamer supplies—they are the best.

18. *Does the Y in your dream, which you describe as* (recapitulate the description), *remind you of anything in your waking life?* As when bridging from people in dreams to waking life, it may be necessary, or desirable, to follow this question with others like

"Does the Y, which is (recapitulate again), remind you of anyone or of any part of yourself?"

19. *How so?* As with any image the dreamer has bridged, asking the dreamer to clarify and confirm by "unpacking" the perception is vital.

Feelings: Descriptions and Bridges

20. *How do you feel at this moment in the dream?* This question can be asked at any point in the interview. I especially like to ask it right at the end of the first telling of the dream, while the dreamer has been brought by the story to the last moment. Frequently the dreamer fails to reveal spontaneously how he feels when, for example, at the very last moment in the dream, the ferocious lion is shot in the chest with a bullet. The dreamer could feel relief, gratitude to the gunman, or dismay and unexpected sadness. We must know which he feels, and so must he. It is good to ask how the dreamer feels at any point there is reason to suspect the existence of unexpressed or unappreciated feeling in the dream.

21. *Tell me more about this feeling.*

22. *Tell me about a time (or the last time) you felt this way.* These last two invitations are useful when the dreamer is reticent or having trouble recognizing and exploring feelings.

23. *Does this feeling of* (recapitulate the description) *remind you of anything in your current life?* By now the dreamer should be familiar with the feeling and may have already bridged it to a waking situation.

Action: Descriptions and Bridges

24. *Describe the major action or event in this scene.* This is where the people and objects find their dramatic context and bridging efforts that may have failed earlier may suddenly succeed. To make this happen, ask the dreamer simpleminded questions. If he has just told you that he was hiking in the Alps wearing his bedroom slippers, ask, "Are bedroom slippers what humans usually wear while hiking in the Alps?" Then ask him why or why not. You can recapitulate these answers by themselves, or you can recapitulate them as part of the following bridge question.

25. *Does this action* (recapitulate the description) *remind you of any situation in your life?* For example, "Is there anywhere in your life where you are hiking in an extraordinarily challenging environment with only your slippers that leave your feet unprotected and vulnerable to frostbite and other hazards?" The dreamer might respond, "It reminds me of my new job environment." Then you would ask the dreamer to unpack the bridge with the following question.

26. *How so?* The dreamer might then describe more fully how the partners in his new law firm are a bunch of sharks, and he has been acting as if he were associated with a group of benevolent mentors. As he continues noting other parallels, he may come to think that his behavior is not appropriate in his current work environment.

27. *How would you describe the central plot of this dream?*

28. *Does this plot* (recapitulate the description) *remind you of anything?*

Summary

29. *Shall I summarize all the descriptions and bridges made so far, or would you like to do it?* Either the dreamer or, more often, the interviewer strings together the descriptions and bridges in the sequential context of the dream action. This can be done at the end of the dream interview, or as you go along scene by scene. Ask the dreamer to correct you if your recapitulation doesn't sound just right. Sometimes the dreamer suddenly has more to say on an image in this phase of the interview.

30. *So in this part of the dream* (this happened), *which you described as . . . , which reminded you of* (bridge). *Then* (this happened) *etc. Does all this remind you of anything else?* Take your time in this phase. Even when the metaphor or analogy is obvious to you, it is important to resist the temptation to provide the dreamer with the interpretation. These last two steps are more difficult than the preceding ones, because they require discipline and practice in accurately summarizing a whole scene or the entire dream interview without slipping in your own ideas.

31. *Now, how do you understand your dream? Tell me the whole dream, adding the bridges and commenting on what you understand and what remains unclear.* Remember to leave interpretations to the dreamer. The interviewer's job is to ask questions that will clarify or point out inconsistencies. In cases when the dreamer is unable to make important connections, suggesting possible hypotheses regarding possible bridges may be helpful. However, this step is fraught with danger and should be used only as a last resort. Leaving the dreamer to puzzle out how it all comes together can yield better results, depending on the dreamer and the situation. Be alert during this summary phase to anything new or any deference of detail. This may be significant and require reexploration.

Let's take a look now at the use of these questions in another interview with Diana. Like those of us in her dream study class, you may have wondered just how a psychotherapist fell for the con man, Jeff, who swindled her out of $40,000. Well, Diana looked back in her dream journal and found two telling dreams. Here is one that she dreamt one month after meeting Jeff and two weeks before marrying him:

I am climbing. A woman is close beside me, exuberant but inattentive. She makes me gasp at her foolishness. My "appropriate fear" keeps me holding tight, climbing slowly. She falls. What could I have done to prevent it? Nothing. There is a gathering around her by the time I get down. Ron is taking charge. He makes a bed for her. His wife, Jill, is in the house, somewhat depressed after the arrival of their new baby. She is slim and gorgeous looking. A boredom seems to possess her. She flips listlessly through a magazine. Ron takes over the care of the baby. Although he is gentle and supportive, he is unable to reach or move her. He even prepares dinner. Except for Jill, we all help with dinner. Her eyes are pale blue and a weak smile is the most excitement or emotion anyone gets out of her.

After supper, we clean up. I go out to the car to find the injured woman beside her car offering to drive us to the movies in it. Ron insists he drive her car for her. The three of us pile into the car. She and I start speaking in French about the movie we are to see while we wait for Jill to get the baby bundled up. Then she, Mark, and Milly get into the car, too. Ron is surprised at the depth of our discussion, and soon, with great liveliness, he joins in. **(EXUBERANT FOOLISH WOMAN)**

INTERVIEWER. What is this exuberant, foolish woman like?

DIANA. Well, what comes to mind is . . . moving too fast. As I reviewed all the dreams I recorded from the time I met Jeff, looking to see if my dreams had offered me any warning signals that I missed, I said, "Damn, here it is." Here is the foolish, reckless youth who doesn't pay attention to her safety, and goes over the edge.

I. Does the way this exuberant, foolish woman was acting remind you of how you were acting at the time of the dream?

D. With Jeff. I was planning to marry this guy after having known him for only one month. It was a foolish, reckless, and speedy movement that was not comfortable to me, but I kept doing it.

I. Does this foolish movement remind you of anything else?

D. Yes. Of the relationship I had with a younger man. I was reckless in that one, too. I moved too fast.

I. What was your "reasonable fear" in the dream like? Was it reasonable?

D. Yes. There's a huge part of me that feels that when people go slowly or cautiously, they are wimps. It's a sign of weakness rather than of wisdom. So there's always been a dichotomy between the daredevil and the wise, cautious person in me.

I. I'm still confused. In the dream, were you being wisely cautious or were you being a cautious wimp?

D. I was being wisely cautious. But in my waking life I was acting more like the reckless woman.

I. In the dream, you say you could have done nothing to prevent her fall?

D. I don't think she would have listened. She was on a determined course. And that was true of me. My sister and my aunt both had expressed some trepidations about this man and I just . . .

I. Who is Ron, the one who has made the bed for the woman who has fallen?

D. Ron is the husband of my friend Jill.

I. What is Ron like?

D. Ron is . . . how shall I describe him? I've always thought he was a wimp. He's a feminine man. He's quite wealthy. He is a man who would cook or take over caring for the baby. I mean, he is kind of attentive, and he takes full responsibility for things. He wouldn't be someone who would do something dangerous. He's cautious, contemplative, slow.

I. Does he remind you of anything or anyone?

D. No.

I. In the dream, Ron takes on the responsibility of making a bed for the woman who has fallen. How do you feel about that?

D. I appreciate it.

I. What is Jill like in waking life?

D. She doesn't work. She is always searching for the thing that is going to give her some liveliness. She's not so much the mannequin as she plays in the dream, but yes, I would say that she's someone who hasn't found her place in the world.

I. Jill looks gorgeous, but . . . ?

D. Jill is . . . maybe this has something to do with what I see as the role I would get into as a wife. The mannequin woman who has the finely done nails. Soon after childbirth she has her body back, she is skinny, has her hair done. Yet there is no quality of life or loving about her. She's bored, she's listless . . .

I. Tell me again what Ron is like.

D. I think of feminine men and me. I rejected the feminine qualities of my father. I wanted him to be a macho man, out in the world and successful. He wasn't. My mother was. So Ron, like feminine men and like my dad, is nurturing and responsible, not just an aggressor, a doer in the world. My boyfriends have always been, at least on the surface, aggressive doers.

I. Does the family scene with Ron and Jill remind you of anything?

D. Again, I'm always afraid that I'll turn into the woman at home. I would lose my spark and wouldn't have anything interesting about me. I'd be doing my nails and keeping my body thin! That is my image of married life.

I. So does the scene of the mannequin wife and the wealthy, nurturing husband bring anything else to mind?

D. Well, at the time of the dream, I thought Jeff was this big, successful millionaire with whom I could settle down and have children. He was offering me that.

I. But Jeff wasn't like Ron was he? [Even though at this point in the interview, I suspect that Ron may be highlighting qualities of Jeff that Diana resists recognizing, I do not say it. Instead, by phrasing the question this way, I hope to encourage greater clarification.]

D. No. Although Jeff *had* offered that if I wanted to have the child I was pregnant with from my affair with the younger man, I could.

I. Not that Jeff would take care of it . . . ? [Again, I am baiting her. I take the position of her resistance and leave her free to correct me if she wishes.]

D. But in a way he would. He promised to support me if I decided to have the baby.

I. Tell me about Ron's making the bed for the woman who had fallen.

D. He did it so that she could be attended to and taken care of. They would fix her up and make sure that she would be okay.

I. Interesting.

D. The fallen woman is myself. I had the abortion and here comes Jeff into my life offering to make me a bed and heal me. I never ever wanted to have an abortion. What a horror it was to have gotten myself into that situation.

I. So the first part of the dream in which the girl falls reminds you of?

D. My reckless relationship with the younger man, my abortion, and my reckless tendencies.

I. And the family scene with Ron and Jill?

D. It reminds me of Jeff who will take care of my fallen, foolish self and of a lifeless future as a wife who does not work.

I. What happens next?

D. We're going to the movies. I speak in French with the injured woman about the movie we are to see.

I. What sort of language is French?

D. It's a romantic language. The language of my youth. It is culture. Ron is a very cultured man.

I. What does speaking this romantic cultured language remind you of?

D. It takes me back to my youth. To a time when I had a very good life. I lived at my French school. My family was wealthy then. It was a time when I had a lot of power, and there was excitement in my life.

I. What do you think about the wounded woman wanting to drive her own car?

D. She was acting stronger than she was.

I. Remind you of anything?

D. Yes, I definitely was wounded by this thing with the young guy, the baby, and all that. But I was not going to allow it to get me down. I was determined to charge full-speed ahead and get my life going again with Jeff.

I. Enter Ron again. He insists on driving. What is he like? Is he Ron the wimp, or Ron the cultured?

D. In this dream, there is no Ron the wimp. That's the way I used to think of Ron. I no longer thought of him as a wimp at the time of the dream.

I. Okay, he's Ron the what?

D. Well, he's the caretaker.

I. The caretaker. Is he dull, exciting, interesting?

D. He's dependable. He gets interesting . . . I mean interested.

I. The caretaker gets interested. Does that remind you of anyone?

D. Yes, I'd say so. When I went through the abortion, Jeff was pacing up and down. I had apparently passed out after the operation and was taking much longer to come out than expected. He had fantasies that I was dying.

I. Did Jeff get interested in the part of you that speaks French?

D. Yes. He loved it that I was well connected in the city and that I was cultured. At the time I thought he was very cultured; now I realize he was not.

I. Would you like to summarize the dream or would you like me to?

D. Would you? I'd like to hear all this together. I'll let you know if you go off course.

I. It seems that in the dream you are looking at some of the ways Jeff, like Ron, is (or seemed to be) a rich caretaker who has come to save you after the abortion and the pain involved with that. Perhaps also to save the reckless woman in you and give her a good life. [Diana nods in agreement, so I continue.]

There is, however, a fly in the ointment, and that's Jill. And you are not sure the life of a millionaire's wife would be all that great. At the end of the dream, Ron takes the wheel much as Jeff took on the organization of your life as he became attracted to your cultured, powerful, French-speaking self.

D. That about sums it up, doesn't it?

As you can see, by answering relatively nonleading questions, the dreamer can discover what her dream means for herself. It took a few rounds of questions to bridge Ron, but in the end the connection was clear. Diana was able to use the dream to look more closely at her recklessness, her desire for a wealthy caretaker, and her fears of becoming a listless millionaire's wife. She also had a glimpse of the effect her mother's and father's styles had on her choice in men.

The questions from the cue card were sometimes modified to fit the tone and rhythm of the interview. I find that maintaining a normal conversational/interview tone is very important in putting the dreamer at ease. The order of the questions can be varied to fit the structure of the dream and the particular interviewing strategy you are using.

BASIC DREAM INTERVIEW
STRATEGIES

If you have already experimented in conducting a dream interview with a dream partner, you will have noticed that keeping in mind the core steps of the interview (eliciting a good description, recapitulating, bridging, and summarizing) is not as easy as it may seem. The questions on the cue card help a great deal in the actual practice of the interview, yet as you can imagine— if you've not already discovered—dreamers' responses can be very surprising and at times rather confusing and disorienting. Then there is the problem of the especially loquacious, shy, or defensive dreamer whose responses don't appear to be particularly enlightening. Learning to cope successfully with these difficulties in interviewing other dreamers is the best possible training in learning to understand the dreams of one of the most challenging dreamers you will ever work with—yourself.

Following are several basic strategies that will help to facilitate your dream work. If you practice using these in conjunction with the cue-card questions, you will be able to take full advantage of the advanced strategies to be presented in a later chapter.

STRATEGY 1.   *Amplifying the feelings.* When the dreamer is not forthcoming about his feelings, opinions, or judgments in his descriptions of any dream element, you must get him to amplify what little he *can* express so that both of you can get a better picture of what is going on. Try to give the dreamer permission to exaggerate his feelings by asking him to do so, "for just a moment." Tell him you could imagine having strong feelings about such a thing. Tactfully tease a dreamer you think would respond well to words such as, "Come on, now. I'll bet you have some feelings about that." If a dreamer seems on the verge of tears thinking about a particular image or part of the dream but has no response to being asked what he is feeling, try asking something like, "What is the saddest part of this scene (or image)?" or "If your tears had words, what would they say?"

STRATEGY 2.   *Guessing the absurd or the opposite.* When a dreamer has trouble finding words to describe a dream image or action, it is sometimes helpful to make a guess that you are quite sure is wrong. When you suggest an absurdly silly or clearly inappropriate descriptive word, the dreamer is almost always jarred and responds with a quick and telling correction. This is an amusing and enjoyable strategy. For example, one of my clients just couldn't find much to say about turnips beyond describing them as a boring vegetable. I asked her if they were a favorite dessert among humans. She replied, "Good heavens, no! You only eat turnips if your mother forces them down your throat. They are disgustingly bland." Now the dream we had been discussing, in which one of her prospective employers offered her turnips, shed new light on certain turniplike aspects of this career opportunity. These qualities had been overshadowed by her desire to move up the career ladder even if the new position were not as exciting as she would like.

STRATEGY 3. *How is it different from . . . ?* When a dreamer can describe an image, but only vaguely, asking him how the Volvo he dreamt of differs from a Mazda or a Corvette will help him home in on the qualities he sees as unique to Volvos. Think what category of things, people, feelings, or action the dream falls into and ask how it is different from another thing, person, etc., in that category. If the image is a cat, ask how cats are different from dogs. If the image is polo, ask how polo is different from soccer, horse racing, or football.

STRATEGY 4. *Unpacking.* We have already mentioned this strategy because it is difficult to conduct an interview without employing it. When a dreamer makes a bridge, asking why that dream image reminds the dreamer of this or that in his life is extremely helpful. The dreamer's explanation will allow both of you to verify, modify, or disqualify the bridge.

STRATEGY 5. *Corralling the dreamer.* When your dreamer becomes loquacious or tangential in his descriptions, you can help him refocus his energies, return to relevant material, and keep on track by saying something like "Let me bring you back to the dream." You may have to interrupt some dreamers with a line like the above or risk wasting much time and losing your way in the forest. When you interrupt the dreamer, it is often appropriate to reassure him that he has done nothing wrong; his job is to say what comes to mind in response to your question, it is your job to corral him when he seems to move too far from the dream.

Freud and Jung wanted a full personal history (anamnesis) of the dreamer and a detailed description of the current life situation as background information for dream work. Freud then asked for copious free associations; Jung, for more focused associations. I agree with Boss that relevant history and current situational material will be offered by the dreamer or can be selectively elicited as the dream poses its issues. The interviewer asks highly focused questions that, in most cases, bring out the necessary relevant information in the emotional and conceptual context of the dream. This can save time, and encourages the dreamer, rather than the interpreter, to point out relevant bridges or parallels between waking and dreaming realities.

It is true that in corralling the dreamer you risk cutting off a line of thought, feelings, or associations that could lead to relevant and useful material. But, as a rule, even if you do make a mistake by corralling the dreamer too soon, you will get stuck at the bridge and realize you must return to get a fuller description of the image. A good interviewer is part bloodhound. With practice you will learn to follow the scent of the dream and not allow anything to get you off that scent.

STRATEGY 6. *Sheepdogging.* A decade ago or so I demonstrated the dream interview method in one of Arthur Hasting's classes at the Transpersonal Psychology Institute. Arthur, who is a very sensitive psychologist and skilled student of dreams, later told me that I reminded him of a sheepdog. In the class, I was working with a particularly defensive woman and had to use all my wits. Arthur said, "You work like a sheepdog: you gently get her to lay out a description, then try to get her to go over the bridge. But if she looks like she is going to resist, you back off immediately and go at her from another image. You warm her up through her description then try again to get her to the bridge. If that attempt fails, you go to another image or back to a formerly explored one, each time backing off just before her defenses rally and she might bolt. After a while she has laid out so many suggestive descriptions that you've got her. She crosses the bridge because it seems the only thing to do." It was eight years after this discussion before I first went to a county fair and saw sheepdog trials. Arthur was right. An interviewer needs to be insistent and focused on getting the dreamer to cross the associative bridge, but he must be agile and back off quickly when resistance is high. He must also know how to use a number of strategies.

STRATEGY 7. *Restatement.* Simply restating the dream action or the dreamer's description of a dream element can be a powerful strategy. Diana's response to my repeating "the caretaker gets interested" at the end of her dream interview on the "Exuberant Foolish Woman" dream precipitated a bridge between Ron and her fiancé, Jeff, that had badly needed confirmation. Here are a few ways to work a restatement into the interview: "So then such and such happened, right?" "Wait, let me write that down." "Let me see if I've got that straight," and "It's interesting (odd, curious) that . . ." With your tone of voice you can use these lines to gently invite useful comment from the dreamer.

Now we shall take a close look at an interview with Diana to see how various steps of the interview were facilitated by the use of some of the basic strategies. Diana had this dream a few days after the "Exuberant Foolish Woman" dream, about a week and a half before she married Jeff. The interview occurred several months later.

> **I go to meet my brother,** Kevin. He is living with a friend in a run-down house, camping out. There are many sexual overtones between us as if we're having an affair. He's trying to find a spot where we can be private. He's apologetic. In a little while, a girl/woman whom he has been dating comes over. She asks me directly if I'm going to have an affair with him. I am shocked by her frankness and forwardness, but I admit that it is true. At the same time, I acknowledge that we can never be a couple. There would be too much social fallout. She is glad I recognize that and says that she thought I was pretty crazy before she talked to me about it.
>
> In the next scene I meet my sister, Lyn, and my mom to have my makeup done by a woman who is a psychic makeup artist. She has already done Mom. She puts

makeup and blush on my face then walks away to talk
to Lyn. I overhear the conversation. She is shaking her
head and claiming that I'm trying to do my makeup
like Mom. She says that it has holes in it; that I need to
do mine according to me.

The third scene is a rescue one, with a dog who is a
highly trained rescue artist.

(KEVIN, MAKEUP, AND THE
RESCUE-ARTIST DOG)

In the interview that follows, I shall note in brackets both the
interview step attempted and the strategy employed by the interviewer. Describing and breaking down dream interviews in
this way is an instructive exercise that helps you sharpen your
skills as well as see that there is always more than one way to
approach an interview; you must often choose one of a number
of equally promising paths. To accomplish the basic steps of the
interview, you will have to choose which strategies and which
questions seem most appropriate at any given moment. If you
make an unfortunate choice, you will know it sooner or later
when you get stuck, at which point you can return to the trouble spot and try something else. Knowing how to recognize and
abandon a tangential path or dead end is perhaps just as important as knowing how to continue on a promising one. You will
notice in this interview that I abandon my first line of question-
ing.

INTERVIEWER. [I thought that the obscure last image
was the punch line to the dream, and that we would
save much time if we could unlock it at the beginning of the interview, so I took it up first.] Do you
remember what kind of dog the highly trained rescue artist, in the last scene, was? [Eliciting a description.]

DIANA. No.

I. Do you remember anything at all about the dog or how it acted? [Eliciting a description.]

D. No.

I. What is Kevin like in waking life? Is he your only brother? [Trying to elicit a description of a more promising image.]

D. He is my second brother and I have been infatuated with him since I was a little girl. He was the big, strong, older brother; convivial, handsome, athletic. I can remember, back in high school, his coming home from the paratroopers in his uniform and my sitting on the bathtub watching him shave and listening to his adventures thinking he was such a hero. There has always been a lot of affection between us, and as I get older, there is kind of a sexual overtone. It's unspoken, but it drove Jeff crazy. Kevin, like Jeff, is a *puer,* or eternal child, to the *n*th degree.

I. In what way? [Invitation to unpack spontaneous bridge.]

D. Oh, like never being responsible about money, about time. He goes from job to job and never really settles down. He is now in the drug world. [Unpack.]

I. Do you see him much? [Eliciting a description of the relationship.]

D. Once every two or three months. He breezes through town to see everybody, runs up bills and leaves. Everyone is angry with him. He arrives and the conviviality is there for a while, but the anger starts to build up because he is a freeloader. [Description.]

I. Has he always been a freeloader? [Eliciting a description.]

D. There was a turning point somewhere. He was going along the committed route, got married, had children. He followed the prescribed pattern. Actually, he had impregnated a woman from a Southern family when he was in the army and that is what led him to marry—to be decent. They had a child. But then he said, "To hell with this," and left his wife and child. [Description.]

I. You say you've been infatuated with him since you were a girl. What are the things you like about him? [Eliciting a description.]

D. He's a cross between being a hero in the world of athletics and physical prowess and a real gentle spirit, real loving. He's naive and, at the same time, he's not very responsible. [Description.]

I. What would be an example of his irresponsibility? [Invitation to unpack the description.]

D. Recently, he said he would pitch in and help me arrange a dinner party, but then he pulled out at the last minute, breaking his promise. [Unpack.]

I. [The possible bridge to Jeff's broken promises of help, of excitement, security, and love does not seem to occur to Diana. It seems so blatant that she must be working at not seeing it, so I do not attempt a bridge, but wait for the issue to surface again later. This is an example of sheepdogging.] Is Kevin, in fact, loving? [Eliciting a description.]

D. On an affectionate basis, he offers love. He'll get stoned or have a beer, that kind of sentimentality.

I. Is anyone else in your family like him? [Invitation to bridge.]

D. My dad had a similar kind of sentimentality. Dad was different in that he definitely had a commitment to the family and to doing things right. Then he had the nervous breakdown, and he sort of limped along after that. [Bridge.]

I. [Kevin also had a commitment to family until he

said, "To hell with this." Jeff pretended to have a commitment to family, yet, apparently, Diana does not see that possible bridge yet.] What was your father's nervous breakdown like? [Eliciting a description.]

D. Severe depression, manic-depressive. But what it looked like then was that he was doing the right thing—having the big house in an exclusive area, having the career, the wife and kids, redecorating the house, keeping up appearances as the business was crumbling. He was caught between pride and bankruptcy. He didn't tell Mom about any of this. She just kept on spending. He became an alcoholic. [Description.]

I. So your Dad had a breakdown and limped along. Kevin is your hero, but he's having trouble. Does this remind you of anyone? [Recapitulation and invitation to bridge.]

D. Well, falling for Jeff, for me, was a case of saying "Please be the hero that none of the men in my life were." And he touted that. [Bridge.]

I. Kevin is living with a friend. Can you describe her? [Eliciting a description.]

D. No, other than she is the prototype of the women he picks, who are girl/women [Description.]

I. There are sexual overtones between you and Kevin and then she comes in. What is she like? [Recapitulation of action to put Diana in the mood for further description, then eliciting that description.]

D. She's possessive of him, you know, the way cats stake out their territory. I don't remember very well what she looks like, other than that she's got a hard body, like those very slender women who have that eternal girl look about them. [Description.]

I. What makes her a girl? [Eliciting a description.]

D. She hasn't fully developed herself yet. [Description.]

I. [A bit of sheepdogging here. A likely bridge to herself might make the important follow-up question hard to answer, so I elicit this description first.] What does she see in Kevin? Why is she with him?

D. He's romantic, very sexual. He says all the cooey words that a woman likes to hear. The fact that she's still a girl means that she's not in a position to challenge a man. So he is safe, and she has someone to love her. [Description.]

I. Hmmm, and the way she is a girl/woman. . . . Remind you of anyone? [Invitation to bridge.]

D. You bet! That sort of caring, the neediness, the cooing without the challenge, not getting angry, not being confrontational—that's me! [Bridge.]

I. Is this the kind of woman Kevin requires? [Eliciting a description.]

D. Oh yes.

I. So there is a part of you like the girl/woman who is a match for men like Kevin. Remind you of anything? [Recapitulation and invitation to bridge.]

D. Sure. I am that way with Jeff who is like Kevin. I guess I am still attached to Kevin and keep picking men like him. [Bridge.]

I. What does the girl/woman mean when she says, "I thought you were crazy before I talked to you"? [Eliciting a description of action.]

D. She recognizes that I have an awareness of the situation and that I don't think it will work for me to be my brother's mate. I go from the emotional to the rational and make a wise decision. Before that, she thought I was on a crash course to follow through with something that wasn't appropriate and marry Kevin. [Description.]

I. So in the dream you have wisely decided not to marry Kevin who you say is like Jeff. [Restatement with previously established bridge.]

D. If I had understood this dream, I wonder if I would have made the same decision in waking life and decided not to marry Jeff.

I. You say the marriage idea is not going to work. [Restatement for emphasis.]

D. It was very clear in the dream that it would not work.

I. What is a psychic makeup artist? [Eliciting a description.]

D. Someone who embellishes people and is also a psychic. [Description.]

I. What is a psychic? [Eliciting a description.]

D. Someone who sees the larger picture, who sees the future. [Description.]

I. Is this a trustworthy psychic? [Too leading a question, but it just slipped out. I should have asked Diana, "What sort of psychic was she?" to elicit her words. In any case, Diana nodded in agreement, and I moved on.] She made up your mom first. What is your mom's makeup like? [Eliciting a description.]

D. My mom's makeup is . . . (here Diana seizes the pun). I would describe her during my childhood years as very much the Athena woman: out in the world, doing business, running an efficient household with not much tender loving or femininity or romanticism. A religious woman, dedicated to her children, but removed in a way and sort of righteous. [Description.]

I. And what was her makeup in the world? [Corralling and eliciting a description.]

D. Oh, that everything is fine, I'm doing fine. The big saying that Mom introduced to our family was "Rise above it." If there's anything that bothers you, rise above it. Transcend all feelings. [Description.]

I. So that was the face that she showed the world? [Restatement.]

D. Right. No confronting, ever.

I. The makeup artist says you've been making yourself up like your mom, that your makeup has holes in it, and that you need to do your makeup according to you. Remind you of anything? [Recapitulation and invitation to bridge.]

D. This reminds me of my difficulty in confronting men—the cooing and my not being able to really confront the situation and find out what is really going on. I think, too, of my difficulty in recognizing and expressing my feelings. I think of me and my mom not being confident, having to cater to someone else, not being decisive. I really have been acting as if I had my mom's makeup. But I have other potentials. [Bridge.]

I. What are the holes in the dream? [Eliciting a description.]

D. Well, every time I feel I have to cater to someone's mood, that's a hole. I don't decide for myself what's going on. I depend on the other's mood and actions. [Description.]

I. So your mom's makeup on you leaves holes? [Restatement.]

D. Right.

I. Do you remember anything at all about the last scene with the rescue-artist dog, the setting, the feeling, the situation? [Eliciting a description.]

D. I only remember that I needed to be rescued. I don't even know from what. [Description.]

I. Our time is up. See if anything occurs to you about the dog as you transcribe and review the interview, okay?

Diana had done a lot of work already with important issues concerning her brother, father, boyfriend, and mother. When I read the transcript of the interview, I realized that I was unable to get a good bridge to the dog because I had failed to get a good description first. I telephoned Diana as soon as this occurred to me and asked her, "What are rescue dogs?" She replied that they save people from various situations. When asked, "What is a rescue *artist* dog?" Diana answered, "One that pretends to or plays at rescuing! And that fits my brother and my fiancé, Jeff, to a tee."

■

CHAPTER
FOUR

EXPLORING THE
DREAM SETTING

Consider the various places your dreams have taken you. To your childhood home, perhaps? To a high-school gym? A forest, or a city alley? To a country you've never seen, or the middle of the ocean? The setting in your dream can give you important clues to the meaning of the entire dream. As Jung said, "The description of the locality is very important; the place where the dream is staged, whether hotel, station, street, wood, under water, etc., makes a tremendous difference in the interpretation."[1] The setting usually signals the emotional mood of the dream action and thus provides its context. If you can recognize the metaphor expressed in the setting, you will understand what area of your waking life you are exploring in the dream.

Not all dreams have clear settings. In some, the action occurs in no particular place or in an ill-defined one. In these cases, you simply move on to the other dream elements, which usually suffice to express the dream message. Often one dream will contain more than one setting, indicating a shift in mood and or a shift to another arena in your life where the issues treated in the dream play a role.

To explore a setting, try asking yourself or your dream partner questions 5, 6, 7, 8, and 9 from your cue card:

5. *Describe the opening (or next) setting of the dream.*
6. *What is this place like in waking life?*
7. *What is this place like in your dream?*
8. *How does it feel to be in this setting? or How does it feel as you stand (or sit) there?*
9. *Does this* (recapitulate the description) *remind you of anything in your waking life?*

These questions, supplemented if necessary by similar ones tailored to a given dream, will assist the dreamer in identifying the metaphoric bridge between the dream scene and a particular waking situation. In each case, only the dreamer can provide the information necessary to understand the scene.

Most dream settings fall into six categories: buildings, which include institutions, houses, hotels, monuments, and rooms; geographical locations, which include towns, cities, states, countries, and continents; natural settings, such as parks, forests, mountains, and meadows; vehicles, which themselves may be in a larger setting; time, of day, year, season, or century; and events, such as a party, wake, graduation, wedding, war, or earthquake. There are, of course, other settings, but consideration of these six types will prepare you to apply the setting questions skillfully to any setting you come across.

BUILDINGS AND INSTITUTIONS

In 1973, I dreamt that I was being sentenced to four years in prison. I saw myself in a cell with books on my plain desk. I said, "That's not so bad, I'll get a lot of reading done." I awoke, horrified at my acceptance of such a fate. I described a prison to myself as a place which constrains one terribly, deprives one of freedom, makes life unbearably regimented, and distorts all of one's perceptions of the outside world, with which one loses touch. I've always thought that the best one could make of prison would be to read voraciously. I immediately recognized a bridge to my trouble in choosing a graduate school for my four-year doctoral program. The programs with the best academic reputations looked like parochial, true-believer prisons to me then. When I realized that I could die before ever getting out of the prison, I decided to look for a more progressive and eclectic program and not to settle for a prison term in a rigid program. Often, as in my prison dream, a stated length of time, or a specific time is used to describe a place and thus furnishes an important clue to its meaning. We will see several examples of this as we proceed.

Schools

Facing a similar issue, one of my students Vivian incubated a dream asking if she should switch from her graduate program in religion and psychology to one in clinical psychology. That night she dreamt:

> **I find myself in the art school** I attended in France. I see one of my psychology teachers from my current program holding a candle in the dark hall. She is wearing a long magenta dress. She wants me to follow her. It is as if she has something special to show me. She looks very tall, but when she turns to me, we are eye-to-eye. She whispers into my ear, "Clinical psychology." I look at her with a puzzled face. I tell myself, "But I will not have any freedom." **(PUZZLING ADVICE)**

Does this dream sound familiar? Might it have a similar interpretation to what I arrived at for my prison dream? Let's look at what the interview revealed. Vivian described the art school as a very rich experience, playful, well structured, hard work, and a very good training program. She learned a lot there, but wished the students had been less conservative. She said that in the dream she was aware only of the positive aspects of being in the school. The teacher in the dream taught in the religion and psychology department of her current school. Vivian said that the teacher's being extraordinarily tall in the dream made her seem elegant, imposing, and important—more so than in waking life.

She described magenta as her favorite color, the one that connects the two ends of the spectrum, and that reminds her of royalty. When she described the clinical psychology program, she said that it was more demanding than her current one and that it was very solid and more focused, much like her art school program. The clinical program also had the advantage of providing her with a license to practice psychology, which the other did not. But, as in the dream, in the interview Vivian said that she had so much more freedom in her present program that she hesitated to make the switch.

One key to this dream is the credibility of her image of the teacher she pictured as tall, holding a candle, and wearing magenta. Was she getting advice from a source she could trust? Her dream portrayed the teacher at a height and in a color the dreamer admired, and the teacher held a source of light in a dark hallway. The other key was Vivian's appraisal of the quality of her art school program, which was highly focused and solid like the clinical psychology program. The dream did not decide the issue for Vivian, it clarified the conflict that made it so hard for her to make a decision. Vivian realized that what she had to decide was not which program was more rigorous and practical, but rather how much freedom she was willing to trade for a more solid program.

Places of Worship

Another institution commonly dreamt of is the church or temple. Sometimes the dreamer will find herself in a generic temple with no other specifics to offer. Such a dreamer then must tell us why humans go to temple, what kinds of humans do this, and why. Then, if she tells us how she values this environment, whether she goes to temple in waking life, and how she feels in the dream temple, we will probably discover why and how she used the image of the temple for her dream.

Beverly dreamt of being in a Catholic church looking for a book by Mary Baker Eddy. Unable to find it, and not really wanting it anyway, she goes across the street to the Lutheran church. There she sees a friendly, social group but is pressured to declare her membership. She realizes that she does not belong there and leaves, crosses the street, and gets into her car. She notices that her brother has left her California smog certificate there, and she thinks how thoughtful he is. But she realizes that he doesn't have to take care of her anymore. She could now easily obtain her certificate without his help, and besides, her car doesn't need a new certificate until next year. She notes it is late in the day and wonders how she could have been inside so long. She puts the car in gear, and starts home along sunlit streets of a neighborhood that is bright, free, like a blend of the Haight Ashbury and Noe Valley districts of San Francisco. She confidently knows exactly how to get home. (The Churches)

Beverly is especially skilled in dream work, and our interview, which took place during two private consultation sessions, required no special strategies because she was able to provide good descriptions that got right to the point. Here are the highlights of our interview:

INTERVIEWER. What is a church?
BEVERLY. A place to commune with God. A place to turn inward. By definition, for me a church is a cloistered place, sheltered from anything real.
I. What is a Catholic church like?
B. The buildings are awe inspiring and have a wonderful expression of communion with God through music, art, and architecture. Much mystery and ritual. Awful too. The Catholic church insists that someone, a priest, must play the intermediary between the human being and God. It is very authoritarian and rigid.
I. Who is Mary Baker Eddy?
B. She founded the Christian Science church and was a self-healer who taught right thinking. Her teachings

are rather dreary in that if you don't get well, you are not doing it right, you should try harder, etc. This reminds me of my dad and his emphasis on self-healing and the power of the mind. Sometimes it is easy to get carried away with self-healing when an aspirin would do.

I. What, then, does being in this Catholic church scene, reminiscent of communion with God through art in a cloistered setting, looking for a Mary Baker Eddy book, remind you of?

B. Everything in my life used to be like that. I followed authorities looking for self-healing and growth. I lived an inner life, alone and cloistered.

I. The Lutheran church is across the street, nearby?

B. Yes, I go there next.

I. What is the Lutheran church like?

B. I know absolutely nothing about Lutheran churches, however my prejudices are extreme. Judging from a Lutheran I know, I would say that it is the most doctrinal of churches, yet is very procommunity. The community, however, is closed and horribly moralistic. "You are a *bad* person if you don't do such and such." As in my childhood with my father and grandmother, "You are a bad person if you are not busy all the time doing good." I guess I've always believed that you can't have community without having to conform to rigid morals.

I. How do you feel about being pressured in a friendly way to declare your membership in the community?

B. I don't like it and decide that I don't belong here.

I. Does the Lutheran church scene with its community, morality, and pressure to join remind you of anything?

B. It reminds me of how I have seen certain possibilities in life. Either I cloister myself and focus on growth and God through art, authority, thinking right, and exerting enormous effort or I can have community at the terrible price of conforming to a rigid morality.

I. Has there ever been a group like the Lutherans in your life that offered you friendly community but exacted a moralistic conformity from you?

B. Yes! I used to be involved with a very moralistic group of spiritual healers who had extremely fixed ideas about what was right and wrong, good and bad.

I. You decide neither the Catholic nor the Lutheran scene is right for you and you go to your car. You realize that your thoughtful brother need not make such efforts to take care of you anymore, that you can now handle things that used to fluster you?

B. Right. I wonder how I could have stayed inside so long.

I. "How I could have stayed inside so long?"

B. Yes, I'm breaking out at last after spending so much of my life focusing inward. I want to be outside in the world.

I. In the dream at this point, the setting is sunlit streets in a neighborhood that is a blend of the Haight Ashbury and the Noe Valley districts of town. What is the Haight like?

B. Bright, colorful, a place where people do what they want to be doing. It used to be the hippie area during the 1960s. But here there are no connotations of drugs or excess. One can live here without moralistic constraints on feelings.

I. What is Noe Valley like?

B. It's a healthy family district with a good sense of community. As a blended image, this neighborhood is unusual for me: bright, definitely outside, free,

colorful, and has a healthy sense of community—
children are playing happily in the street. I like the
new direction my life is taking as I focus on the
world out there in my photography and in my social
life.

As you can see, we would not have gotten far with this
dream if we had not taken the time to explore the settings from
the point of view of someone who was unfamiliar with them. I
lived in Noe Valley for ten years and would have described it
very differently. Beverly's ability to express her opinions,
especially about the churches, without beating around the
bush made my job much easier. You can see how important it is
not to judge or try to correct a dreamer's descriptions of an
image. Clearly, the truth about how Lutherans really are is irrelevant. Only the dreamer's impressions went into creating her
dream, and only they will help us to understand it.

After having transcribed this interview, I vaguely remembered
something Beverly had written in her day notes some time ago.
A bit of research through her file brought me to the day notes
she had made in her dream journal about two years before the
dream "The Churches." Here is the entry I had been looking
for:

> *Day Notes.* Last Tuesday, at the end of our spiritual heal-
> ing group session, I received a dressing down by Belya,
> the reigning guiding spirit, during which he enumer-
> ated all my shortcomings, which were apparently in-
> terfering with my healing work. I was shocked and
> hurt, as I had no idea I was "in my head," etc. I was very
> angry. I was angry on Wednesday and still angry on
> Thursday.
>
> This afternoon, I decided I had no fear of Belya, and
> I would keep my self-esteem. Worked hard at the office
> all day. Philip came over for dinner and to go over the

healing group books with me. I am now treasurer of
the board for the group. I have discovered that keeping
the accounting records and understanding them will be
a lot of work. It once again brings up the issue of my
assuming drudge work. Being responsible for the
records makes me feel important now, but will be a
drag later, no doubt.

As her day notes illustrate, Beverly's dream "The Churches"
announced the beginning of her liberation from long-held beliefs and attitudes that had, in many ways, been limiting her
ability to enjoy her life.

Houses and Rooms in Houses

Returning to one's childhood home in a dream is something
probably all of us have done. A young, handsome, and extremely bright schoolteacher named Wentworth dreamt that he
was in his parent's house, which, in the dream, is also a school-
room. The principal keeps putting him down, saying, "You are
stupid, and you don't know how to teach." In describing how
he felt in his parent's home, what his father was like, and how he
felt as a teacher, Wentworth was able to make all the important
bridges. He recognized that his anxieties about his teaching
were more than a little influenced by the fact that in his class-
room he felt as if he were back home under the critical eye of his
highly perfectionistic father. He realized that he fully expected
his school principal to judge him just as his father did.
Wentworth saw how, in a way, he has not left home yet. He still
carries his father's attitudes wherever he goes and he uses them
against himself. (The Father-Principal)

In a dream that has recurred since childhood for thirty-five
years, a physician named Cynthia dreams of living in a fixer-
upper house that is unkempt. In the latest version of the dream,
she now no longer worries about how much money it will cost

to fix up the house, but makes lists of things to be done. However, the contractors never come. She is dreadfully unhappy. (The Fixer-Upper)

Asked what it feels like to live in such a house, Cynthia said that it is awful; you can't have friends over, parts of the house don't function at all, and you never feel comfortable and "at home." Cynthia grew up in a series of such houses because her father made money by fixing up and selling their homes. Asked if there were any part of her life that felt like that, she said she had just dreamt for the first time that a room, the living room, was finished and she could have visitors. She thought that this must be connected to the fact that at the same time, she had just started getting comfortable with a man she was dating. Using the sheepdog strategy, I came around to this question a few times before Cynthia began to recognize more explicitly how parts of her private inner life have felt like the dream houses—uncomfortable and not ready to welcome others inside. The feeling of dreadful unhappiness in the dream reflected her desire for a comfortable interior she could enjoy and share with others. She bridged the "contractors who never came" to the parts of herself that resisted rolling up her sleeves and getting to work on putting her house in order. That the living room was finished suggested that she had nevertheless made enough progress to let someone into her life at least as far as the living room, where visitors are welcome. The more intimate and private parts of her emotional house were not yet fixed up.

Many people love to tell their dreams of being in a strange or familiar house and discovering wonderful new rooms. Most dreamers bridge this experience to situations in their waking lives in which they are opening up to new aspects of themselves and to new possibilities in their lives. As usual, the specific details of the dream indicate the particular situations involved. Dreams of cleaning out a basement require that one ask the dreamer, "What are basements?" "What are they for?" "How do you like them?" and "What is the one in your dream like?" If a dreamer says that basements are distasteful, moldy places into which one throws the junk one can't quite throw away, the bridge is likely to have to do with an area of the dreamer's life that she has decided to clean out in spite of the distastefulness of the long delayed task.

Attics are often described as being like basements: storage places for junk. However if you use Strategy 3, discussed in the last chapter, and ask how an attic is different from a basement, the dreamer is able to be more precise. The answers may vary, but a common response is to describe an attic as a place where one might keep family treasures of nostalgic and sentimental value, whereas a basement tends to collect worthless junk. You can imagine how these two settings could set the mood for very different explorations.

As common as the above descriptions of basements and attics might be, it is absolutely vital that the dreamer is invited to provide her own description without any suggestion from the interviewer. Even if the interviewer and dreamer share the same impression of, say, a basement, the effort the dreamer makes to find the words to describe one will help her get in touch with her feelings about basements and will provide the key words with the greatest impact for the dreamer to be used in the recapitulation and bridging phases of the interview.

When Dr. Flowers and I present the dream interview method in lectures or training workshops, we often ask the audience to volunteer their definitions and descriptions of a living room and of a bedroom. We remind them that we come from another planet and need a rich description. What do we hear? That living rooms are "rather staid, boring, formal places where children and their messes are forbidden to enter" or "They are for show, for entertaining, not for feeling comfortable and relaxed" or "They are the heart of a house. The central place where the family and friends gather and have fun, watch TV, toast marshmallows in the fire, read." Bedrooms are described as "a tranquil place to sleep" "headquarters central; a private place with a big bed for sleep, TV watching, phone calling, sex, and dreams" "a lonely place where one is sent as a child for punishment or to sleep all alone" or "my one oasis of peace and privacy in a big and busy family." Even with the simplest of images, one never knows what a dreamer will say on a given day, after a particular dream. My psychiatrist husband, Steve Walsh, in commenting on how well this approach lends itself to psychotherapy in general commented, "In therapy, as in dream work, the assumption of common ground between yourself and another person is one of the great delusions."

In asking questions about houses and rooms, one must explore any noted architectural style or design, the person to whom the place belongs, and the time in waking life that one lived in or visited the place. A Victorian room sets a different mood than an art deco, late orange crate, or punk styled one would. Ask the dreamer to describe the decor, how she likes it, and what sort of people would want such a room. Then you may discover with her the bridge to the part of her life that is like her description. If your dreamer tells you of finding herself in Grandmother Thomasina's house, you will never know the feeling of the house if you don't find out what Thomasina was like. First ask the interview questions designed to elicit descriptions of people, then you can ask the setting questions, "How does it feel to be there?" etc. The "proprietor" of the place is usually its most important descriptive quality. This quality often indicates attitudes the dreamer has learned from or shares with the proprietor. For example, if Thomasina was a family mediator and peacemaker who was both firm and patient, the dreamer might say that the dream image of having been away too long from this wonderful house of her Grandmother's reminds her that indeed she has been out of touch with these qualities in herself since she took on her new management job.

If you ask the dreamer, "Between what years did you live in, or visit this place?" she will be able to enrich and make more precise her description of the setting. A person having trouble

in a current marriage might dream of being in one of her childhood homes. By asking when she lived in the one presented in
the dream and what was going on in the family at the time, you
will usually discover much. Generally speaking, the dreamer
will be in a house in which she experienced some fear or conflict
relevant to her current situation. For example, the dream house
might bring back the memory of how her parents always
fought in those years and began their separation. The insecurity
of that past situation may describe perfectly the dreamer's hidden feelings of insecurity in her current situation.

To Jung's description of the house, which "generally means
the habitual or inherited attitude, the habitual way of living, or
something acquired like a house, or perhaps the way one lives
with the whole family,"[2] I would add that one should be ready
for surprise meanings and equipped to explore the style, people,
and time that make the bridge of meaning specific and useful.

Public Places

Dreamers often find themselves in public places. When an interviewer asked Amber to describe the concession booth she stood
in throughout a dream she replied, "The booth is empty." And
to the question, "What is a concession booth like?" she answered, "It is a temporary structure that separates one and one's
goods from the crowd. Nothing can get to me. I am guarded
and safe." After a recapitulation of this description and a bridging question, Amber said that this reminded her of how she
lives her life and relates to the world. Her concession to the
world of relationships is to join in by observing through a limited opening like the one in a concession booth.

When I had a daily radio show on dreams, a woman named
Lina called one day and said that she was troubled by a recurring dream in which she is making love to a man who keeps
getting younger and younger until he is only twelve years old!

She is angry at him for not having told her he was so young. Then she is in an emergency room where a doctor asks her how she feels being a child molester. She awakes horrified. (Child Molester)

I asked her to pretend that I come from another planet and need to know why she was angry with her young lover. She said that she was not the sort of person to make love to such a young person. One should not do that. I asked why not and she replied, "Because a young boy could not handle the pressures of such an intimate relationship with an older woman. It would overwhelm him. It's just not right and entirely inappropriate." To save time, I asked her if she had a son. The emergency room setting suggested to me that this was an urgent matter, close to home. Lina said yes, that he was twelve years old, and that she certainly never molested him. We established that she was divorced and living alone with her son. I asked if she ever confides in her son. Enthusiastically she replied, "Oh yes. Why, he is my confidant, the man of the house. I tell him all my problems, everything. He is so good and so wise. I love him very much." I asked if she might ever be inappropriately intimate with her son on an emotional level. Did her problems and her dependence on her twelve-year-old son ever seem to overwhelm him? At first, she thought that just perhaps this might be so. But as we continued to explore the scene in the emergency room she came to recognize that in a way she has been molesting her son and that she needs to remember that he is only twelve years old. The emergency room setting got her attention.

Sylvie dreamt of going to the Princeton University Club. In waking life she was a graduate of the university but had disdained joining the club. In the dream, she enters and joins. Describing the club she said, "By joining I am saying that I, too, can join a society that functions at a high level of achievement." This set the stage perfectly for the later appearance at the club meeting of a macaw, which Sylvie described as an exotic, beautiful, wild bird. She said she had always had a love affair with macaws and that it was so very sad to see them kept in cages. After a little more interviewing, she saw how the macaw was a metaphor for her powerful, exotic, creative self that she had long kept in a cage of timidity. The fact that the dreamer was afraid that the macaw would misbehave by leaving droppings in the club's Oriental carpets suggested to her how much she inhibits herself for fear that she will do something wrong and suffer terrible criticism. (Princeton Macaw) Dreams are good at showing us how we carry fears and anxieties from childhood that, because we fail to recognize and reexamine them, continue into adulthood and distort our perceptions of the present.

If you or your partner dream of a place that is hard to describe in terms of style, time, or ownership, ask, "What kind of person(s) would live (work, stay, etc.) in such a place?" The dreamer can usually answer this question, and it almost always yields helpful material. In fact, these descriptions are so telling, I often ask the question even if other descriptions already gathered seem adequate.

GEOGRAPHICAL LOCATIONS

Turning to dreams that place us in Japan, Alaska, Florence, or New Delhi, we ask the same general questions remembering that we, the interviewers, come from other planets and have no preconceived notions about such places. Francesca dreamt of being in Los Angeles. To her surprise, she saw that LA now has two rapid transit systems in place, but that it still has the problem of the homeless. She described LA as the city she grew up in, with smog and pollution. She bridged this to the unhealthy family environment she grew up in, which was polluted by her father's sexual abuse. The dream fact that LA had installed a rapid transit system led her to say, "At last, they're getting on the ball and dealing with their problems." This, restated, reminded her of her own progress in psychotherapy dealing with the scars from her relationship with her father. But LA still had not dealt with the homeless problem, and Francesca described this as an outrageous problem that must be dealt with now. In the dream the crowds of homeless people threatened to devour her happy, high-spirited son, Jim. She bridged this to her own failure to look at how insecure and homeless she felt inside. In spite of the fact that her family had always clothed and fed her, she felt unloved, could not trust her parents, and felt, in fact, homeless. Early in her life she had lost touch with the part of herself that was high-spirited like Jim. She saw that it was time to deal with her feelings of homelessness if she wanted to save the Jim within her. As the one in charge of her inner Los Angeles environment, she had done good work, but there was more to do. (LA Homeless)

The question "What kinds of people live there?" is useful only if you can convince the dreamer to give you her frank, stereotype-oriented impression, as Beatrice did regarding Hawaii in the following dream.

> **In Hawaii a young Hawaiian boy** and I are riding in the backseat of a car. Jan Wilson is driving. On the right I see a path with many white-robed men walking up through the woods. The highway is crawling with cops who are blocking the entrance to these woods. I think, "It must be the Bohemian Grove—what are they doing *here*?" As we drive on, I realize that Jan is driving badly. Then we see an amusement park with an extraordinarily high Ferris wheel and I think how I'd like to be on top of the Ferris wheel—what I might see from there!
> **(HAWAIIAN FERRIS WHEEL)**

What are the major settings in this dream? Hawaii, the backseat of the car, the entrance to the woods, the Bohemian Grove, the amusement park, and the hoped-for setting of the Ferris wheel. One could argue that the highway is a setting, and that the Ferris wheel is a dream object that permits a certain vantage point, but the interviewers in our class dealt with the settings as listed. Here is how the interview went.

INTERVIEWER. What is Hawaii like? [Eliciting a description.]

BEATRICE. It's a beautiful, relaxed, fragrant island. [Description.]

I. What is the Hawaiian boy beside you like? [Eliciting a description.]

B. I don't really know.

I. What do you think boys from Hawaii are generally like? [Using the sheepdog tactic.]

B. Oh, they are laid-back, more physically than intellectually oriented, and are just generally more relaxed about things than the Americans on the mainland. [Description.]

I. Does this boy who is laid-back, physically oriented, and generally more relaxed remind you of anything or anyone? [Invitation to bridge.]

B. He's not like me or my sons. Actually, he reminds me of what I'd like to be like, more relaxed about things. [Bridge.]

I. What is it like to sit in the backseat of the car? [Eliciting a description.]

B. Okay for a while, but later I realize there is a problem, that I'm not in control. [Description.]

I. Who is in control? [Restatement.]

B. Jan Wilson.

I. What is Jan like? [Eliciting a description.]

B. Very energetic, very unattractive, but socially active and very admirable. She's so positive all the time! She takes care of herself, yet is a leader. Her children do everything right—or else. She's a bit strict. [Description.]

I. So she is energetic, unattractive, socially active, admirable, and rather strict. Remind you of anything? [Invitation to bridge.]

B. I'm like that! I am all those things, including unattractive and rigid. [Bridge.]

I. And she is the one in the driver's seat. [Restatement.]

B. I'm afraid so.

I. Describe the white-robed men. [Eliciting a description.]

B. They remind me of monks or Ku Klux Klan members. [Bridge.]

I. What are monks like on earth? [Eliciting a description.]

B. They are ascetic, disciplined, spiritual men who give up family life to follow a religious path. I would have been a female version of a monk had I not chosen to have children. I miss the solitude of my years in a convent, but am glad I did not choose that route. [Bridge.]

I. What is the KKK? [Eliciting a description.]

B. A group of despicable men who think themselves morally superior to all. They think they have the right to lynch blacks. [Description.]

I. So the white-robed men who look like spiritual, disciplined, ascetic men, who give up family to follow a religious path, also seem like KKK members, who are despicable men who think themselves morally superior to all. Remind you of anything? [Recapitulation and invitation to bridge.]

B. My brother. He is brilliant. He has been my intellectual trainer, but he thinks he is morally superior to all. He has high standards. I knew I could never meet his standards of beauty, and at an early age I agreed with him that I am unattractive. In a way he lynches those who don't meet his standards. [Bridge and unpacking.]

I. The men walk through the woods. What are the woods like? [Corralling and eliciting a description.]

B. The woods are life to me. They are very comfortable and alive. [Bridge and description.]

I. What is the Bohemian Grove? [Eliciting a description.]

B. Woods that belong to a club of wealthy men who run the country. Every year they hold a two-week encampment and relive boys' camp. There is an ersatz spiritual tone to the event, but basically these men have no feminine values and are mostly interested in control and manipulation. Actually my brother is like a Bohemian Grove club member in his judgmental, superior ways. My brother's way is not my way; it is hateful to me and destroys life. [Description and bridge.]

I. How does Jan's way compare to your brother's way? [Eliciting a description.]

B. Jan is the part of me that follows my brother's dictums and tries to win his approval. I try to do things right and make sure my children do things right; I am socially active and try to look positive all the time. And that part of me is in the driver's seat. The part of me that wants to relax and enjoy the beauty of the woods, of Hawaii, of life is stuck in the backseat. [Bridge and unpacking.]

I. How do you feel about the fact that the men are in the woods? [Eliciting a description.]

B. They are preventing us from entering the woods. The cops are their agents hired to keep everyone out of the woods, and I don't like this at all. [Description.]

I. So there you are, wanting to get into the woods that make you feel comfortable and alive, but the white-robed men who, like your brother, are controlling and manipulative men, who think themselves superior to all, have hired cops to keep you out. [Recapitulation.]

B. I can't get into the state of mind of the woods as long as I let my brother and the part of myself that has internalized his rigid, superior, judgmental attitudes take over the woods. I have bought into his game, and the rest of me is paying the price. [Bridge and unpacking.]

I. Then you realize that Jan is not driving well? [Corralling.]

B. Leaving it up to Jan who keeps trying to please my brother is no way to run my life. [Bridge.]

I. What is an amusement park? [Eliciting a description.]

B. A place for fun. My favorite ride is the Ferris wheel. [Description.]

I. What are Ferris wheels like? [Eliciting a description.]

B. They are wonderful. My friends think it strange that I like them so much. Most people hate the idea of being stuck in the air if the thing breaks down. They don't want to have to wait while nothing is happening and they think it dull. But I love it. I don't mind delays. There is no purpose to Ferris wheels but pleasure and amusement. I live constantly under the driving pressure to do and accomplish. But the Ferris wheel is freeing. It has no reason, no purpose that is serious. It induces a state of mind that relieves me from my internalized brother's and family's belief that everything must have a reason and a purpose. [Description and bridge.]

I. Why would you like to be on top of the Ferris wheel and look at the view? [Eliciting a description.]

B. It feels so good to be on one, looking out over the expansive view. Maybe a little amusement and Hawaiian relaxation would give me some perspective on my life as I drive myself in the name of Jan's needs. I am amazed to see how much my need for approval from my brother has shaped my view of myself and my life and has kept me out of the beautiful woods. And to recognize how much my brother shares with the KKK-like Bohemians who play at being monks is unsettling. [Description, bridge, and summary.]

Each setting played a significant role in this dream, and the dreamer's descriptions of them helped her see what she was investigating through the dream.

You may have noticed that dreamers will occasionally bridge before they get to a description. To verify the aptness of such bridges one must pay careful attention to the unpacking of the bridge. Dreamers will also sometimes bridge after a restatement or a recapitulation. Going with the flow of the conversational tone of the interview will keep it lively and avoid the stilted effect created when the interviewer insists on asking every question in order. Sometimes not all questions are necessary and the interview moves along more quickly. This becomes more frequent as the dreamer gains experience in the interview technique and is more forthcoming and more terse. If you find that the omission of a question or step caused a snag, you can always return to the relevant image and explore further.

Natural Settings

When exploring natural settings, your questions will usually be of a more general nature than when exploring neighborhoods, states, or continents. In Beatrice's dream of Hawaii, we also had to identify the metaphor of woods. When you work with a dream where the dreamer is in a field of flowers, on a mountain peak, or beside a creek, asking how the dreamer or how humans generally feel in such settings is a good idea. Then you can find out how the dreamer feels in the dream.

Perhaps the natural settings that fascinate people most are those of oceans or large bodies of water. There are plenty of preconceptions about what water means in dreams. Some say it is the unconscious; others, the spirit; and others, the emotions. Well now, that just depends, doesn't it? Don't you suppose that a person who dreams about scuba diving in the Pacific will have a story different from that of the person who dreams of drowning in the Aegean Sea? What about the person who saves a friend from drowning under the ice in the Antarctic? What about the sailor who dreams of going back to the sea again? And what about the dreamer who is washing dishes, or finds herself in a fishbowl? We would have to find out the specifics about the water in the dream, and the dreamer's waking and dreaming relation to that water, before we could say anything about what it means.

Kirstin, a mother of two grown sons, had a dream about a tidal wave.

> **I am on a beach.** Two women are walking ahead of me. It is slightly overcast. I am feeling unsure about being there, perhaps I should be back home on the other side of the hill with the children. One of the women looks like Lori, my husband's twenty-one-year-old daughter.
>
> I am glancing over my shoulder and as I face forward, I see a huge tidal wave wall of water in the distance rapidly approaching the beach. I am frightened and tell the women I must get back to the children. Then Lori woman says it is useless, I will never get there before the wave hits. I say I am going anyway and start running.
>
> As I am running, I decide not to look back because it will only add to my fear. I begin to wonder whether the

wave will crush me immediately or throw me against the rocks when it hits and whether I will be able to hold my breath long enough to surface and survive. So I begin taking big breaths to prepare for survival.

The wave finally hits and I can't believe it—it is like being under a bathroom shower with just a little spray of water—I am not drowning! I look around and see other small waves coming and keep running. I am afraid I may not survive the next time.

(THE TIDAL WAVE)

Kirstin described a beach as a place to relax and enjoy oneself, and bridged it to her new phase in life now that her children have left the nest. An overcast beach reminded her of the pall her son's forced marriage had cast over the family. The engagement party was to be held at her home this weekend. She had made all the arrangements and dealt with a very unhappy husband, a difficult daughter-in-law-to-be, and unhappy siblings and parents-in-law. She was running herself ragged trying to make a pleasant occasion out of a wretched one. No wonder in the dream she felt she should be back home. Kirstin has slipped back into her role of caretaker of all her children, including the adults in the family. Kirstin described a tidal wave as a huge body of water that springs up very suddenly and can't be stopped. The one in her dream was huge and powerful. That she decided not to look back, she thought, referred to her past. We asked what force might have existed in her past that is now threatening her survival, springs up suddenly while she relaxes, and might crush or suffocate her. Kirstin said she had felt threatened by the invasion of the families for the weekend. She feared being overwhelmed by their demands as she has allowed herself to be in the past. She unpacked this bridge further, saying that three of her children had arrived and, to her surprise, they went to visit friends for part of the day and generally took care of themselves for the next few days. The day before the party was not as hectic as she had feared, and she even had time during the weekend for dinner with her husband when the children had evening plans. She had feared an overwhelming invasion that would suffocate her or thrash her against the rocks, but it turned out that it was like the spray of a shower. But Kirstin was still too recently out of her "supercaretaker" mode to relax. She had to keep running, because she never knew when those little waves would turn into a tidal wave of demands and obligations that she would not be able to stop.

TIME

The element of time is often overlooked as a setting in dreams. One could consider some references to time as further descriptions of settings of place, and I often do. But sometimes time and date are worth investigating in their own right.

Statements like "I was back in the Middle Ages," "This dream takes place in the time of the dinosaurs," or "I am in the year A.D. 2500"—followed by action in no particular place—use time rather than place for a setting. If the dream took place in the past, ask what it was like back then; this usually elicits a good response. Then, of course, one must ask what, specifically, it was like in the dream. For dreams that take place in the future, you can ask what it is supposed to be like then and what it was like in the dream. The answers to these questions will usually describe the mood of the dream and set the scene for the rest of the investigation.

Some authors write that a dream set in a past time signals a past life lived by the dreamer. Being unable to travel through time myself, I can't say whether or not this is true. However, in my experience, dreamers often miss a great deal if they assume their dreams to be simply flashbacks to past lives and leave it at that. Whenever I have interviewed such dreamers and asked the questions suggested above, we have found that the time describes a period of the dreamer's current life, or an area or web of attitudes in this life. The material fits into the dramatic structure of the dream and presents the dreamer with practical insights into her current relationships, work, or life patterns.

Santuzza had a dream of this nature.

> **I am in London.** It is the mid-1800s. I am in a manor house looking across a canal at a similarly lovely home. I am aware that the lord of the house across the way has decided he wants me and if he cannot have me, he will make certain that I die. He has at least two killer dobermans.
>
> My brother, Jaquino, lives with me and was aware of this problem. He knows I have adamantly refused to have anything to do with this man. Knowing this, he left on a business trip. I rush downstairs to make sure the door is locked. I see those vicious dogs racing toward me with an order from their master to kill.
>
> I find a very old groundskeeper and tell him of my dilemma. He tells me we could escape to an abandoned carriage house nearby. It is decrepit, but if we don't go there we will die. We go to the carriage house.
>
> (LONDON DOBERMANS)

In the interview, when Santuzza described London in the 1800s, she said that it was alive with social activity, elegant picnics and the like. It was a superficial but pretty life. Male-female roles were pleasant and well defined, if not very substantial. There was a sense of great abundance of a past era in the dream. She then described the lord of the facing manor as very possessive and difficult, just like her former husband. Her brother was "a beautiful 1960s sort of person, laid-back and mellow, who keeps his life working smoothly." He told her in the past that he was smart enough to know when he could not help her out of a problem she had to solve for herself. At this point, she could bridge the major dream images. The financial settlement between her and her former husband, Winston, had remained unresolved for years. Winston was still delaying the sale of their resort home that would provide the funds for the settlement. Santuzza was anxious about maintaining her former abundant, nineteenth-century London lifestyle. She had displaced some of her dependency needs from her former husband to her brother and needed to start solving her own problems. One was her continuing and painful entanglement with her former husband in regard to the settlement. In the dream she sees the destructiveness of this relationship and reluctantly decides that it is better to drastically scale down her lifestyle and live in a carriage house than to be dinner for the vicious dogs. This, by the way, is what she later did in waking life. But before she could bring herself to take this step, she had the following dream.

> **I am in Paris.** Norman, my son's friend, is with me. He is in a frenzy, having problems with schedules, and so on. However, they are problems that apply to 1988 and are totally inappropriate because we are in postwar Paris. Our time, climate, and issues are of another decade.
> (POSTWAR PARIS)

We discover that Norman is an artistic young man suffering an identity crisis, wondering if he should leave his town and family's influence. He is high-strung and at this time frantic, wondering what to do with his life.

Santuzza told us that the postwar Paris of her dream is an incredibly beautiful town, full of art. It has recently emerged from the darkness of the war and the occupation. In the dream, it feels like she has returned to it to enjoy it for the first time in many years.

As you might imagine, after the recapitulations, Santuzza bridged Norman to herself in her currently frenzied state of wondering what she would do with the rest of her life now that she was divorced and her children had grown up. Her picture of a hopeful, liberated postwar Paris reminded her of having just emerged herself from a depressing marriage and divorce period and of the beauty of the life all around and within her. She said, "We are in Paris every day of our lives, if we want to be." She was impressed at the clear inappropriateness of Norman's frenzy. "Can't he see that right now we are in a beautiful place?"

If we had assumed that the time settings of these dreams had to do with past life memories, we would have lost the opportunity to learn some things that could make a big difference in the dreamer's life.

Frequently, time is expressed in dreams as a season or, as it was in Beverly's dream of the churches, as a time of day. Beverly realized in her dream that it is late in the day, and she did not miss the metaphorical connotation that more time has passed in her life than she has realized. If it is late in your dream, ask yourself where in your life you feel it is late.

Beatrice, who had the dream Hawaiian Ferris Wheel, had another dream a few weeks later about being back at Grinnell College in the spring. Her descriptions of Grinnell and of spring were both important. As you will see, Grinnell in the spring is unlike Grinnell at any other time in the eyes of our dreamer. Beatrice described Grinnell as a wonderful, beautiful, liberal, and intellectually exciting place that was too isolated geographically, being in the middle of Iowa. In her first years she had loved it, but when she returned after having spent some time in Europe, she found it too small and constricting. With such a divergent description, the interviewer is left wondering which image of Grinnell is relevant to the dream. As is usual in most dreams, asking the dreamer how she feels in the dream usually clarifies things. Beatrice said that Grinnell in the spring emphasizes everything she loved about the place, the art and music, and the intellectual life. When we asked her to describe spring as a season on earth, we heard that spring is a time of heightened emotions, of abandonment, and permission to be free and enjoy life. Spring lightened her sense of the weight of intellectual life. By now, we in the dream study group could see, as she could, some parallels to Beatrice's Hawaii dream and to her efforts to work on her conflicts regarding the roles of achievement and pleasurable relaxation in life.

In some dreams, a specific date in which the action occurs is at least as important as the place. In Ruth's dream it is the day before the Fourth of July.

> **I have a paper due** on the Fourth of July. It is the day before and I am just sitting around the house. Rob is coming to pick it up and give it to the teacher. I have not even tried. I feel bad. I will get Rob in trouble. I try to bullshit a paper, but it doesn't work. Rob leaves a pretty yellow-flowering plant with me. He knows what is going on. He must be angry at my not being ready. He will return later tonight so he can deliver the paper tomorrow. He says I am okay because I keep correcting myself when I blow things and that's really good.   (**PAPER DUE**)

Ruth was studying her dreams while on vacation from college. She identified the Fourth of July as Independence Day. She guessed her paper might have something to do with her struggle for independence from her family. Rob "is a psychology major who does a lot of thinking and feeling. He is caring, intelligent, and gets things done." Ruth had been resisting taking a close look at her codependent relationship with her loving, but overbearing and critical father. She was living at home that summer in regular conflict with him, but she couldn't get herself moving on the independence work that the part of her that was like Rob wanted to accomplish.

VEHICLES

Vehicles in which dreamers find themselves may also act as settings, even when they are themselves embedded in a larger setting. An example of this would be dancing on the *Queen Elizabeth II* while crossing the Atlantic. We would want to know what life is like, or supposed to be like, on this ship and what it is like to be dancing there in the dream. There is always the possibility that the name *Elizabeth* rings an important bell for the dreamer, in which case we would have to explore that. We would also want to know if the ship is on a normal, regular route, or how this one is different from its other routes. What is it like to cross the Atlantic? And what is it like to cross it while dancing on such a ship?

Santuzza dreamt of sailing during the period of her identity crisis.

> **I was on a yacht in San Francisco Bay.** Fritz and Suli were as dressed up as they would be for the opera. Very ostentatious. They disrobed and dove into the bay. Fritz was wearing a silk scarf. I dove in to check on a child I thought was swimming near a barge. When I tried to surface, Fritz was holding me down with a pole. I dismissed the thought that he was trying to drown me, although he was holding me down purposely. It occurred to me that he wanted me to retrieve his silk scarf. I could not believe that his possession was worth taking the chance that I could lose my life!
> **(GOING UNDER FOR FRITZ'S SCARF)**

Santuzza described being on a yacht in the bay as the fashionable thing to do, but in fact, she found it a whole lot of work and rather boring. Fritz, she informed us, is a sleazy, rigid, money-oriented surgeon, who cares nothing for his wife. Without exploring all of the images and issues in this dream, we can see that the yacht sets the mood. From this point of reference, Santuzza could bridge Fritz and his wife to one aspect of her former life with her materialistic husband. She could also see that her attachment to Fritz and his money was a threat to her well-being, if not her life.

Violet, a mother of grown children and separated from her husband, had a very different dream about being on a yacht.

> **We were invited to go on a yacht** for its first real boating solo. It was to be very special, a big party, as the people who owned the boat had put everything into it. They had done the very best they could possibly do. My son, Michael, and his wife, Florence, were going to help. Somehow their car had to be moved out of the way, but this could not be done until the boat started to move out of dry dock into the water. Something about releasing some pressure.
>
> My family was with me, we were all dressed up for the occasion. The boat was all white and beautiful with glass, crystal, and rich wood everywhere. It was glorious—much larger and more spacious than I had anticipated. It was a wonderful experience. I said, "Everyone should experience this once in a lifetime." But the boat wasn't on open water yet. We had to proceed very carefully, with everyone's help, through shallow water for a while. This was a little harrowing as we would occasionally hit a rock or bog down for an instant worrying if the boat had been damaged.
>
> From a distance, I could see that Michael and Florence had succeeded with the effort to free their car. They and their friends all proceeded to go away. *Finally,* I thought, maybe we're ready to go more freely and without obstacles, and with more water under us. Then we came to a narrow channel and had to follow that,

staying within bounds. We were coming to a bay—
deeper water and more freedom at last.

(OUT OF DRY DOCK)

As Violet explored the beautiful yacht into which the owners
had put everything and with which they had done the very best
they possibly could, she thought of her life and the quality she
had built into it. Like her, it was getting ready for its first solo
voyage, just as she was moving toward greater freedom in her
life. For decades she had been tied to the demands of her husband and children, and now there were only a few more obstacles between her and much greater freedom. She had to adjust
her relationship with her son, Michael. She had to move a little
before he could break free. She knew she had to stay within
certain bounds as she moved toward freedom, but she could do
it. On the ship with her were family members who were now
acting as companions rather than dependents. Her freedom ship
was moving her into a bay, not into a lonely ocean.

People who dream of being in airplanes that crash often fear
that the dream is psychic and that they should not fly—not
soon, at any rate. While such dreams may come true, as we read
from time to time in the papers, in fifteen years of working with
a great number of dreams, I have yet to hear such a dream that
turned out to have foretold the future. In asking the dreamers of
such dreams what it felt like to be in the doomed plane, what
the plane was like, and so on, I have found that the dreamers
find themselves describing career projects, relationships, or
their own sense of self-confidence, which, when looked at honestly, is in fact at great risk of crashing. In a variation on the
plane crash dream, Alexi told me of being in a plane he thought
would crash. In the dream, he decides to bail out. When I asked
him if there were anything in his life he thought was about to
crash and from which he was planning to bail out, he said that
was a pretty good description of his marriage. He had decided
on a divorce.

Automobiles are popular dream vehicles. When the dreamer drives her own car, which looks just like the waking car, she is usually taking charge of a transition in her life, as Beverly was in her dream of the churches. When someone other than the dreamer is in the driver's seat, there is usually trouble ahead, and the interviewer should pay the greatest attention to who is driving, how the dreamer feels in the passenger's seat or in the backseat, and how things are going. If the car (truck, bicycle, or limousine) is in some way unusual or is no longer the dreamer's current one, it is smart to lavish plenty of attention on its description. A dreamer who is driving a car she had in her college days may be acting in her current life as she did back then. This may or may not be to her advantage. The way to find out is to ask what she was like when she used to drive the dream car. If the car is a particular vintage, model, or color, this is worth investigating. If the dreamer makes a point of "dream-driving" a car of a particular year, it is because she has specific feelings and memories associated with that year. If she dreams of a 1956 Chevy, we want to know what '56 Chevys were like. If she has no idea, ask what Chevys are like and if the year 1956 brings anything special to mind. We need to know if her first boyfriend had a '56 Chevy, if she has just restored one, if she was married in 1956, if she thinks Chevys are underrated cars and notes that she was born in 1956. We'll never know if we don't ask.

Francesca, a banker who was reconsidering her career choice, dreamt of riding in an open mountain train that was like a roller coaster. A man in front of her was trying to hold her in place by holding her hand. The man behind her was insisting that she look up at a statue of a man exposing himself. She had been on this ride before and was not amused by the statue that she had already seen. The roller coaster with the long uphill climb reminded her of her efforts in the long climb to financial success, and the man behind reminded her of her intrusive and abusive father. The man in front of her felt like her former employer, who was trying to hold onto her by offering her another important position. In the dream, Francesca decided to get off the roller coaster. In the interview, she recognized how she had kept herself on an emotional roller coaster and a long professional climb as she struggled to escape her critical father through professional achievement, but she found herself working closely with a man who was overly dependent, like her father. (Mountain Roller Coaster)

My husband, Steve, awoke one morning with this dream:

I am riding in a big, tall, tour bus. Except for the driver, I am the only one in the bus, which, on the inside, is like a huge empty living room with a lower level where the driver is. I am lonely. Through an open door, I can talk to the driver a bit, but the driver is busy driving on this very winding, curvy road like the one to Muir Beach. When the dream camera shows the action from outside, the bus looks like a big high tour bus making its way along the winding road. It leans from side to side as it goes around the curves.

From the inside shot, I am there alone in this big living room. I worry a little about being in such a high bus that leans as these buses do on the curves, but things seem to be going just fine. Mostly, I am aware of feeling lonely.   **(LONELY ON THE BUS)**

Steve started by describing these buses as so high that he is always surprised they don't turn over as they lean out of curves. Then, before I could catch him, he bridged his loneliness in the dream to a sense of existential loneliness he had felt lately. "You know, we are all finally on a lonely voyage in life," he said. Well, true enough, I thought, but this philosophical gem seemed to be lacking something. I said, "Okay, but could you tell me a little more about these big tour buses?" I was brushing my teeth, and Steve was combing his hair when he finally moved out of his interpretive mode of trying to figure out the dream (because he thought he had already done that) and shifted into the descriptive mode. He said with some amusement, "Actually, I've always been surprised how a little person is able to control such a big monstrosity." We both laughed with sudden recognition. Steve often teases me about being a little person with a lot of power and control. He then said, "Are you the little driver with whom I talk through the open door, but who is too busy working to provide much of the social interaction I want and need? These last two weeks, you've been downstairs in your office at the computer writing your book all day and all night, while I've been alone upstairs in our big living room. I was especially lonely this weekend. Our little fight last night probably had more to do with my loneliness than with anything else."

EVENTS

Do you remember ever having been in a war, in a tornado, or in a snowstorm in your dreams? Events like these can be the settings for exciting dreams. You can approach them with the basic cue-card questions and take advantage of their expressiveness. When exploring events, it works well first to ask questions about the event as an object—for example, "What is an earthquake?"—and then ask, "What it is like to be in one?" followed by "What is the one in your dream like?" and "How does it feel to be there?"

Dreams of being at a graduation or a wedding may indicate that the dreamer is examining her feelings about some achievement or transition or about love and commitment; but what she is dealing with specifically we will not know until we know how she feels about such events and how they are pictured in the context of the dream. Here is a dream of an alumna of Princeton University, named Tina, who dreams of marching under unusual circumstances in the annual reunion parade, or "P-rade," through the campus.

> **Mom is going to die soon.** I take her out, and we have a good time. A few days later, she dies. I am glad to have been with her recently. She is in a coffin at a place where the P-rade will pass by. As I arrive at our class's spot along the P-rade route, I note that I've not cried yet—not let Mom's death sink in—for I had things to do. I march in the P-rade with my class. In the crowd, I look for and pick up a new baby, which belongs to a relative. As I hold the baby, friends from younger classes, former professors, and journalists who have interviewed me in the past greet me. I particularly notice a journalist from the magazine *Pacific Currents* who says hi. I walk on, and at last, I let myself cry. I feel sad, but relieved to be able to cry.   **(P-RADE)**

Tina and I have worked with dreams since we were undergraduates together, and it took only one question for her to see what her strange dream was about. I asked her, "What is a P-rade?" Even though I had marched in more than two dozen of them myself, I could not know what they are like for her. Tina replied to my alien's query by saying,

> The P-rade is made up of all the alumni who have returned for their reunions. Every class dresses in its own particular and peculiar orange-and-black costumes. The P-rade is led by the oldest class, joined, class-by-class, by the younger classes, who line the P-rade route and cheer on the classes that go before them. Lots of people think it is silly, but it really is a pageant of life. You see pass before you the very old guys who are proud just to be able to walk or to ride in a golf cart if they can't walk. Then the fellows in their seventies and sixties come by. They have a certain comfort about them. The middle-aged group is more mixed, some seem very impressed with themselves, others are here

to have a good time. As we fall in, it is clear that the younger classes get wilder and more enthusiastic. I wonder if the seniors who look so young are really old enough to be in college. Yet I remember being a senior myself and looking at the class five years out. I thought, "Will I be as old as they are?" They seemed an eternity removed from me.

I see what the dream is about now. I am putting my mother's impending death in the larger context of life that I see parade before me at every reunion. The new life in the baby is included in the cycle. My mom has been an invalid for years, and I have been postponing my grieving for her as the mom I once knew. I have kept busy in my career and somewhat detached from her. We were very close. Even the title of the *Pacific Currents* magazine underlines the theme of the currents of life. Even my mother's coffin has a place in the P-rade.

Many people fear that if they dream of someone's death, that person will soon die. While this may occur in rare instances, I have never seen it. Like Tina's mother, the person who dies in the dream lives on well after it. The death is almost always a symbolic one.

Children who dream of being caught in a war, if asked to describe wars, in general, and the dream war, in particular, will usually be able to bridge to a similar waking situation about which they often have difficulty talking with adults. Often these children's dreams express their distress at being caught in their parent's marital conflict. Adults who dream of war may be dreaming of a time in their past when their parents were warring, of their own marital or interpersonal skirmishes, or of the inner battles going on inside them. The only way to find out exactly what is going on is to ask and not to assume one of many possibilities.

HELP KEY

◘ *When a dreamer responds to your questions with "I don't know" or "I have no idea,"* smile, relax, and use your sheepdog judgment about when to come at the problem from another angle. The exception to this rule is in cases where the dreamer describes a "given" in the dream. For example, if a dreamer says, "Suddenly we were in Persia," it is pointless and irritating to the dreamer if you ask how she got there. With practice you will come to recognize these givens. In the meantime, if you stumble on one or two, the dreamer will say, "I don't know, it just happened that way in the dream," and you can say, "Oh, I see," and move right along. Later we shall look into how these givens are part of the dramatic structure of the dream and how they make associative sense.

◘ *If the dreamer gives you a divergent description that goes in two or more conflicting directions,* you can avoid much confusion and loss of time if you get a brief description going in each direction, then quickly look to the dream context to see which aspect of the image is being emphasized. Follow that line of description and see if it results in a solid bridge. If not, you can go back and see if you narrowed the description prematurely. For example, if Earl tells you that Boston is a socially conservative town but one where he feels free because he went to college there, ask about both aspects. Both might be relevant, i.e., a place that is conservative at one level and liberating at another, or Earl may find that as he enriches

his description, the quality of freedom through education may fit best.

☐ *If the dreamer begins to describe the physical appearance of
the church, plane, house, etc., and you feel the most useful part of the description will be in its functional and feeling aspects,* let the dreamer warm up to the image
through what is often a useful physical description,
but don't let the dreamer bore you both to tears
with a long, lifeless description.

☐ *After an invitation to bridge such as "Does this Lutheran
church remind you of anything in your life?" the dreamer
may ask if you mean does she know of a place that looks
like the church or a place that feels like the church.* It is
safest at such times to be open to both possibilities,
saying, "Both the physical and the emotional connections would be interesting if they come to
mind." Most often, it is the feeling connection that
will make the bridge, but now and then the physical similarities with another place will add useful
information. Be careful, however, not to let the
dreamer get lost in the literal, physical bridging effort. It often leads nowhere, and frustrates the
dreamer. Keep her to a brief search on the physical
level and, if necessary, say, "How about emotionally (or metaphorically); do you see a bridge?" This
approach works well when the same sort of thing
occurs in bridging the people, animals, and actions
in dreams.

□

CHAPTER
FIVE

PEOPLE IN DREAMS

My beloved, admired friend and high-school principal, Si Romanis, found a wonderfully quick-paced jazz song from the thirties which I play at the opening of some of my lectures. The title, "You Meet the Nicest People in Your Dreams," is a refrain that in its last appearance adds, "You meet fine people, grand people, the most rambunctious people in your dreams, yeah, man." Besides the nicest and the most rambunctious, you also meet the most frightening, mean, and enigmatic people in your dreams. Think of the array of actors who have played starring and supporting roles in your dreams: neighbors, friends, and enemies from work, or from third grade; family members; deceased relatives; benevolent and evil strangers; prime ministers; rock stars; football players; and ballet dancers. Then, of course, there are those characters who are a blend of two or more people, and some who transform themselves into different people before your very eyes.

The styles, roles, actions, thoughts, or feelings of people in your dreams can highlight certain characteristics in them that you may have underestimated. They may highlight similar qualities that you are not sufficiently aware of in yourself or in someone close to you, who is more like your dream character than you realize. By manifesting the often hidden dynamics in your relationships with people in waking life, the people in your dreams may also play roles that can help you to explore and improve your relationships with the flesh-and-blood people the dream figures remind you of. To find out whether a dream person represents a part of the dreamer, an aspect of the dream figure, or someone else, or some force or dynamic in the dreamer's life, hold your suspicions in abeyance and ask yourself or your dream partner the following questions from the cue card.

10. *Who is X?*
11. *What is X like in waking life (or in general)?*
12. *What is X like in your dream? What is X doing in your dream?*
13. *Does X, whom you describe as* (recapitulate the description) *remind you of anything in your waking life?*
14. *Does X, who is* (recapitulate the description), *remind you of anyone in your life, or is there some part of you that is like X?*
15. *How so?*

Let's say Samson dreams of Jimmy Carter. Samson describes Carter as a man who did not let criticism break his spirit, as a man who continued to serve his country after his presidency, whereas most men in his position just live off the fat of the land. If Samson can then bridge these qualities to the path he might take after his upcoming retirement from a high-pressure, disappointing career, you've scored a significant goal and can go on to the next image in your interview. If, however, your initial questions do not elicit such a good description, you will need to come up with special questions for special situations.

TYPES OF DESCRIPTION REQUIRING SPECIAL QUESTIONS

Inadequate Descriptions

If, in answering the question "What is X like?" the dreamer tells you a string of anecdotes about X, such as the time X did this or that, or how X is the type of guy who drinks Perrier at a football game, you can corral him, interrupt him gently, and ask, "How would you describe a guy who does the sorts of things X does?" or "What is a guy who would drink Perrier at a game like; what does that say about him?"

Dreamers who paint anecdotal pictures are usually having trouble describing this particular image and, in some cases, are people who have not learned how to give good, terse verbal descriptions. You can assist these dreamers by asking, "What stands out about X?" or by asking for three adjectives that best describe X. Reassuring the dreamer that he can always modify the description later will make the choice of only three adjectives seem like less of a life-and-death matter. The exercise of choosing three adjectives forces the dreamer to think more clearly, evaluate the relative importance of the dream character's attributes, and find words that best express the most telling qualities of the figure. The resulting adjectives will get things going and will usually be the most useful form of description for your recapitulation and bridge work later.

The strategy of guessing the absurd or the opposite is an amusing one that often energizes the interview by injecting a welcome bit of humor. It is also effective in jarring a dreamer into a recognition of just what he *does* think about a given person. For example, a dreamer can think of nothing much to say about a vaguely disliked woman named Jeanne at work. After hearing you ask if Jeanne is a supportive, grandmotherly co-worker, he might fire back with, "Ha! She's more like a snake in the grass who intends to bite her way to the top."

Negative Descriptions

Sometimes dreamers give descriptions in the negative form. For example, "Well, he's not warm, not someone I have had much rapport with." Such a description could probably fit a dozen people in the dreamer's life. We need to know what X *is* like to be able to make a positive identification in the bridge. After such a response, say "I see" and ask "If X is not warm, what *is* he like?" and "Why do you think you have not had much rapport with him?" This will usually do the trick. The "I see" response is very important—one must be careful to accept, not reject, whatever the dreamer says. After all, the dreamer is trying to cooperate and is usually unaware of the lack of specificity of certain responses. The negative description can actually be a useful warm-up for the dreamer as he begins to explore the character. By responding to a negative description with "Yes, *but* what *is* X like?" the dreamer will be likely to sense your impatience, and feel scolded. By saying something like "I see," you politely accept what has been said, and even if you must interrupt, your tone of voice can suggest that you have another question in mind, not that the dreamer is wasting your time.

For example, Vera dreamt of winning two tickets to spend a day and an evening with two famous football players. Her first description of football players was, "Well, they're not the kind of guys I'd talk about existential dream work with." A novice interviewer asked, "What else wouldn't you do with them?" to which the dreamer responded with a blank stare. That was not the point, and the remark yanked the dreamer out of a close and rather concrete experience of her dream and of football players. The question "Why not? What are they like that would make it unlikely that you would talk about existential dream work with them?" resulted in the description, "They are big and powerful and very protective, but not well-educated, so we would have little to talk about. They'd make better bodyguards than dates." As it happened in the dream, the tickets and the date were a ruse to get Vera out of her house while someone stole all of her belongings. Later, she was able to look at how she tended to pick boyfriends who acted more as bodyguards who kept other men away from her, but who often left her feeling empty and robbed of companionship. (Football Player Decoy)

Dreamers who give negative descriptions are often trying to avoid saying something critical about the figure who appears in the dream. The dreamers will usually open up if you encourage them to blurt out whatever they really think about X—you promise not to tell! Also, it is important to some dreamers that you let them know you understand that X may be a fine person, even if this dream is focusing on one of his worst flaws.

Critical Descriptions

Once you have succeeded in eliciting a frank, if brutally critical, description of a disliked dream figure, you are in dangerous, sensitive territory. If the figure portrays hateful characteristics shared by the dreamer, or by someone close to the dreamer whom the dreamer needs or loves, he may experience your recapitulation or bridge as an accusation and close up and become defensive. The dreamer is more likely to be open to looking at the possibilities and ramifications of such a bridge if you do the following things, after eliciting a good, honest, lively, critical description:

1.   Recapitulate the description with the same charged spirit and words the dreamer used, being extremely careful not to add any of your words or judgments, even in jest. If the dreamer just described the dream character Theo as a slimy, cheating, exploitative scoundrel, don't recapitulate this by adding a summary statement like "So he's a real skunk." You never know if the dreamer is about to bridge Theo to her beloved scoundrel boyfriend. Your added descriptions, even if they are not as negative as the dreamer's, can sound like a damning judgment of someone the dreamer does not want to see too clearly.

2.   Before bridging, say to the dreamer, "If you were a psychologist, what would you say might lead someone to become a slimy, cheating person like Theo?" To answer this question, the dreamer is forced to look into what she knows about people like Theo with an understanding, rather than a critical eye. Most

dreamers will respond that the disliked figure has suffered this
or that recently or in his childhood.

3. Immediately bridge this "psychologist's explanation": "Is
there anyone you know, or a part of you that has suffered (recapitulate the explanation)?" It will be much easier for the
dreamer to assign or acknowledge the pain that led to the development of the hated qualities than the qualities themselves. That
is the next step.

4. Now, or later on in the interview, invite the dreamer to
make a bridge, with a recapitulation that softens the sharpest
critical words and emphasizes the understanding explanation.

This "If you were a psychologist" line works with almost
everyone, even children. I am struck with how frequently my
novice clients and my students underestimate the sensitivity of a
dreamer in situations like this. It is an interviewer's duty to protect the dreamer from the unnecessary shame and loss of face so
easily inflicted by an expression of the interviewer's judgments
and his insensitivity to the dreamer's self-judgments. Having
done the best you can, it never hurts to ask the dreamer if he
feels embarrassed or uncomfortable working with this material
or if he feels pushed or judged. If the dreamer conducts his own
summary, listen carefully for signs of forgetting, denial, awk-
wardness, or embarrassment in the sensitive sections. You
might want to reassure the dreamer that you are not shocked
and congratulate him on his straightforwardness and courage in
dealing with these issues.

In cases where the bridge from a disliked dream figure is going to lead directly to someone close to the dreamer or, indeed,
to the dreamer himself, you will greatly inhibit the dreamer's
ability to be frank if you give any hint at all as to where the
bridge might go before you get a full description. Encourage
the dreamer with your facial expressions, your gestures, and
you words to focus for now only on the description of the

dream figure in the dream and in waking life. One of the most rewarding advantages of the interview method is the reduced defensiveness and increased forthrightness in dreamers, who are encouraged to think concretely and descriptively about the images *before* considering any metaphorical, interpretive possibilities.

After I referred one of my students, Beverly, to a psychologist for psychotherapy, she dreamt of having a guest teacher in her writing class. In describing the guest teacher, she said he was brittle and moved too fast. She added that he didn't check in enough with the students to see if they were following, but that he was teaching some very important material, and that she would have to find a tutor to help her learn the material at her slower pace. My student bridged the guest teacher to the psychologist to whom I had referred her. Had she realized where the bridge was leading, she would have been less free with her criticisms of the psychologist, whom she knew was a good friend of mine. Her examination of her discomfort with the psychologist led her to discuss with him her feelings and desire to improve their communication. Remember, definitions are least defended and most candid before the dreamer thinks of the possible bridges.

Divergent Descriptions

Divergent descriptions are more common regarding people than settings. A spouse might be described as kind, attentive, brave, brilliant, sexy, maddening, stubborn, and infuriatingly flirtatious. Descriptions of people the dreamer knows well, especially mothers, spouses, and siblings, can be long and branch off in many directions. The dream context and the dreamer's recent waking experience with the dream figure will usually suggest a particular path to pursue. For example, if your sister is saving you from drowning in quicksand, you should explore the qualities in her that the scene suggests. If she is stealing your boyfriend, you should look at another side of her personality.

The tone in the dreamer's voice as he describes the various aspects of the person may suggest that his most intense feeling is related to a particular cluster of attributes, and if these seem to complement the role the person plays in the dream, it is probably a reliable clue as to which aspect to concentrate on. If you are still in doubt, ask the dreamer which way he thinks you should go with the description.

Descriptions of Little-Known People

What if the dreamer says, "How can I describe X? I don't even know him well (or at all)." You can answer, "That's all right. Think about what little you do know or have heard about X, his looks or style, name, reputation, family, or business. What do you imagine he might be like?" Easily frustrated dreamers respond well to, "It's great that you don't know much about X. That makes our job easier. The little you know is the relevant part, and will save us the trouble of weeding out extraneous associations."

Blended and Transforming Images

Blended images of dream people are fun to work with. As with blended images of any other dream element, get a description of each aspect, in this case, each person suggested in the image. Then ask the dreamer to describe the composite person. Transforming images in which a single, distinct dream person turns into another person are among the most fascinating events in dreaming. Here, we need a description of the person as he first appears in a given context. Then we need to pay special attention to the feelings and action that immediately precede the transformation. Next, get a good description of the transformed character in his context. Bridging after each step will usually reveal the surprising meaning. The dream "George Bush's Architect," in which President Bush turned into the dreamer's client, is a good example of this phenomenon.

BRIDGING AND INTERPRETATIONS

Bracketing Premature Bridges and Interpretations

If your dreamer tends to cut short the descriptive phase and leaps to a bridge with statements like, "Dora represents . . ." or "Dr. P. says Dora represents . . ." or "Dora is my feminine self . . ." or "Dora is my anima or shadow," beg the dreamer's indulgence and go back and get a good description first. Such bridges are premature and often prefabricated. However, these descriptions and interpretations can be useful sources for questions you might want to ask later, and they might suggest some sound bridges. Therefore, I encourage my students to "bracket" them, or make a note of them, for possible later use if the descriptions lead in their direction. Psychological terms mean different things to different people and are often used as a safe parking place for unexamined material. If the dreamer uses a psychological or astrological term as part of a description of an image, it is important to get a good description of it, as if you had never heard of such a thing before, so that you can employ its descriptive (not diagnostic) power in your recapitulation and bridging.

Subjective versus Objective Interpretations

Many people are confused about how to know if the dream person is to be interpreted on the subjective level as a part of the dreamer or on the objective level as part of someone in the dreamer's life. Some people say, as did Gestalt therapist Fritz Perls, that every image in the dream, including every person, doorknob, plate of food, and garage door represents a part of the dreamer. I think this an extreme position, as untenable in the real world of real dreamers as Freud's insistence that almost all dreams are the disguised expressions of an infantile wish. Jung said that a good rule of thumb was to consider the likelihood that any figure with whom the dreamer is currently in close contact in waking life would be on the objective level and/or the subjective level, but that the other figures would most likely be understood best on the subjective level. In my practice, things often work out this way, but I prefer to leave the assignment of interpretive level to the dreamer. If a good description is elicited and recapitulated, the dreamer can usually tell for himself where the bridge fits best.

Sometimes the image is an accurate caricature of both someone in the dreamer's life and of the dreamer himself. In cases where the dreamer seems to assign the dream person's qualities defensively to someone outside of himself, but you have reason to think that a subjective interpretation would be more accurate, you might go with his choice for the time being. Wait until the objective interpretation leads the interview into a cul-de-sac or until you can use the sheepdog strategy and ask for more descriptions from another angle, which would invite a fresh bridging effort.

Sylvie had a dream in which she is visited in her retreat house by John, her spiritual teacher, who does a Tarot card reading for her. [This she bridged to her teacher-self helping her look into her soul.] Later, John brings in a girl and a shy guy. John and Sylvie go to the window and either he or she says something about wanting to be out in the real world. Through the window they see girls riding bareback on wild horses. Sylvie thinks how she would like to ride. [She bridged the horses to her yearning for energy and power.] Then she understands that the shy guy is in love with the girl but that they have broken up. The girl had been very wild when the two met—she had emotional problems, was into drugs. She had changed a lot during their time together. [Sylvie bridged the girl to how she used to be a few years ago.]

The guy is having a hard time getting over their breakup, but he is trying. [So far, no bridge at all to the guy.] John tells the guy to dance. He doesn't want to, but although he is shy and hurting, he gets out on the floor with John or the girl and begins to dance. John's telling the guy to dance reminded Sylvie of how in waking life John teaches his students to talk and dance in front of a video camera to practice being strong, clear, unselfconscious, and unafraid. Finally, we were ready to ask her if this shy, hurting guy (who was trying to get over breaking up with a formerly troubled girl and who was trying to participate and dance as the teacher instructed) reminded her of anything or anyone. She said he reminded her of her "male" [according to her beliefs about maleness] and, therefore, less fearful self that had turned inward and helped her wild, troubled self with meditation and other spiritual practices. The male in her had been very attached to the part of herself that no longer needed his ministrations. She would have to get over the breakup and find a new identity in the real world now that she no longer had to spend all her energy healing the troubled girl within. (Shy Dancer)

It is not uncommon to find a dreamer using a figure of the opposite sex to highlight a quality within himself, so you can't depend on any simple formula regarding the sex of the dream image to indicate the subjective or objective nature of that image.

Now let's turn our attention from special situations that occur while working with people in dreams to the various kinds of people who appear in them.

TYPES OF PEOPLE WHO APPEAR IN DREAMS

Famous People

Images of famous people whom the dreamer does not know personally are among the easiest images to understand. A dreamer can usually provide a stunning description of the famous person's character without being troubled by having too much information to choose from. What the dreamer knows about famous people is usually well defined, stereotypical, and rather highly charged. Thus for the purposes of the interview, the descriptions come quickly to the point. If the dreamer protests that he does not know the person personally and, therefore, is unable to describe how X really is, reassure him that you understand this and that all you need to know is what impression the dreamer has of what X is like in waking life. Say something like "Why don't you just tell me what you have heard about this person? What is his reputation?"

Victoria, a homemaker and artist whose children are full-grown, dreamt the following dream on her deceased mother's birthday.

> **I was waiting in line to enter a restaurant.** I noticed a little girl in a yellowish dress standing with her family. I said, "Oh, what a pretty dress you have!" She didn't seem to believe me. She didn't respond.
>
> Then the mother started stroking my face, as if soothing away the wrinkles. She taught me how to do some sort of needlework on my dress. I enjoyed that.
>
> Later, the mother and child were gone and I was standing there with the father who was *Zubin Mehta*! We were standing very close, perhaps he was embracing me. I said, "I know all about you! I've read everything about you." He seemed very interested in me, and as we talked, I knew we would soon make love. I was very excited about it. Zubin Mehta, of all people! I knew it would be wonderful, and I knew that this would decisively end my relationship with Monte.
>
> (ZUBIN MEHTA)

In the little girl, Victoria saw a picture of herself and the difficulty she has had since childhood believing that she is attractive. The mother reminded her of a friend whom Victoria described as mature, calm, and very giving as both a wife and a mother. This description, in turn, reminded her of a potential in herself, a way she would like to be. She told us that this friend had given birth to a son the same time Victoria did and that they both enjoyed nursing their sons for a long time but found that their husbands and older children became jealous of the attention they lost to the nursing infants. Unlike Victoria, the friend gave up nursing and took her husband off on a trip to Hawaii. Victoria felt that her friend had made the wiser, more mature choice. Perhaps if she could develop this potential in herself, she would be a happier, more contented person.

While an orthodox Freudian analyst might well say that Victoria's encounter with the Zubin Mehta-like father expressed a repressed childhood wish to kill her mother and have sex with her father, in the dream, Victoria admired and enjoyed the mother—it would be quite a distortion to suggest that a murder took place off the dream stage! And the way Victoria described Zubin Mehta did not remind her of her father: she described the Indian conductor as "dynamic, a demon, full of energy, power, vitality, bombastic, furious, pure fire!" When asked what this description brought to mind, she replied, "People have said that of me, when I let myself go, which isn't too often. But that fire does come out in my art. I should do more. Oh, I feel so alive just thinking of his energy!"

Five years later, Victoria's Zubin Mehta is still a powerful, meaningful, and motivating image for her. Had we simply interpreted her dream for her and decreed that Zubin represented her wished-for father, we would have foreclosed the likelihood of her recognizing Zubin Mehta's qualities within herself.

It is not uncommon for a woman to dream of an unrealized aspect of herself in the person of a famous man. Some suggest that this is because there are relatively few famous women who display qualities other than beauty, dependency, nurturing, and other conventionally "feminine" traits. If a woman is looking for role models that emphasize power, strength, vitality, success, etc., there are indeed famous women who qualify, but there are many more well-known choices among males.

Emma, a sensitive executive in her forties, dreamt that Arnold Schwarzenegger was trapped in a cave. He had been held captive by Russians his entire life, so he didn't even realize he was a prisoner. Arnold had been made to feel inferior because he was different from his captors in that a single horn grew out of his head. Emma said that Arnold, in waking life, is gorgeous, strong, disciplined, and a hard worker whom she likes and admires. The single horn, like that of a unicorn, underlined how special and magical he was, a unique and gentle creature. She was struck how in the dream, the captors really didn't want him to know how special he was. They criticized him for being too Nordic and for not being Russian, like them. Emma had lived in Denmark during the height of the Cold War and told us how the Scandinavians had feared a Soviet takeover. She described Nordic people as strong, independent, and fiercely attached to their own cultures and myths. The Russians she described as far more powerful, evil, and wanting to crush all individuality. Emma could easily see that whereas she identified herself with the individualistic, mythically oriented Nordic peoples, she identified her parents with the Russian captors.

As we worked with the other scenes in the dream, Emma began to see how reluctant she was to take credit for her own specialness, her strength, her discipline, and her magic. She had adopted certain familial and social attitudes that kept the Arnold Schwarzenegger within her captive for so long that she, like Arnold in the dream, never realized her own strength, magic, or beauty. Happily, after a few adventures, Arnold bravely escapes from his cave and comes out into the world. (Arnold Schwarzenegger)

A lawyer named Adrianne dreamt that Danny Thomas was on his way to entertain some children and invited her to come along. When I asked her what Danny Thomas was like, she said that he was a great family man, a philanthropist, generous with his time and money. In fact, in the dream he was dressed in a black hat and black coat, which Adrianne said is how Mafia men dress, and although they have an awfully sinister side, Mafia men are great family men. Adrianne said that Danny was like the good side of *The Godfather* image, and his daughter grew up free to explore and make a great life. He also reminded her of her boyfriend: On a recent vacation with him, she had begun to appreciate how much he loved his daughter. She said she felt well fathered by him herself and was grateful that he was willing to take care of her. Her exploration of this dream image helped Adrianne to see more clearly and to better appreciate the Danny Thomas qualities in the man she was considering marrying. (Danny Thomas)

Victoria dreamt of giving Ronald Reagan a kiss on the mouth. She took his head in her hands and drew it close to her so that she could kiss him—even though she was a Democrat. She was thanking him for having taken her on a tour of something. Who is Ronald Reagan and what is he like? Victoria informed us aliens that as a politician he is too conservative, but as a person, he is strong, straightforward, optimistic, and gutsy. She attempted a bridge, saying that her husband is conservative like Reagan, but withdrew it as she thought of all the complaints she had about her husband. She returned to her description and said that Reagan is a model for her who has shown her how to take things in stride, to be optimistic and gutsy, to have courage and humor. She profitably assigned a subjective interpretation to Reagan, but we wondered on the basis of other dreams, her personal history, and other parts of this dream if she wasn't resisting seeing a parallel to her husband. We asked her if she might want to consider again her earlier bridge, but she roundly denied any connection. It is possible that she would have gained some insight by opening herself to that possibility, but there was no point in our insisting. Even if we were on the right track, she had to find her way to that bridge herself. (Ronald Reagan)

Politicians are especially popular dream figures for many of the journalists I know who report on political issues. They use these images just as other people do, to caricature or highlight particular qualities in themselves or in people they have personal relationships with, much as psychologists and psychiatrists sometimes dream of those patients who evoke particular webs of feeling and association. There are times, of course, that journalists' dreams of their politician subjects and psychologists' dreams of their clients are an exploration or a resolution of problems in the actual journalist-politician and the psychologist-client relationships, but I suspect that these cases are not common.

If a person tells of a dream in which a famous actor appears playing one of his waking-life stage roles, then the interviewer need be less interested in the actor's waking personality than in the personality of the character the actor plays in the dream. If, however, the actor in the dream is playing a role never played in waking life, it is the personality of the waking actor that must be described before you can appreciate why he would be playing such an unlikely role in the dream. Ask yourself, "What is emphasized in the dream, the person of the actor or the role he plays?"

Adrianne, now married to her Danny Thomas boyfriend, had a dream in which a Woody Allen sort of guy played a starring role. She described him as a really weird guy, not put together, bumbling, short, stooped over, wearing thick glasses, and carrying lots of junk. As she went on describing this misfit she interrupted herself and said, "Okay, this is my husband. He is a little weird and clumsy, but once I get through the external stuff, he is very special and talented." As Adrianne continued to unpack the bridge, there were parts that just didn't fit. Her husband was not particularly short or stooped nor did he wear thick glasses. We were about to chalk the inconsistencies up to a dream's need to paint any character who was supposed to convey the image of Woody Allen with these characteristics. But one especially sharp group member had suspicions about the dreamer's quick bridge, based on past dreams in which Adrianne dealt with her feelings about marrying a fellow who was not as handsome as Robert Redford. This interviewer's curiosity had not been satisfied by the bridge to Adrianne's husband. She still wanted to know why the dreamer had taken such pains even in the dream to describe Woody Allen, so she asked, "Is there any part of you that is short, stooped over, wears thick glasses, and carries lots of junk?" To everyone's surprise, Adrianne's eyes lit up with the pleasure of recognition, and we knew that somehow this elegant, beautiful, bright lawyer had seen herself in Woody Allen. She said laughing, "Well now that you mention it . . . I am too short, my dance teacher has been showing me that I am slightly stooped over, when I take out my contact lenses, I wear extremely thick glasses, and I am carrying a lot of old junk feelings and attitudes left over from my childhood. And I do get to feeling awfully self-critical and clumsy and weird at times, although most people don't know that. I really do have a Woody Allen side to me." Having recognized her own clumsiness and weirdness, Adrianne had a chance to look again at how much of her criticism of her husband's clumsiness was an intolerance born of her projecting onto him qualities she preferred to ignore in herself. (Woody Allen)

Mythical Figures

It is very tempting when one dreams of fairy-tale characters or mythical beings to run to the nearest reference book to look up a scholar's description of the figure in an effort to discover its meaning. Nothing could be less productive. We need the dreamer's description, not the scholar's. We need to know how the dreamer would have described the image upon falling asleep before the dream. If he has looked up the image since the dream, it can be very difficult to obtain a dream description uncontaminated by someone else's ideas. The dreamer employed the image as he knew it before the dream, and this is the association that will tell us what the image meant to him. The Jungian practice of mythological amplification, in which the analyst draws from his special knowledge of mythology and tells the dreamer what a given figure means in folklore, is based on the belief that this explanation will enrich the dreamer's appreciation of the image. If the image is amplified by the analyst or by the dreamer's reading before he has carefully described it from his original perspective and bridged it to his waking life, I think the amplification is counterproductive. It distracts the dreamer from his own impressions and often seduces him to look at his dream experience as an exercise that relates him to mythical, abstract, philosophical realms rather than to his real, lived-in world. I witnessed this happening countless times during the three years I traveled in Jungian circles in New York and Zurich. However, if one first honors the dreamer with the chance to tell his dream and the chance to reflect on it for a week, he might then profit from hearing someone else's story without the risk of forgetting his own experience. The most skilled Jungians appreciate the need to honor the dreamer's experience and do not introduce their material until they feel it would do no harm.

In a dream about the commander of an armed force, Rosalind described him as blond, curly haired, and like Peter Pan. In the dream she becomes this commander. We asked her to describe Peter Pan and she told us, "He was a commander who lived in never-never-land and refused to grow up even when he fell in love. He refused to come back to the real world because he didn't want to get old and think about all those boring adult things. I am like that. I want to stay forever young and innocent. No commitment or aging or growing up for me! Just like the commander in the dream, I have trouble commanding, being my own authority. I am too much attached to my father." Rosalind was dealing with the Peter Pan personality she had developed as a way of coping with the fears of adulthood she had learned early in life, when her older sisters fell out of favor with their parents. (Peter Pan)

People from the Past

One of the most curious things is that we sometimes dream of people we haven't seen in years as vividly as if we had seen them yesterday. Have you ever wondered why in the world you dreamt of Jayne from your second-grade class, or of Dr. Preller, your favorite professor from college? Why do you dream of deceased people as if they were alive? And how can you realize and accept—while dreaming—that they are dead, but nonetheless acting quite alive in your dreams?

Usually, these figures from our past work the same way all the other images of people do in dreams: They are our best characterization of a part of ourselves or of an aspect of someone in our lives we need to understand better. Adrianne had a vivid nightmare that brought back some amusing memories.

I am in my old convent school. Some new people move in. They are young men like Patrick and Paul. They want to play rock music and do so. Of course, they make too much noise. One nun is livid. I tell her that I'll tell them to turn off the music in order to keep her away from them. I explain to the men how the place is constructed of bare glass, wood, and stone, and everything resounds. So even footsteps can be heard. Very hard to be quiet here.

A lot of us seem to be up on another floor. This is not allowed. Sister Petronilla is coming and will be mad. How can we avoid getting caught? There is a woman, all dressed in pink, who can't stand it. She wants to hide more than anything. She has gone into an adjoining empty room. I'm in there with her. The only thing in there is a very shallow closet. She can't fit there, but I jokingly say I'll put her there. She is going nuts. As Sister Petronilla enters the other room, we all look out of the doorway into the hall. Many of us try to sneak past her. The pink woman gets past her. Then, as I make my move into the hall, Sister Petronilla steps back into the hall at the same moment. She is furious and lines everybody up against the wall. I act as if I don't know what is going on and ask if she is feeling okay. She is fuming and is going to discipline everyone.

(SISTER PETRONILLA)

Here are the highlights of our interview. I have included, in brackets, the interview steps, notations on the strategies employed, and any comments I thought might be instructive. An annotated dream interview such as this one is not only a useful teaching tool but an immensely useful learning one as well. You might want to annotate a transcript of an interview you taped while working with a dream partner. This interview will give you an idea how to proceed.

INTERVIEWER. That is quite a dream! [Congratulatory acknowledgment of the dream story.] Tell me, what is a convent school? [Eliciting a description of a generic setting.]

ADRIANNE. A school that trains high-school girls to be part of the Army of God, very hierarchical, constrictive, hypocritical, filled with rules, and negative in attitude. [Description.]

I. What is the one in your dream like? [Eliciting a description of a specific setting.]

A. It is like the one I went to and fits my generic description. [Description.]

I. Who are the new people who move in, and what are they like? [Eliciting a description of people.]

A. Patrick, an old friend, is a sweet, no-nonsense guy, and Paul is a sweet, sort of klutzy guy. [Description of the people. This seems a brief, but potentially sufficient, description.]

I. So they are both sweet and one is a no-nonsense fellow while the other is sort of klutzy. [Recapitulation.] Is there anyone in your life who is sweet, no-nonsense—[Invitation to bridge to people is interrupted.]

A. I've got it! My husband. Patrick and Paul describe his sweetness, klutziness, and his no-nonsense attitude perfectly. [Bridge to people. This may be a premature bridge, but the enthusiasm with which it is made makes it seem like a direct hit.]

I. So Patrick and Paul, who remind you of your husband, have moved into the convent. [Summary.] Is there any way that your husband has moved into a very hierarchical, constrictive environment full of rules? [Invitation to bridge. The potentially more painful words, *hypocritical* and *negative* have, for the moment, been omitted.]

A. Well, my husband has moved into my psychological environment, by marrying me. And there is a part of me that is pretty rule-bound and constrictive, like the convent. [Bridge and unpacking.]

I. Why would these two sweet guys want to play rock music? [Eliciting a description of action.]

A. They just want to have fun and be themselves. [Description of action.]

I. Why do you want to keep the nun away from them? [Eliciting a description of action.]

A. Because I am embarrassed that such an awful nun is here. [Description of action.] That's me! The nun is a picture of all the "shoulds" that I use to constrain myself, in my relationships, in my career, and within myself. [Bridge to person and unpacking.]

I. Aha. Is it very hard to be quiet enough to please the nun in this environment? [Summary and implied invitation to bridge to feeling of the need to be good.]

A. Oh yes. The nun in me is hard to please—the slightest infraction of the rules resounds. [Bridge to person and feeling.]

I. Why are you all not allowed to be up on another floor? [Eliciting a description of action.]

A. Just a silly rule. [Description of action.]

I. Who is Sister Petronilla, and what is she like? [Eliciting a description of person.]

A. She was our principal. She had a nervous breakdown. We knew we could drive her up the wall. I fomented a revolution in the school. She was afraid she would be considered unable to control her girls. She was afraid of holding her turf. She tried to live by the rules, but did so superficially, not from her inner, natural self. She was heavily judgmental, vindictive, and controlling. She had a strong need to look okay and not get criticized. [Description of person.]

I. [The interviewer, as sheepdog, decides to wait a while before trying a bridge from this highly charged image.] Why will Sister Petronilla be mad? [Eliciting a description of feeling.]

A. Because we are breaking her silly rules. [Description of feeling.]

I. So you all want to avoid getting caught. [Summary.] What is the woman like who is dressed in pink? [Eliciting a description of person.]

A. She looks like a flapper, a free spirit. To hell with the rules! She wants to have a good time in life. [Description of person.]

I. What is she up to in the dream? [Eliciting a description of action.]

A. She wants to stick her head in the sand. [Description of action.]

I. How is she feeling? [Eliciting a description of feelings.]

A. She is extremely embarrassed. She is supposed to be perfect and any criticism is intolerable. She cannot bear being flawed. [Description of feelings.]

I. She is extremely embarrassed because she is supposed to be perfect and cannot tolerate flaws or any criticism. [Restatement, less challenging than an invitation to bridge.]

A. I am like that. I am so embarrassed to be caught not being perfect. This reminds me of the dream that showed me how many critical voices I carry inside me. The pink flapper is the rebellious side of Sister Petronilla. Both are saddled with a need to be perfect and cannot bear criticism. One enforces the rules, while the other breaks them, neither is free of the tyranny. [Bridge and unpacking.]

I. What happens next? [Eliciting a description of action.]

A. The rest seems pretty clear to me now. I realize I can't keep my free spirit in the closet in our empty hideout room, and eventually we are all caught. We try to hide, to sneak by, we don't confront the problem directly. Sister Petronilla, my rule enforcer, still rules; my rebellious pink flapper doesn't really escape from the tyranny of my Petronilla-like attitudes. [Bridge to rest of dream.]

Adrianne then summarized the interview and our study group members joined her in reflecting on the extent to which we each carry a bit of Sister Petronilla in us. The driving need to be perfect and the exaggerated fear of criticism shared by the flapper, Sister Petronilla, and, of course, the dreamer drives us to seek out rigid systems of belief and behavior. In these structures we find the promise of safety from criticism if we act and think as the system decrees; if we do right, we will be approved of and perhaps even praised. The flapper slips by only temporarily, her terror of being criticized keeps her tied to the convent's system.

If you or your partner dream of someone you have not seen since you both were children, but who in the dream is now, like you, an adult, go back to what you last felt and knew about that person for your description. A forty-five-year-old client who dreamt of Louise's daughter had last seen Louise ten years ago, when her daughter was only a few months old. In the dream, Louise's daughter was as old as the dreamer. To elicit a description of this dream figure, we first asked the dreamer to describe Louise as the dreamer remembered her, then asked for a bridge. As it happened, Louise reminded the dreamer of her own mother's most courageous and persistent self. Louise's daughter was then easily bridged to the dreamer herself. When asked to describe an adult figure who another client dreamed was screaming at his wife, the dreamer replied, "How should I know what he's like, I only knew him as the block bully." To this I said, "That's exactly what I'd like to hear about. What was he like when you knew him?" This led to an invitation to bridge: "Is there a grown-up bully screaming at your wife anywhere in your life?"

Pamina, a bright and passionate woman who had a terrible self-image, having grown up with a mother who did not know how to nurture and encourage her, had the following dream about one of her mom's old friends:

> **I am dancing with Rosina.** The dancing is full of beauty and tears of joy. She truly loves me. We share such joy. It is a totally exciting, wonderful experience.
> **(DANCING WITH ROSINA)**

Rosina was a woman who "truly did love" Pamina and expressed her affection. Pamina said, "I wish she had been my mother." The dream came the day after Pamina made a breakthrough in recognizing for the first time how different her own beloved daughter was from her. This new insight reminded Pamina how she appreciated it as a child that Rosina recognized her unique qualities and let her be herself, not a clone of her mother. Pamina felt her dream reflected and reinforced the previous day's breakthrough. The dream also gave Pamina the gift of experiencing the feeling of being loved for herself in a joyous celebration of dance.

Sybil, a gorgeous businesswoman who had always suffered from her jealousy of other women's looks, clothes, and men, brought to our private sessions a number of dreams in which she was envying other women's dresses. In these dreams, she was exploring and acknowledging her jealous feelings and looking into how she had developed them. Then she had a very helpful dream of a high-school friend. Sybil dreamt that her envied high-school friend, Sheila, "was showing me her beautiful party dress in her room, and I was so jealous. But then I finally noticed that my dress was even prettier and suited me far better." Sybil had spent so much of her life envying girls like Sheila; now at last she was beginning to see that she, too, is pretty and has her own style. This dream was, of course, dealing with more than prettiness; it was helping Sybil to readjust her self-image and increase her confidence by opening her eyes to who she is, whereas earlier she could only see who she was not. (Beautiful Party Dress)

Some people who are mourning the death of a loved one report dreams of the deceased that are unusually vivid and sometimes seem more real than other dreams. These dreams often follow a general pattern, and we will take them up in the chapter on common dream themes. Here I would like to consider the dreams that feel just like other normal dreams but that include deceased friends and relatives in the cast of characters.

When presented with these figures, you need only ask, "What was the deceased person like when he was alive? What was his personality like?" Once elicited, the description is usually quite satisfactorily understood by recapitulating and bridging it as you would any dream person. The fact that the person in the dream is dead in waking life may be quite immaterial if his qualities were exactly those necessary to express a part of the dreamer or of someone in the dreamer's life. The feeling and action context of the dream should indicate if the fact that the figure is dead in waking life is a relevant descriptive feature, perhaps suggesting that the qualities embodied by the figure are indeed, or almost, dead in the dreamer's life.

A figure who is dead in the dream itself is another matter. If the dreamer knows the corpse, she needs to describe its former personality and how she feels in the dream about the death. Once this material is bridged, the dreamer must look to see if the qualities of the deceased have died in herself or in some aspect of her life or relationships. If, as is common, the dreamer has no idea who the corpse is, she must depend on the other elements of the dream (setting, objects, feelings, and action) to provide the necessary clues.

Remember, as with any person in a dream, the dreamer may be dreaming about his or her actual relationship to the dream figure—alive or dead.

Family Members

Some married couples say that their spouses are frequently with them in their dreams as companions, not necessarily active in the dream action, but just there in a pleasant way. This is quite a different role than that usually played by family members in dreams. Usually they are main characters and play either very positive or very villainous roles. For example, look at Ben's dream:

My mother was preparing the Thanksgiving turkey. She asked each of her children to contribute one of their own body organs for the stuffing. In the dream, this appeared to be an old family tradition. My sister refused to meet my mother's demands and left the house. I began to cut my throat so I could reach in for an organ. Then the thought occurred to me, "Maybe I don't have to do this," and the dream ended.

(MOM'S TURKEY)

Ben, a graduate student, was in psychotherapy when he had this dream. His sister's refusal to acquiesce to his cannibalistic mother's demands in the dream and in waking life began to suggest to him that he had some options vis-à-vis this domineering woman. The dream helped him recognize that her demands were not only extreme, but mortally dangerous to anyone who complied, no matter what tradition might dictate.

Tina dreamt of meeting two women who were to be her college roommates. She described them as selfish provincial snobs who shunned her overtures to be friendly. In the dream, Tina decided that she had had it. She had put up with too many critical, bitchy roommates in the past, and either the university must assign her new roommates or she would insist on moving to another room or dormitory. She had spent too many years in the past with critical roommates and now knew she did not have to put up with such treatment. Tina had no idea why she should dream such a dream, but found herself preoccupied by it for the next few days. She understood the dream as soon as she answered her interviewer's first question, "What is a roommate?" Tina described a roommate as "someone who is in your inner circle, who is supposed to be supportive, dependable, and fun, or at least pleasant to be with over long periods of time and on a rather intimate level." Having said this, Tina bridged the critical roommates in her dream to specific women in her life:

her mother, certain troubled roommates, and a variety of envious women, including her sister. She said she felt waves of anger at their covert hostility, which she could never assuage as long as they resented and envied her for her gifts and lifestyle. She was angry at herself for having so long and so futilely tried to placate them and win their approval and love. This dream precipitated her decision to redefine her relationship with her critical relatives and to seek out intimate friends who were happy enough with their lives to delight in her successes and share a supportive friendship. She had finally realized that she could neither heal nor win the approval of women who resented her for the best parts of herself, and after appreciating the meaning in this dream, Tina changed the nature of her relationships. (Roommates)

When Rosina was a senior in high school, she told me a dream that upset her so much that she had remembered it since its occurrence five years earlier. She saw her younger brother chopped up in a trash can. While I could have launched into a discussion of sibling rivalry with her, I thought she would get a lot more out of a brief interview. I asked her why people chop up other people. She said, "Because they are mobsters or very angry." What do humans put in trash cans? "Stuff they don't want," she said. She described her brother as "a pain in the neck." Asked how she felt when she saw her brother in the trash can, she said she was very sad. I asked, "Why? What would you have missed about your brother if he had died when you had the dream?" She replied that he was a lot of fun, he stuck up for her when it was really important, and he laughed a lot. Then she added that she had become much closer to her brother when she was in the eighth grade, which was the year she had the dream. Now she saw how the dream might have affected her feelings at the time and thought there might be a connection between her dream and the change in her attitude toward her brother. (Brother in Trash Can)

One woman had a long involved dream about her sister, who

was identified not by name but by her role as sister. We asked her, "What is a sister?" and she burst into tears. As she described a sister as someone who loved you through thick and thin, with whom you can share your secrets, your hopes and fears as well as your trivia, she realized for the first time that she did not have such a relationship with her sister, who was envious and critical. Their relationship was only superficially intimate, and the dreamer began to see in the rest of the dream why she had been "neglecting" her sister. It is amazing to see how sometimes one question will unlock the meaning of an entire dream. (Sisters)

When I asked Margaret to describe her husband, who starred in one of her dreams, she put up one block after another. I just couldn't elicit a good description from her, so, in sheepdog fashion, I went around to the dream action and asked her to describe that. She said that in the dream he turns on the water in the backyard and floods the entire yard. "What is a backyard?" A private family place for relaxation and recreation. "What is wrong with flooding a backyard?" I queried as a Martian might. Margaret said that this rendered the yard unusable and temporarily ruined it. Then after a summary of what we knew so far, she was able to bridge saying that her husband "floods our private family life with his extreme reactions of anger, and he closes off communication. I am angry now, as I was in the dream, when I think how he has repeatedly done this to us." (Flood in the Backyard)

Of course, family members in dreams aren't limited to evoking our recognition of qualities we have underestimated in them, nor to showing us a part of ourselves that is like one of them. Sometimes, relatives highlight qualities of other people in our lives and of our relationships with them.

Victoria dreamt of seeing her uncle Bill, whom she greeted coolly. She said she didn't hug him, or even shake hands. Victoria described Uncle Bill as a father substitute of whom she was fond. He was an alcoholic, but he was a dear, sensitive man who did not merit such cool treatment. Victoria bridged these feelings to the way she was feeling about her vacationing psychiatrist, who had failed to respond to the letter she wrote him. In this dream, Victoria had the opportunity to reconnect with the likeable parts of her uncle and, through him, with the things she valued about her psychiatrist that her hurt and anger had obscured from view. Her feeling that her uncle did not deserve such shabby treatment came out in the interview questions about feelings and was the key to her reconsidering her judgment of her psychiatrist. (Uncle Bill)

Friends, Colleagues, and Acquaintances

Amber, an editor, told us that the man named Bob in her dream was the production manager at her newspaper. In describing him, Amber said, "He's too laid-back on the job to oversee the production effectively." In an earlier scene of the dream, Amber was acting like a laid-back high-school student, putting off studying for her college exams. After summarizing the part of the dream that preceded the appearance of Bob and pointing out the similarities between her and Bob's dream behavior, Amber began to see something new about herself. Although she convinced the world and herself that she was busy as a beaver, Amber was, in fact, neglecting her more serious work of self-study, which she bridged with the college-level exams. She had been spending too much of her time on minor busy work at the high-school level, and as far as her self-study was concerned, she was letting Bob manage her life. As is often the case, our colleagues enter our dreams to teach us something about ourselves, not just to remind us of what we think of them during the day. (College Exams and Bob)

Lucia dreamt that her boyfriend preferred to sleep with Johanna, a colleague of hers at the teaching hospital. In the dream, it is understood that Johanna is an "old friend" who has come to stay with Lucia and her boyfriend. Lucia described Johanna as a quiet, shy, gentle woman. Yes, she saw those traits in herself, although they had receded in recent months. To the question, "Is there any way that your boyfriend might prefer those traits in you?" she replied that he probably missed the gentleness and the quietness that she now rarely showed him. (Boyfriend Prefers Johanna)

Friends and acquaintances in dreams, like colleagues, usually need only to be well described before the dreamer can see them as powerful metaphors. Emma's dream of a particular friend is a case in point.

> **Suddenly I am in a room** of a house with my girlfriend Chris. We look into an adjacent room filled with men who seem to be related to me in some way. Chris is laughing at them and thinks they are ridiculous. They are peasantlike. They are caring for a beautiful baby. They have given the baby too much orange sherbet and the baby is throwing up. Chris says men are like that. My mother appears and says that she really is the one who gave the baby too much sherbet.
>
> (ORANGE SHERBET)

The old-fashioned style of the house made Emma feel like she was in Chris's bailiwick. "Who is Chris and what is she like?" Emma said that Chris is a friend who is pretty and very manipulative. She is Germanic and enjoys keeping control of people and situations. She acts as if she is superior, but underneath she feels quite inferior. Chris is the one who is laughing at the peasantlike men whom she finds ridiculous. Peasantlike men are unsophisticated, coarse, and inferior, according to Emma. The baby is beautiful, but has been given too much orange sherbet. Emma tells us that orange sherbet is cooling and sweet, and she eats it because it makes you thin. Chris, who feels superior to the men, blames them for the baby's vomiting, and says that men are like that, i.e., unsophisticated, coarse, and inferior.

The surprise comes when we discover that the problem is not the men's fault, but the mother's. When asked, "Is there any way your mother overdoes it with trying to make the baby sweet and thin?" Emma noted that she had, indeed, adopted her mother's unhealthy emphasis on being sweet and looking good for men. Chris's attitude of superiority toward men felt very familiar to Emma, who had learned to control and manipulate men at an early age. She still often operates this way with men and, of course, feels superior to them "because the peasants fall for it." As a result of this dream, Emma began to recognize that her superior attitude toward men was not born of men's lack of sophistication, although it exploited men's unsuspecting naïveté in certain areas. Rather, she began to see that her superior, manipulative attitude derived from her deep-seated sense of inferiority vis-à-vis men. This feeling of inferiority led Emma, as it does so many women in our culture, to use covert, underhanded manipulation to assert her needs and desires.

Strangers

Strangers in dreams are usually not as difficult to work with as one might think. Even if the dreamer does not know who a stranger is, there are usually plenty of clues in the stranger's setting, appearance, or behavior to identify him for the purposes of the dream. Adrianne dreamt:

> **A young woman goes to college.** Students are supposed to arrive a month early to get oriented, get books, and start reviewing. The woman wants to get a typewriter and a tape recorder so she can review her languages. In fact, she wants to go through all her books before classes begin. I think this is silly.
> (COLLEGE PREPARATION)

When Adrianne described this woman as ridiculously over-concerned with preparation, she could bridge to her own problem of needing to be perfect (this is similar to one of the bridges in "Sister Petronilla"). The waking situation that tied into the dream was Adrianne's feeling that she needed to learn absolutely everything about the new career she was starting before embarking on it. She saw this need as a reflection of great insecurity and fear of criticism.

An unknown boy and his dog, who had both been sadistically burned by a girl in Colette's dream, were quite a puzzle until, in the next scene, we see the boy and his dog lying together on their sides. "They don't look burned, but they do look devastated—hurt or wounded—but it doesn't show physically." With this clue we could ask if the boy and his dog reminded her of any hurt or wound that didn't show on the outside. And as you might guess, the answer was a firm yes, having to do with hidden hurts unresolved since childhood. As we shall see in the next chapter, suffering dogs often reflect the suffering, but clearly innocent, parts of the dreamer that have been or are being mistreated by the dreamer himself or by others.

Beverly, who had the dream of the Catholic and Lutheran churches, dreamt about seeing photos of a real trip she had taken with her spiritual healing group to observe spiritual healers. In the photos, she saw strangers all dressed in white, with white faces and hair who looked as if they were trying to be ghosts. As she continued to describe these strangers, who seemed bizarre and silly in their trench coats as they aped being ghost-detectives, she began to recognize the members of her friendly healing group who were so interested in investigating spiritual things. This was not a comfortable bridge for Beverly, for at the time of the dream she was still under their spell and quite dependent on them for her social life. But the dream did help her see some of the silliness and pretense of those in the group, and led her to several more dreams on the subject that eventually contributed to her leaving the ghost-detectives' circle. (Photos of Ghosts)

Nationalities, Races, and
Specific Categories of People

The thing to remember when exploring dream characters identified as members of particular categories of people is that the
interviewer must elicit from the dreamer his honest thoughts
and feelings about that category of human beings. I have found
that most of my clients are more willing to speak frankly about
embarrassing sexual images and issues than they are about their
attitudes toward different races and nationalities. Some are even
reticent to let you know what they really feel about certain occupations, for fear of looking narrow-minded. To overcome
this reticence, the interviewer can reassure the dreamer that we
all carry the weight of prejudice in ourselves and that this prejudice may be deeply embedded from our social training or it may
be superficial, based on an awareness of social stereotypes that
do not have a great influence on our heartfelt attitudes. It is
common to have the deepest conviction that every human being
should be honored equally and that one should work to attain
that goal in this world and, at the same time, to carry certain
unacceptable prejudices somewhere inside oneself. In dreams
we use these stereotypes as a metaphoric shorthand to portray
particular characteristics that are really a part of our own personalities or part of someone or something in our lives.

In asking the dreamer questions about such images, it is important to pay special attention to the generic descriptions. Tell
the dreamer you are not interested in a polite, liberal description, but in the stereotypes associated with the image. Be sure to
elicit the stereotype before exploring the specific image in the
dream, then consider the description of the stereotype as one
aspect of the full description to be recapitulated and bridged.

In Amber's dream about putting off studying for her college
exams, she was critical of Bob, whom she described as too laid-
back and not productive enough. In the dream, Amber was critical of an article Bob had written, but then discovered she could

not blame Bob for it because Bob had only adapted the article, which had been written by a man named K. Singh. Amber had never known a man by this name, but she knew at this point in the interview that he was the key to finding out what was behind her own lack of productivity. We applied a question we would ask about a stranger: "Because you don't know anyone by this name and because you never see him in the dream, all we have to go on is his name. What can you tell us about such a name?" Amber, who had lived in an ashram for three years, replied that it was a Sikh male name that meant lion. We asked, "What are Sikh males like?" She described them as "rigid, dogmatic, and rule bound." She bridged, saying that this K. Singh was like the lion in her who wanted to take over Bob's job and dictate how it should be done. Now we could see how Amber's Bob-like behaviors were, at least in part, an adaptation or reaction to the rigid, rule-bound Sikh lion within herself. The next dream she brought into our study group dealt head-on with the driving force behind both her Bob and her K. Singh tendencies.

When a dreamer gains insight about a conflict within himself and is able to hold on to that insight and incorporate it, his dreams will move on to examine the deeper levels and ramifications of the conflict before dropping it from the dream agenda.

Keeping in mind that no two people can assume that they share exactly the same stereotypes about any group, and that any individual may arrange his description of a group differently according to his mood or dream context, we always ask the dreamer to describe the group as if for the first time. A dreamer who described the Japanese as introverted, spiritual, and introspective in one interview, later described them as rigid, conformist, and too submissive to authority. Each description was evocative of meaning in its own dream context and illustrated different aspects of a single underlying issue: the dreamer's spiritual quest.

One reason we insist that interviewers in a group keep their thoughts and opinions about specific dream images to them-

selves is demonstrated by the description of Persians provided
by two different dreamers. Madeline told us that Persians, like
Indians, are friendly, hospitable, spiritual, and simple and more
open, humble, and honest than most other people. When Beatrice had a dream about a Persian woman, she described Persian
women as caricatures of the female sex: They anoint themselves,
wear beautiful clothes, and keep themselves hidden from all
men save their husbands. They are the property of the one man
they serve—which Beatrice didn't like—but she added, "They
are very sensuous. I am drawn to them, too. If you cut everything but being erotic out of your life, you must get very good
at it." Madeline and Beatrice used the image of Persians in very
different ways. It would have been disorienting and disruptive
for either of them to impose her impressions of this nationality
on the other.

Racial stereotypes are most difficult to elicit from dreamers
who consider themselves liberals and who are sickened by racist
attitudes and policies. My colleague Loma Flowers is black and
I am white. At our dream center we teach people from a variety
of races how to work with dreams and often assemble them in
groups. It is both sad and funny to see how we have to work to
get new students to trust us and the other students enough to
reveal their racial stereotypes. Adrianne, a white lawyer, dreamt
of a young black male friend unknown to her in waking life.
With a little encouragement, she described her image of young
black males: "They are cocky, and full of an obnoxious bravado
that comes from insecurity. They tend to be aggressive and
brimming with hostility." Adrianne bridged this figure to the
way she was when she began to practice law. She still felt
ashamed and embarrassed about her bravado, inappropriate
hostility, and aggressiveness in that period. She could see now
how much anger she felt in those days. The rest of the dream
pointed to the difficulties she was currently having with this
part of her personality.

People will also cast dream figures as male, female, gay,

straight, thin, or fat to highlight a particular web of association and feeling. Dream stereotypes act as a kind of mental shorthand.

Beverly dreamt of gay men and described them as nice fellows who would never be interested in her and never be husband material. She bridged them to the older men in her work environment whom she had, in a way, used as husband substitutes. Blond females in the dreams of women who are not blond often receive brutal descriptions such as "Blonds are superficial, dumb, incompetent, and lack sexual discretion," "Blonds are man thieves," and "Blonds look good from a distance, but if you look closely at them, they never have beautiful facial features, their features are rather bland." Often, the dreamers who give a version of the sexy dumb blond are actually dreaming of the sexy part of themselves that they judge critically. Men who dream of blonds often have a very different group of descriptions to offer that, if they are similar in "factual" description, tend to contain a greater variety of emotional responses. Kirstin, a pretty blond, dreamt of a brunet and described such creatures as "attractive women who can let it all hang out. They can say what they want and get away with it. They are far more powerful than blonds."

People with particular occupations can have surprising references, as well. Albert's dream is a good example:

> **I am on a ship** with a friend who is a crewman like me. I feel that we have illegal aliens aboard. They shouldn't be there, but everyone tolerates them. A new chief petty officer arrives who is going to make trouble and crack down. The new chief says no more fooling around. No yoga. Then he says yoga is okay but no TV, no ball games all day long. I have a package about a foot long and a foot wide shaped like a loaf of bread. I think that I can get on the new chief's good side if I give him the bread. **(NEW CHIEF PETTY OFFICER)**

Albert commented that he didn't like his years in the navy—
too much discipline—but he knew how to get by and keep his
officers happy. He bridged the illegal aliens to "illegal" parts of
his own personality that were unpleasant and destructive, but
that he and his friends had tolerated for years. His description of
a chief petty officer was the major key to the dream: "A chief
petty officer is the boss. He is the one who really decides what
happens on a ship. I guess that's my wife!" The rest of the
images fell quickly into place. His wife decided that Albert
should be shaped up. She dragged him to therapy to fix the
parts of him she disapproved of (the aliens), insisted that he
cease and desist from behaviors that she did not consider productive of personal and spiritual growth. But Albert knew how
to deal with these no-nonsense officers—offer them a lot of
something they like, and they'll get off your back for a while.
Bread, or money, and lots of it seemed to be the thing that
would appease this officer, Albert's wife. To provide this pallia-
tive in waking life, Albert saw that he had to manage his money
better to better manage his wife.

People of Particular Ages

When the relative or specific age of a dream character is mentioned, you can be sure that the age is an important aspect of the
character and will assist the dreamer in recognizing the metaphoric significance of the image. Amber's dream image of a
French girl did not make sense after she answered our first
question about what the French are like. She said they were a
pleasure- and fun-loving lot who were very earthy and preoccupied with material things. She could not make a bridge until
we asked her what French girls were like. Then she told us that
French girls like the one in her dream were still being formed
and were very impressionable and vulnerable to the influences
of their materialistic culture. Now Amber spontaneously
bridged by saying, "I grew up in the American culture that is

like that, and like the girl, I am still impressionable." In the
dream, the French girl had been taken under the wing of a
woman whom Amber greatly admired. Amber suggested that
there was hope yet for her overly materialistic self. (French Girl)

Clara dreamt of a boy of a specific age for a specific reason:

> **A fourteen-year-old boy** is playing ball inside. He looks
> like he has had a serious accident. As we talk, he makes
> light of it. His leg is in a cast, but he says he is working
> with the Spaulding Company to get back in shape. I
> ask him how long it will take, and he says another
> thousand miles. He seems quite diligent and deter-
> mined.   **(THE FOURTEEN-YEAR-OLD)**

In this scene, there are seven major clues to help identify this
dream figure:

1. The boy is fourteen.
2. He is playing ball inside.
3. He has had a serious accident.
4. His leg is in a cast.
5. However, he is training with Spaulding to get back
   in shape.
6. He says it will take another thousand miles to get
   back in shape.
7. He is diligent and determined.

Asking Clara to describe each of the elements that make up
the clues will maximize her chances of making a good, solid
bridge. In general, I like to ask about the specific age last of
all, because age usually acts like a punch line that is hard to see
before the dreamer has appreciated the specificity of the image
that the other clues help to establish. In Clara's case, there
seemed to be a part of her that played ball inside, rather than in
the outside world. She was recovering from emotional wounds,

was a bit constricted as a result (the cast), but was training with the best (according to Clara, Spaulding makes the best, bounciest, most resilient tennis balls) in her tour of various therapies. She was impatient to be in top form and thought another thousand miles a long way to go, but the boy was diligent and determined to pull it off. After having elicited all this information, we asked Clara the standard questions about specific ages: "Fourteen years ago puts us in what year?" Then, "Is there anything in your life, or some part of you that is like this boy who is (recapitulation) and that is now fourteen years old or that began in 19–?" Clara responded that it was in that year, fourteen years earlier, that she made a career choice, which she was in the process of modifying significantly. At last, she had her foot in the door. With further reflection, Clara could look back to the year the dream boy was born and see if there were other important choices she made about herself that were particularly evident in her career choice.

Specific ages are not always references to the part of the dreamer that is exactly that old, as in Clara's dream. Amber went to bed one night very disgruntled with her marriage. She had this dream.

> **Someone had a baby boy** that was growing very fast. He was under two and already over five feet tall. He was very intelligent, as well. The children in the neighborhood gave him a hard time, but I thought he could be taught so as to catch up with the age group that he *looked* like he belonged in.   (TALL BABY)

In this case, we asked Amber to describe what humans are like who are under two years old. She told us that they are just beginning to walk and need lots of nurturing and encouragement in learning all the basics. Then we asked what was wrong with the treatment the baby received from the other children, to which she responded that children are cruel to big children who are younger than they look. The children expect them to act as old as they appear because the children do not understand or have sympathy for developmental limits. We asked Amber what she thought about her proposed dream solution to this problem and she said it was entirely unrealistic. She bridged this to the way she criticizes her husband, whom she has tried too energetically to educate in matters of feeling and self-awareness. This bridge was not easy for her to admit. Amber told us that it would be very difficult to give up her unrealistic expectations of her husband and understand that he was only just beginning to recognize his own feelings. She now realized that he needed encouragement, not a crash course in self-understanding.

Heroes and Villains

The Nazis, vampires, witches, Darth Vaders, angels, gods, Gloria Steinems, John Kennedys, Charles de Gaulles, and Joan of Arcs serve the same functions in dreams as do other people, and yield their secrets to the same questions. Again, remember that one man's heroine might be another's villain, and one cannot assume that the interviewer and the dreamer see the same good or bad things in the same person. Almost always, the very words a dreamer chooses to describe a character are the exact ones that will most quickly trigger a good, sound bridge.

When Dora dreamt of a terrible, evil presence behind a door, she described it to us as "Something very evil that might get me, or change me into something awful. It might make me disappear. It is much more powerful than I." Armed with this description, Dora could bridge it to her paranoid, psychotic mother, whose effects on her she had not yet dealt with effectively. (Evil behind the Door)

Nazis are popular dream villains. Mary Ellen described them as isolated people with a narrow vision of the world. They have no feelings and do not allow others to have them. They are vicious because their only interest is power and control, and they live by rigid rules and formulas. In the dream, the Nazis had her trapped in Lola's house. Lola was described as a friend who was very creative and very driven. She overworks terribly, and is obsessed with being independent. Her drive in her creativity, her work, and her need for independence has become unhealthy and isolating. It is not surprising that in this emotional setting, highlighting the Lola characteristics of her personality, Mary Ellen felt trapped in a small house with no room to hide from the Nazis who were pursuing her. Mary Ellen suffered the same obsessive drive as Lola and was similarly isolated. The Nazis were winning. By the end of the dream, they may have killed her, she wasn't sure. Dismal dreams like this one, which end badly with the actual or probable death of the dreamer, often indicate an urgent need for intensive psychotherapy. Mary Ellen needed help in battling the Nazi attitudes she turned against herself and that could kill her creative spirit and make her life an isolated nightmare. (Trapped by Nazis)

Heroes and heroines are far easier to work with than villains, and just as important. People can learn through pleasure as well as through pain. Insecure people who underestimate their gifts often dream of heroes who exhibit the qualities they ignore and fail to develop in themselves. When working with such dreams, it sometimes helps if the interviewer gives the dreamer permission to throw modesty to the winds and acknowledge whatever traits he ascribed to his hero as ones he too may possess.

Interviewers

When the interviewer appears as himself in a dream, the dreamer often needs a good deal of encouragement to describe the interviewer frankly. If the interviewer has established a good atmosphere and relationship, there is hope that the dreamer will feel comfortable enough to speak his mind, at least in part. The interviewer must usually make an extra effort to elicit possible critical thoughts the dreamer may prefer to omit from his description. As the interviewer, talking about yourself in the third person can make it easier for the dreamer. For example, I would ask, "What is Gayle like? What is she doing in the dream?" If the context of the dream gives me any reason at all to suspect some negative material is missing from the description, I say things like "It's okay, you can tell me what you don't like about me. I can take it. And if I can't, don't worry, I'm married to a great psychiatrist who will put me back together again." A little humor can go a long way in easing anxiety. In the end, after the description, recapitulation, and bridging, we see once again that the interviewer in the dream represents an aspect of the dreamer, someone in the dreamer's life, or an issue in the dreamer-interviewer relationship.

HELP KEY

- *If the dreamer can't come up with specific words to describe a well-liked dream character,* try asking, "What would you or the world lose if X died?"

- *When a dreamer responds to your recapitulaton of his description of a dream person's personality with the statement "I used to be like that,"* say, "I see. Now you had this dream this week, and dreams usually deal with a current issue in one's life. Do you think there might still exist a small vestige of these traits somewhere in your current personality?" If the answer is no, but you suspect the dreamer is being resistant and not acknowledging that he is still somewhat this way, you might tell him that dreams tend to exaggerate to get a point across; then ask if there isn't even a trace of these characteristics left in him.

□

**CHAPTER
SIX**

ANIMALS IN DREAMS

As a rule, the easiest dream images to work with are those of land animals, birds, fish, and insects. If you remember to elicit a description directed toward a Martian, you will probably find that the dreamer will have no hesitation in providing you with a concise value-colored description. Most dreamers do not feel the need to protect the reputation of an animal, nor do they fear your censure if they criticize one. The key question to ask about animals is "How would you describe the personality of an X?" The first time a dreamer hears this question, she will be surprised and may protest. If you say something like "Well you know what X's look like (or how they act, or what they are known for), what would you guess their personality might be like?" your dreamer will then be able to give you the information you need. You will hear some exquisitely memorable descriptions, I assure you.

You will find that many of the questions you have learned in the chapters on dream settings and people will come in handy when working with dream animals. You will also find that as you develop your interviewing skills, you will enjoy coming up with your own questions tailored to the many special situations dreams present. I hope that by now you have found a dream partner with whom you can practice different interviewing techniques. This will not only be fun but very instructive. The following dreams involve all sorts of animals and should provide ideas that you can apply in your own interviews.

QUEEN BEES

Angela is a very pretty, bright, and talented blond who is vibrantly alive and optimistic. She is the sort of blond many women have been conditioned to envy and hate, but have trouble finding cause to criticize and, finding no justification for their negative feelings, must struggle with their uncomfortable envy. This response from other women has had its effect on Angela, as we see in her dream about a bee. In the dream, she and a friend are trying to put up a partition in a room to block out a queen bee, which is flying about. Angela notes that in so doing they will block out the fireplace area, as well. In the next scene, someone is preparing to kill the bee. This is so upsetting to Angela that she cannot bear to watch. (Queen Bee)

Angela awoke and thought the dream must have something to do with her interest in acupuncture. I was surprised, but then, after all, a bee could stick one with a needle. I doubted this hypothesis would stand for long because I suspected Angela would describe the bee's sting as something other than medicinal or healing, and because the plot suggested something very different to me. Because this was Angela's dream, not mine, I acknowledged her hypothesis, and bracketed hers along with mine, filing them for possible reference during the interview.

I asked Angela to describe a queen bee. She said that she is unique in her hive. She receives special food, is the only one who can lay eggs, is forty times bigger than any other bee, and receives preferred treatment from the day she is born. Asked if there was anything in her life like a queen bee, Angela admitted that her mother had always preferred her and given her special treatment, calling her "the golden girl." She then went into how this had not made relations with her sister easy. I asked her if she had tried to block the queen bee qualities out of her room and had turned away when she saw her bee in mortal danger. Angela said yes, she saw this queen bee as an image of her shining special self, which she has tried to push out of her life and do away with because it seemed to be the cause of so much friction and envy in her life. Given her experience with envious women, she was afraid that if she really let her queen bee out, she would lose the love she had and might even overwhelm the men who had been her main social supports. The heroine in this dream is sacrificed because of the dreamer's fear of risking being herself. Her deep sadness at the bee's imminent demise gave us cause to hope that she might yet decide to save it.

BIRDS

In Chapter 4 on dream settings, we saw how Sylvie's dream of the macaw at the Princeton Club helped her recognize her anxiety that her macawlike, exotic, beautiful, creative self might misbehave and be rejected by the members of a club for high achievers.

Amber had a dream about seeing a wounded bird that was brought before her by a snowy owl. A few healthy birds hold and comfort the wounded bird. Amber feels badly, not knowing what to do for it, but then says to herself, "Instead of feeling bad, I should pay attention to what the birds are doing and see if I can't learn something from them." The birds were showing her that all that was necessary was just to be with the bird and share warmth and comfort; that was what the bird needed. Amber described birds as the only creatures who know how to fly, and that for a bird not to be able to fly is an enormous loss. She bridged this to her soul or spirit. The wounded bird she saw as herself, and in the weeks following the interview she became increasingly aware of how much she felt like the wounded bird, which she had described as fragile, vulnerable, and unable to care for itself.

She described the snowy owl as nocturnal, knowing how to live in cold, harsh environments, and not intimidated. The owl in her dream seemed pretty, rare, wise, and caring. She bridged the snowy owl to a wise potential aspect of herself that, through her Alcoholics Anonymous and dream group evening meetings, is presenting her with the need to recognize and attend to the wounded bird within her. She saw her dream as encouraging her to observe the comforting behavior of the healthy birds and try to learn a similar accepting, caring attitude toward herself. (Wounded Bird)

CAMELS

Animals that tend to evoke similar descriptions from many dreamers will strike each one in a personal way. Elvira described camels as irritable animals that are hard to get along with, but they can go a long way without a drink. Elvira was reminded of her own efforts as a recovering alcoholic. In certain ways, she had become something of a camel. Vera described camels as "domesticated, but proud, wild desert animals who go a long way without needing food or water. Camels are completely soundless at slaughter." At this point she bridged to her own quiet acceptance of meager emotional supplies during childhood, to her pride and difficulty in admitting she has any needs, and to her little girl's silence when her father abused her.

DOGS

It is vital to attend to the breed of dogs in dreams if it is known. Again, assumptions are dangerous. A fine psychiatrist who was working with a dream image of a German shepherd pointed out to the dreamer that the dog, being German, was associated with rigid, Germanic attitudes. For all he knew, the dreamer might have had a German nanny who supplied all the love and acceptance her mother denied her. She might well have thought of Germans as robust, generous, fun-loving people. Or perhaps

"German" was not the point. Far more likely, in my experience, is that she would have had something to say about the personality of German shepherds if someone had asked her. I have heard descriptions of these dogs ranging from "vicious police attack dogs that maul anything a honkie cop orders" to "wonderfully loyal companions who have great dignity and love, but who can get overly protective." The first dreamer found that he was describing his brother; as the second dreamer, I was describing my husband. When a new member in one of our long-term dream groups described a Great Dane as exhilarating, slobbering, and affectionate, he blushed in commenting that a special teacher had once compared him to a Great Dane, and he guessed he was like that.

Emma had a vivid dream of two dogs in city hall:

> **A couple is trying to control** a rather wild dog inside city hall. It is not obeying—it is running to and fro and defecating on the floor. It has the proper licenses, however.
>
> I am holding another dog, a schnauzer, in a basket with a blanket wrapped around it. It is very quiet and passive. Suddenly, the unruly dog smells the dog in the basket and grabs it and bites it on the leg. The schnauzer looks at me, upset that she was minding her own business and yet was attacked. She, however, does not have the proper credentials from city hall.
>
> (TWO DOGS IN CITY HALL)

As Emma described the unruly, wild dog the couple could not control, she bridged to her son, to whom she and her husband, as the city hall authorities, gave license to be disobedient. She saw in this dream a picture of how they had been much too permissive and now were paying the price—a fact she tried to deny while awake. The schnauzer was like a sweet, loyal, obedient, passive dog she once had and that now, in this context, seemed to reflect that part of herself. Emma commented that she had been letting her unruly son attack and chew her up emotionally. In reflecting on the dream, she said that she had tried to be too much the friend and not enough the authority to her son.

CATS AND RATS

Cats have been awfully misinterpreted by those who have read or heard that they represent the eternally feminine qualities (whatever they are). Sometimes dreamers describe cats as sleek and feminine, sometimes—many times—they do not. Agatha described cats as "independent and extremely loving when they want to be, but they generally keep their distance. They are clever, complicated, and more interested in a wider range of things than are dogs, who give their love totally without question. Cats only come for food, love, and attention when they feel like it." This description reminded Agatha of her boyfriend Terry; then she said, "All the men in my life are like that. They come to me on their terms when they need something. Like cats, they are never there for me."

Adrianne dreamt of talking to a crying friend in the friend's broken car. When she described this friend as someone who really needed psychotherapy, but who just wouldn't admit it, Adrianne acknowledged for the first time that her car, her way of getting around in the world, had broken down and she too needed therapy. In the next scene, there are two cats and occasionally a rat. She goes down into the basement a couple of times to try to kill the rat. The last time she goes down, she finally realizes that the rat is not a rat, but a third cat. This cat is wounded and she wonders why she should kill it. (The Third Cat)

Adrianne described cats as her feminine self, so we asked her to elaborate. She said they are "strong, lithe, and wonderful. They are me as a woman." Concerning the basement, Adrianne bridged to her unconscious, where she kept the many unrealized and unwanted parts of herself. We asked if two cats in a basement reminded her of anything, but she could not make a bridge. We repeated a recapitulation of her description of the cats and asked about there being two of them, then she recognized the possibility that they were like Loma and me; both of us had spent time exploring her unconscious. She described a rat as a pest that can spread disease and should be exterminated to maintain health. But what was this? She had mistaken a wounded cat for a rat. She quickly bridged this cat to her wounded, feminine, strong, lithe, wonderful self. Perhaps her metaphoric realization in the dream that she needed therapy allowed her to look more closely at what she had thought was a rat and discover that it was instead a wounded cat.

Adrianne's description of a cat is a good example of why an interviewer should never be content with a prefabricated, general description such as "This represents my feminine side." The unpacking of such images, even when the first formulation is generally accurate, will provide you with the specifics necessary to understand the metaphor of the image in a given dream and life context.

Just as with specific breeds of dogs, if you or your partner dream of a specific sort of cat, it will be important to ask questions like "What is the personality of a Siamese cat like?" or "How is a Persian cat different from any other breed?" If your friend dreams of Topkapi, the cat she currently lives with, you will do well to ask about Topkapi's personality directly, because the response will include what is relevant about the breed as it relates to the specific cat.

LIONS

Someone unrolls a rug to show me the lion. At first, I think it is facing front. Then, it is spread out, sphinx-

like. Then I note an Oriental pattern in which I can dis-
cern a female lion's head and body. When I shift
position, I see the lion's form in another place on the
rug. I am very excited about this. Others don't believe
me; they can't see it. Then I realize that everytime I shift
position, I see another perspective of the lion. Someone
talks about how they like it that I get excited about
things.   (THE LION RUG)

Adrianne was delighted by this dream. She bridged the complex, intricate Oriental rug patterns to the psychological patterns she was discovering through her work with dreams. She
described lions as

magnificent beasts who are kings of the jungle. The
sphinx could answer riddles. It is really the lioness who
is the hunter. She has the smarts and agility. The male is
lazy and steals the kill from the females. Lions are sensuous, and have lots of presence. They sense their own
power. One never thinks of a lion wondering about its
role in life, whether or not it's a lion. Lions are beautiful
and without frills; they have lots of substance.

Adrianne was learning to see her lioness qualities from many
new angles, and she loved it.

Beverly dreamt of a lion in a different situation. Her dream
lion was coming down the hall of the home she lived in as an
adolescent. She ran to her parents' bedroom, tried to shut out
the lion, and called to her parents to wake up and help her. Her
parents did nothing, but the lion seemed to have given up, as her
parents had predicted it would. (The Lion Gives Up)

Even while dreaming, Beverly knew the lion was familiar, a
symbol. She described lions as "great, big, huge, slow, and very
powerful, massive things that can kill you. They are unmanageable. Leos are overpowering, very strong, territorial, entitled

people. Lions don't worry about making mistakes." She heard
the recapitulation as a description of the potential in herself that
she had been running away from since her adolescence, when it
became clear to her that her entitled, territorial, powerful self
who did not worry about making mistakes was a threat to the
way she was encouraged to be at home. She felt she always had
to throttle her sense of power: "Every time I got thrilled about
something, there would be no answering thrill from my family.
My family did not do thrilling things." As you may remember
from Beverly's other dreams, Beverly's family emphasized doing good for others, and the children's leonine traits were not
encouraged. The lion gave up. This dream came the night after a
day when, as Beverly wrote in her day notes on retiring to sleep,
"I felt I'd retreated into my small, timid self, and felt incompetent."

In dreams like this, the apparently threatening force turns out
to be a cluster of rejected and feared traits of the dreamer's personality that she tries to keep out of her life. Once the dreamer
recognizes and begins, however tentatively, to accept these
traits, the dreams change and the threatening figures become
less threatening and, eventually, helpful and friendly. Jung commented often on this phenomenon, and I have seen it many
times. It is as if the lion is saying, "Let me in, or else." Fear acts
like a distorting lens, especially in dreams. A good interview
will reveal whether the threatening being is to be slain or em-
braced.

Crystal described lions as "frightening because of their un-
predictability. The females catch the meat and do all the work.
The males growl out the orders—they are the ultimate chauvin-
ists and have several females under their control. Cats are notoriously unpredictable." Crystal effortlessly bridged the lion to
her notoriously unpredictable father who has a controlling,
chauvinistic side to him and likes to growl out orders to his
female family members, whom he protects like a lion. In the
dream,

It is Christmas, and there is a lion loose in the playground. Jeanne, my piano teacher, is there. I don't want
the lion to spoil my Christmas.

(A LION IS LOOSE)

Crystal described Jeanne as a good teacher. She said,
"Jeanne's husband could be my father," because her father plays
such a protective, supportive role in her life, much the same as
the role Jeanne's husband plays in hers. Then Crystal commented that, while she has her own marriage and family, financially she is still married to her dad. She began to think that if
she didn't want the controlling lion part of her loving father to
run loose in her life, she would have to redefine her relationship
with him.

We have just seen how three different people have described
lions and used them in their dreams. To Adrianne, lions are
magnificent beasts who are kings of the jungle. Lionesses are
the smart, agile hunters, while the males are lazy and steal the
kill from the females. Lions are sensuous, have a wonderful
presence, and sense their own power. Lions are confident about
their own identity, and have lots of substance.

According to Beverly, lions are huge, slow, powerful things
that can kill you. They are unmanageable, and like people born
under the astrological sign of Leo, they are overpowering, very
strong, territorial and entitled. Most of all, lions don't worry
about making mistakes.

Crystal sees lions as unpredictable, controlling, and chauvinistic.

Each personalized description evokes a bridge that is
custom-tailored to the dreamer's life. Even when two dreamers
note the chauvinistic nature of lions, they do so in a different
context and give this trait a different shading and priority. In
interpreting a dream about a lion, Jung says, "Lions, like all
wild animals, indicate latent effects. The lion plays an important
part in alchemy and has much the same meaning. It is a 'fiery'

animal, an emblem of the devil, and stands for the danger of being swallowed by the unconscious."[1] Applying Jung's ideas of what lions are like and what lions mean to any of these dreamers' lions would have seriously distorted the understanding of their dreams. The risk of interpreting dreams according to one's specialized knowledge, rather than according to the dreamer's specific knowledge, impressions, and associations, is that of seriously misinterpreting the entire dream, while seducing the dreamer away from her perfectly adequate and relevant knowledge about the image.[2]

SNAKES

Is there anyone who has not dreamt of snakes? Kekulé's reverie of a snake swallowing its own tail gave him the idea for the structure of benzene and gave the world the foundation of organic chemistry.

Most of the snake dreams I have encountered in my practice have been frightening dreams. Rosalind titled one dream "Three Deadly Snakes." The opening scene is a large hall, like that belonging to King Arthur, whom she described as far removed from his people, but a fascinating figure. She then said, "What sort of a jerk could rally an army and great court to establish a unified, peaceful rule and end up with constant war? He was supposed to be sweet and unassuming, but that was his ruin." Rosalind bridged to her father, "a jerk," who had been sweet, but terribly removed from her as she grew up.

In the great hall, she is being threatened by a king cobra, a rattlesnake, and a water moccasin. She described the king cobra in the dream as the one most aware of her. It was intelligent, brooding, and malignant, and reminded her of the brooding depressions that had plagued her for years. The rattlesnake was less frightening, less dangerous, and less complex. These snakes are straightforward—they give some warning before they strike. Left alone, they don't seek to harm humans; they have their place in nature. Although their venom can be deadly, they are easier to deal with than cobras. The rattler reminded Rosalind of herself at work, where she is practicing giving warning before she strikes out with her anger. She was least afraid of the water moccasin, although she described its venom as deadly. She said these snakes live in swamps, in stagnant water, and paralyze their victims. This reminded Rosalind of her fear of her own feelings and how she can become paralyzed by anxiety.

She discovers these snakes in a hall that she associated with her father, for whom she said she felt nothing. There are many unpacked boxes around. This suggested that Rosalind had some unpacking to do regarding her feelings about her unavailable father, who has always left Rosalind the responsibility of caring for her very depressed mother.

In the dream, Rosalind is terrified and tries to figure out how to kill the snakes. The snakes fall asleep, but then an angry woman enters and wakes them with her noisy talk. The angry woman reminded Rosalind of the angry, insecure part of herself she has been learning to deal with in psychotherapy. When she slips into this angry state of mind, she is vulnerable to depressions, which turn her anger inward.

The cobra begins to pursue Rosalind, who realizes that her only chance lies in getting either herself or the snake into the bedroom of a man named Silas, who is exactly like her dad—sweet, good-humored, but absent and ineffectual. She is becoming weak and immobilized by her terror, she can't move, can't will herself to move, but she realizes that she will die if she doesn't force herself into action. She wakes, filled with terror of the king cobra.

Like many women in our culture, Rosalind grew up with a father who was a workaholic and was physically and emotionally absent much of the time. As a girl she longed for more attention from this father, who was sweet and seemed a resource for warmth and comfort. Did she long to have sex with her father? Maybe, maybe not. But we can be sure that she wanted more love and attention from him. Not only did he disappoint her in this way but he dumped the horrendous job of caring for a sick mother on Rosalind when she was a little girl. Her anger at her dad is part of what led her to call him a jerk and say that she has no feelings for him. Her denial of both her anger and her longing for him have led her into a paralyzing conflict. Is the king cobra her father's penis, as some would suggest? Or is it an expression of her anger or her fear of falling into another depression? Does her fear of admitting her longing for her father's love trigger her depressions? The only thing that will save her from this snake's attack is getting it or herself behind Silas's bedroom door. Silas is a man who is just like her dad but whom Rosalind likes and against whom she has no personal resentment. It might make sense to follow the dreamer's lead and see this snake as her father-related depression that she wishes to escape.[3] Silas's bedroom is the solution to Rosalind's problem. Does this suggest that she needs to investigate what is behind the closed door of her positive feelings for her dad,[4] feelings that she has spent a good deal of energy denying? Even if these feelings seem sexual at first, they will most likely generalize to the longing she has felt since she was a little girl who wanted so badly to get love, attention, and support from the one person in her troubled family who seemed capable of giving it.

Gina, an independent businesswoman of unusual gentleness and charm, had a snake dream that she had been unable to understand with her therapist or after several weeks of pondering it.

I have boa constrictor wrapped around my body underneath my clothes. No one but me knows it is there, not even my therapist. The boa's head, which is like a double fish head, is at my heart, poised to strike me with its venom if I do the wrong thing. It squeezes me if I even

think the wrong thing. I am very anxious, for at any
moment, if I do something inappropriate or sudden, it
could kill me or squeeze the breath out of me. I just
live with it like this. No one knows the danger I am in.
I realize I must kill the snake. It makes me sad to think I
must kill it.   (My Hidden Constrictor)

After telling us the dream, Gina said, "My therapist suggested that I carry this around with me in my briefcase to help
me contemplate the archetypal nature of snakes. (She pulled a
large green rubber snake out of her case.) But it hasn't quite
done the trick." We all laughed at the sudden sight of the snake,
which seemed so removed from the dreamer's description of the
snake in her dream. It was time to get Gina to focus on her
dream instead of on other people's dreams or myths about
snakes, which probably weren't boas anyway.

Early in the interview, we established that Gina's experiences
and feelings related to the snake were a secret that no one, not
even her therapist, knew she had. We spent quite a while helping her to give us a rich description of the snake, because she
kept trying to assign it meanings that were in no way analogous
to the threat posed by the snake or to its secret nature.

The description we elicited of boa constrictors followed these
lines: "Boas eat things whole; they are overpowering; they
squeeze their victims to soften them up—and perhaps kill
them—before swallowing them. This one is poised over my
heart, and so can strike with its venom at the most vital center
of my being—the center of my feelings." We asked how it felt to
have this venomous constrictor wrapped around her wherever
she goes. She said it was terrifying, that she always had to monitor what she did and said or the snake would kill her. Up to this
point, Gina could not bridge this image or its associated feelings to anything in her life.

We asked about the odd double fish head of the snake, and in
describing fish Gina spontaneously bridged to her alcoholic

father, who had two particular sides to his personality. At last, Gina began to allow herself to see how her need to be loved by her father had led her to live constricted and ever threatened by his venomous disapproval. No wonder she had developed such a pleasing, friction-free way of relating to people. She didn't dare to be spontaneous, or risk being inappropriate. She had learned early in life that the snake would strike her in her heart. She was living an emotionally constricted life, captive to this snake. This secret fear of retaliation against even thinking independently took its toll on Gina and was especially influential in her relationships with men.

Here is a dream of Beverly's in which she is learning how to deal with snakes:

> **Our group biologist,** who has already had his nose broken, has been struck on the head by the snake. He has suffered only minor injuries, and is now out on his rounds, but will check in shortly. These injuries must be monitored.
>
> We are in a biological station or educational zoo. We sit around the staff member while he tells us about this snake: This is the emerald green python/rhinoceros snake. (The dream camera pans to bare branches just above us where it rests. The zoologist has it on a leash.) It is the only known animal that attacks rhinos. It is heat sensitive and blindly launches itself at the rhino's head. I realize then that, of course, it goes for the nose, which is the most sensitive part.
>
> In captivity like this, or in areas where the rhino is scarce, the snake will attack people, even children, and may kill them. But it is only following its instincts, reacting to the presence of a warm body. So people just need to be more careful when they go into areas where the snakes are and watch the trees and wear hats.
>
> The injured biologist returns for his checkup. He is

also the staff physician. He seems to bear the snake no
malice.   (THE EMERALD GREEN
                             PYTHON/RHINOCEROS SNAKE)

Beverly had no difficulty figuring this dream out on her
own. She looked at her day notes written the night before the
dream and saw that she had just had a gruesome dinner with her
father; his new and very likeable psychologist wife, Toni; some
of Toni's grandchildren; Toni's father, Enrico; and Toni's difficult stepmother, Leonora. Beverly had felt very uncomfortable
and timid at the dinner. The following summary of her self-
interview will show why:

Biologists study living things and are out there in the
jungle. A group biologist studies living things in
groups, as well. This reminds me of my stepmother,
Toni. She is a psychologist and has been like a staff physician to our family ever since she came into it. She sees
more clearly than we do what is going on and has
helped us a lot. The snake is a picture of Toni's stepmother, Leonora, who dined with us last night. The
attributes of this snake clarify the nature of this difficult
woman. She is a python, she wraps herself around you
till you die. She is emerald green. Her husband covers
her in jewels, and this year's jewels are all emeralds.
Leonora is unpredictable and competitive with her
stepdaughter for her husband's gifts of jewels, and she
lashes out terribly at her husband, who is big, heavy,
and thick-skinned, like a rhinoceros.
    Rhinos are oblivious to anything around them when
they charge, like both Leonora's husband, Enrico, and
my dad when they get involved with a project. Enrico's
thick skin and his ability to tune Leonora out must be
what enable him to put up with her. Leonora attacks

her husband where he is most vulnerable, but failing that, she goes for Toni, who seems to have survived her onslaughts with only minor injuries. Like the snake, Leonora is heat sensitive—any warm body will do. At dinner last night I shuddered for fear of whom she would attack next. But the dream zoologist, who is like the scientist in Toni, is showing me how to deal with such snakes. I shouldn't take such attacks personally, they are just part of the nature of the snake, not a reflection on her victims. When I am around people who are like the snake—and my own mother was somewhat like her—I need to remember to wear a hat and keep my eyes on the tree!

Again, the disadvantages of interpreting any image by a fixed meaning should be clear. Sometimes snakes are sexually meaningful in dreams, sometimes they are not. Sometimes snakes are metaphors for unity and wisdom, and sometimes they are not. Even when a snake fits the general outlines of a preformulated meaning, the particular snake in the particular dream will have a more specific and more valuable significance for the dreamer if the dreamer is given the opportunity to explore it unfettered by anyone else's ideas and symbolism.

HORSES

Horses appear most often in the dreams of my clients and students as images of nature, innocence, and power. The power often refers to their natural strength, which the dreamer is entitled to feel and express, but which is often mistreated, lost, or feared. Having said that, I feel the need to warn you against using this observation as a rule. Until you interview the dreamer, you will not know if she is using horses in the same manner, and even if she is, without more specific information available in the dream, this generalization will be of little benefit to her.

Emma dreamt of being on a sailboat in rough seas. The waves were washing over the deck as it tilted from side to side when

> **Suddenly I see a pregnant** brown mare floating on her side in the water on the left side of the boat. There is a man in the water with her who is trying to help this creature back onto the boat in a time of great difficulty and danger. As the boat leans over and the waves rise, the brown mare is lifted onto the deck. Momentarily, she is safe. But then another wave washes her back into the sea.
>
> Now she is to the right of the ship, and the process of the waves lifting her back onto the deck is repeated. She rests on the deck.
>
> (**BROWN MARE OVERBOARD**)

Emma was, at the time of this dream, thinking of starting a new job. She felt that in her present job, and to some extent in her marriage, she was in rough emotional seas. She described horses as giving her freedom. She used to ride a brown horse and said, "Learning to ride transformed me into a person with speed and power." She loved learning to communicate with such an animal. The mare's pregnancy suggested to Emma the state she was in now, getting ready to change her life with a very different job. But she felt vulnerable, about to take a big risk. The man who was trying to help the mare was like her husband: fiery, temperamental, and a strong swimmer who was good in rough seas. In this period, Emma took some comfort and rest in her relationship (sailboat), but was not secure there because the seas were so rough.

After the decision to leave her current job and take a more interesting one that would pay her much more but be extremely challenging, Emma dreamt:

> **There are two horses** in my living room, one brown and one white. The brown horse is lying down and chewing on its foot. It chews and chews, making its hoof all bloody. It is very ill and needs a vet. It looks at me balefully.
>
> Someone is taking care of the horses, and I instruct her to put newspapers on the floor to protect it from the excretions of the horses. I realize that this is not a permanent solution. I decide that the horses really belong in a wooden barn so they will be protected, yet free to roam in the field and live the natural life of a horse.
>
> The white horse is very beautiful, healthy, and interestingly patterned. **(HORSES IN THE HOUSE)**

This time, Emma described horses as great for recreation, magnificent, powerful, strong, and agile. They are work animals and can carry heavy loads. The white horse reminded her of a white horse she had named Princess. Princess was a dreamer, younger, more energetic and superior to the ordinary brown horse. She thought Princess was like her own positive, free-spirited self-image. The brown horse seemed more like her alternate image of herself as a workhorse who could carry heavy loads. And it was true, Emma told us, that she had brought too much of both her work life and her Princess energy into the intimate living space of her family.

In the dream, the brown horse is ill and cannot carry the load, an exact parallel to the way Emma felt at work. "The horse seems to find something wrong with its hoof, and begins to chew on it to get something out. But the horse just keeps chewing and chewing—it was so bloody and horrible! The horse

should have just left it alone. But in his ignorance, his instinct
has gone awry and become self-mutilation." Emma said this
was a good picture of how she obsesses over her shortcomings.
If she perceives a fault or inadequacy in herself, she won't let it
go. She keeps chewing on herself to the point of self-mutilation.

The decision to move the horses to a barn, so they will not
soil the house and will be protected and free to roam in the
fields, reminded her of her hopes that the new job would not be
so hard on her self-esteem and would be less intrusive in her
private life.

Simon, a physicist, dreamt he had a wonderful, spotless
white horse. It was full of exhilarating energy, like the high-
energy, temperamental self that Simon lets out now and then in
waking life. Simon is with a relative, Gene, who is highly prin-
cipled, moral, responsible, warm, and friendly. This reminds Simon of his docile, good-boy self. It seems that Gene and Simon
want to go see a grand mansion, and to get there faster, Simon
leaves his horse in his mother's hands. It turns out that seeing
the mansion is not such an interesting thing to do after all, and
Simon then discovers that his mother has lost the horse. Simon
is beside himself with anger and with anxiety that the horse
could be stolen or lost forever. It takes a long time, but Simon
finds the horse. Now his parents realize for the first time how
important it is to him to have his horse. (Lost White Horse)

Simon's actual parents, his internalized parents, and his social
training had underestimated his need to ride his white horse—
to feel and express his own energy. Simon had acted like the
docile Gene at home, and in his choice of careers. He had en-
trusted his horse to the part of himself that was like his conformist mother, a mother who was unable to appreciate Simon's
need to be alive, even if that meant being different and temperamental. Simon was very moved by the dream experience of this
vibrant horse, which he could hardly believe he had so long
denied in his pursuit of success and a grand mansion.

MYTHICAL CREATURES

When you dream of a sphinx, a unicorn, or a dragon, it is tempting to run to the nearest encyclopedia of mythology or to a dream dictionary and look up the "meanings" others have assigned to it. But there is no need to do so; in fact, there is good reason not to confuse your predream impressions of the creature with the interpretations of other cultures or other authorities. To know why you dreamt of a particular mythological creature, we must know what *your* version of it is. Only that version will promise a conclusive identification of the metaphor. After you have understood your dream and how it relates to your life, a reading of how other people have understood different versions in different contexts can broaden your appreciation of the image.

The British philosopher Bertrand Russell wrote to a friend about a dream that is one of the most beautiful I have ever come across:

> I dreamt that my bedroom was transformed into a vast cavern on a vast precipitous hillside. In the middle of the cavern I lay sleeping on my bed, while all round, tier above tier, innumerable hermits likewise slept. The next room was transformed into a similar cavern on the same hillside, connecting with mine, filled also with hermits, but not asleep. They were hostile to us & might come to destroy us in our sleep. But I in my sleep spoke to my hermits in their sleep, & said, "Brother hermits, I speak to you in the language of slumber, & the language which only sleepers can utter & only sleepers can hear or understand. In the land of sleep there are rich visions, gorgeous music, beauties for sense & thought such as dare not exist under the harsh light of the cruel sun. Do not awaken from your sleep,

do not resist the other hermits by their own means, for though you win you will become as they, lost to beauty, lost to the delicate vision, lost to all that ruthless fact destroys in the waking world. Sleep therefore; by my slumber language I can instil into you what is better than success & war & harsh struggle, & the worthless grating goods which wakers value. And by our magic, as one by one the other hermits fall asleep, we shall instil into them the bright vision, we shall teach them to love this world of gentle loveliness more than the world of death & rivalry & effort. And gradually from us will radiate to all the world a new beauty, a new fulfillment. . . .

In these visions mankind shall forget their strife, . . . & mankind shall come to know the beauty which it is their mission to behold.[5]

Russell offered no interpretations of this dream in his letter to Lady Ottoline Morrell. Nevertheless, the dream speaks clearly to all dreamers who have experienced the bright visions and gentle loveliness of the night. I would suggest that within each of us there are both the waking and the sleeping hermits that Russell describes.

At the second annual conference of the Association for the Study of Dreams, I read this dream as part of my opening presidential address. I hoped it would touch each dreamer and allude at the same time to the grating nature of the rivalry and harsh struggles that have plagued the field of the study of dreaming and threatened to poison its interdisciplinary, eclectic organization.

Later, there came a time when I considered taking off my gloves and dealing with a few of the rivalrous people in the association on their own terms. I had the following dream:

I am on a beautiful seashore and am brushing away some nipping crabs. I also try to brush away a two-foot-tall black furry creature. But then I notice that he has a sign on him that says, "I am an educated being." I am taken aback and apologize to him. We begin to talk, and I see that he is indeed a sophisticated, gentle being with a fine mind and a very loving face. We dance and have a delightful time by the sea.

(THE FURRY EDUCATED BEING)

I asked Dr. Flowers to interview me. When she asked me to describe the little furry being, I had a terrible time. I kept wanting to find a way to say just what sort of creature he was because I felt that I knew, but could not remember what they were called. After repeating several times the description already given in the dream, it finally dawned on me that he was a hermit! The rest of the dream fell into place. I was on the shore between land and sea, between waking and dreaming—this felt like my career. Crabs are irritating but harmless residents of beautiful beaches. Crabs live underground and reminded me of bureaucratic tricks played in organizations. I had come to think that the gentle sleeping hermit style promoted by Russell was too naive to work in the real world and was about to abandon it. But the dream convinced me to take another look at it. Was it smart? By brushing it away and confronting the difficult hermits on their own terms, would I become as they, lost to beauty, lost to the delicate vision?

Through the last eighty years or so, conventional wisdom has taught that people who dream about animals a lot are more immature than those who do not. In my experience with over a thousand mostly healthy individuals, I have not noticed this to be true. Mammals, insects, birds, and mythological creatures usually represent the broad range of things other dream images do in an especially touching and efficient manner. Some of my most mature, sophisticated, and intelligent dreamers include animals regularly in their dreams. So I hope you too will enjoy working with your own and your partners' animal dreams.

HELP KEY

- ☐ *If the dreamer tells you of a blended animal image, such as a snake with a fish's head,* ask her to describe the snake, recapitulate this description, try for a bridge, then do the same thing for the fish, then try for a bridge of the composite image.

- ☐ *If the dreamer is not sure whether to interpret the animal on the subjective or the objective level,* try out each possibility, one at a time, eliciting more descriptions and unpacking any possible bridges as you go.

■

CHAPTER
SEVEN

OBJECTS IN DREAMS

Loma Flowers came up with the idea of opening some of our lectures by asking each member of the audience to write out a description of oatmeal. We ask the audience to pretend we come from another planet and to tell us what oatmeal is and how they feel about it. Here are some of the responses we have received:

"Oatmeal is yucky and sticky. It is a breakfast food I had to serve when I worked in a restaurant. It's ugly, like glue."

"Oh, it's warm, settles the tummy. It makes me feel loved and secure."

"When I was in a Soviet Union prisoner-of-war camp, it was the best thing we had to eat. We had it once a week. When I was little, I loved it. It was warm and good. I was told as a boy that Napoleon ate it on St. Helena, where my uncle was born. So from where I lived in Eastern Europe, oatmeal always seemed foreign and exotic."

"My mom made me eat it. I hated it and resented her power to force it down me."

"I don't like the taste, and it's an awful mess. But it's supposed to be good for you, and I feel guilty if I don't prepare it for my children at least once a week."

"I hated it when my dad made me eat it. But since he has died, I've learned to add cinnamon and dates, and it tastes great. And eating it makes me feel connected to my dad."

"Oatmeal is very colorful. It reminds me of Uncle Joe. The family myth is that Uncle Joe survived on oatmeal after World War II. It was very exotic when I was in high school to have an uncle in Scotland. Then too, I remember a favorite Lucy Perkins story from childhood, *The Scotch Twins,* in which the twins always seemed to be eating oatmeal. I got the impression that oatmeal is about all you need."

Hearing a few descriptions like these convinces most people in the room that even an image as mundane as oatmeal can evoke strong feelings, and that it makes no sense to pretend that anyone other than the dreamer can provide the meaning of an image.

While many dreamers will give similar descriptions of a common image like a purse, which the dreamer has lost in a dream, the slight variations in the descriptions can make all the difference. And then there is always the dreamer who gives you a totally surprising description essential to the meaning of his particular dream. Most women I have worked with describe purses as the thing in which they carry their money, ID cards, and credit cards. However, some will emphasize the credit cards over the ID cards, and some care mostly about their ID cards. Oddly enough, I have yet to hear a dreamer comment that the makeup she carries in her purse comes to mind in this context. Some say losing a purse is a bother, some say it is a nightmare. One woman told me that she hates carrying purses around and would like designers to put pockets in women's clothes so that women, like men, could go about unburdened. This same woman remarked how sad it was to see older ladies who seemed to carry all their sense of self in huge heavy purses, like security blankets. So what does it mean to lose a purse in a dream? For some women, often women whose children have recently left home, it turns out to reflect their anxiety that they have lost their identities as mothers, and that they have thus lost their power and credit in the world. For you or your dreamer, it could mean something entirely different. Let's review the basic cue-card questions aimed at exploring the objects in dreams:

16. *What is a Y?*
17. *What is the Y in your dream like?*
18. *Does the Y in your dream, which you describe as (reca-*

pitulate the description), *remind you of anything in your waking life?*

19. *How so?*

It is important to remember that a good description always includes the dreamer's feelings and value judgments. We would miss a lot if the dreamers who described oatmeal gave us dispassionate definitions like, "Oatmeal is a breakfast food," without letting us know how they felt about it. Even though the question "What is a Y?" begins the investigation of a dream object with the request for a definition, which at times may be extremely useful in itself, most people slip immediately into a personalized description of the object. The definition serves, among other things, to warm the dreamer up to the image. If, however, you find that the dreamer gets carried away with an emotionless, dull, boring definition of, say, a motorcycle as a two-wheeled vehicle made of steel and aluminum, propelled by an internal combustion engine, which runs on gasoline, and so on, you might have to ask a few more questions like:

How are motorcycles different from cars or bicycles?
What are motorcycles like?
Do you like motorcycles, or not?
Do you own one? Why? Why not?
What kinds of people usually ride them?

These questions will usually reveal how the dreamer feels about motorcycles, and will establish a good description.

IDENTIFYING IMPORTANT FEATURES

While we are on the subject of food and vehicles, Cynthia had a dream that used both to good effect:

I am with my boyfriend in his luxurious car. Things are fine, and then I discover that there is a butter melter built into the car on the dashboard. I say, "Gee, this is great, but what are we going to do with it?" I fiddle with it and try to turn it into a tea server. This is not easy; I'm having trouble when I awake.

(BUTTER MELTER)

I asked Cynthia, "What is a butter melter and how does it work?" She had never seen one in waking life, but the one in the dream had a button you could push and the stick of butter would pop down into a receptacle that would melt the butter, then you could turn the spigot of the receptacle and melted butter would pour out! I asked her what she thought about such a device, and she said that it was very luxurious and surprising. I asked her who put it there and why. She explained that it was put in at the factory, that it was built-in, and the car just came that way. (Because the car was the same as the waking version apart from this feature, we did not describe it further.)

"What is butter?" I asked. "It is a fat, and it makes you fat. It is unhealthy, the quintessential fat," said Cynthia. She added that she and her boyfriend, Hercule, are very careful about not having too much fat in their diets. I asked her, "Is there anything about your boyfriend that is like butter, a fat you are careful not to have too much of, but which is built-in at the factory?" Cynthia said, "Well, he yo-yos with his weight, and his tendency to eat foods like butter and to go up in weight is probably built-in at least from childhood. He certainly came that way! You know, I incubated this dream, but I thought it had nothing to do with my question, which was How can I help my boyfriend with his weight management? I think the dream is telling me to back off a bit and allow for the built-in quality of this problem. It wasn't working too well to turn his butter dispenser into a tea dispenser."

Cynthia had another dream in her boyfriend's car, but this time the description of the car was crucial, because the dream version was a modification of the waking version:

Hercule and I drove to our favorite restaurant in a tiny VW version of his big luxurious car. As we dined, the sommelier asked us for a ride. Hercule said that would not be possible because his car seated only one. This situation struck me as funny, because the sommelier would never guess that Hercule was driving such a small car; he assumed Hercule was in his usual large one. The sommelier thought Hercule was trying not to give him a ride home. (HERCULE'S TINY CAR)

Cynthia described her boyfriend's usual car as spacious, luxurious, and comfortable. The one in the dream was small and, like VWs, funky. When asked what sort of people drive such cars, Cynthia said students, who can't afford more car. The main difference between the waking and the dream car is that the waking car is a pleasure car that seats six and the dream car is a struggling student's car that seats only one.

Cynthia described a sommelier as the person who helps with the choice of wine, because he can draw on his broad knowledge of wine and of what is available. I asked, "Why do humans care about wine? Why do they drink it at such a dinner?" Cynthia said wine adds to the pleasure, the comfort, and the festivity of a meal and of an evening. She described Hercule as loving to create and spend lovely evenings filled with the pleasure associated with good wine and good food. Because the sommelier, who was well known to the dreamer in waking life, was not called by name in the dream but by role, it seemed unlikely that we would need a description of the sommelier's personality, but just in case, I asked for one. Pierre was a very giving, gracious, somewhat anxious, and frightened person. I recapitulated and tried for a bridge for the first time at this point in the inter-view: "Is there any way that recently Hercule has been unchar-acteristically unable to accommodate the sommelier who enhances life with the festivity and pleasure of good wine?" Cynthia shrugged her shoulders. I tried again: "Is there any way that Hercule, who is usually the type to drive a big pleasure car, has been more like a struggling student, with no room for the pleasures of the sommelier?" "Now that you mention it," Cynthia replied, "the night of the dream we did go to dinner at this restaurant, but Hercule was distracted, preoccupied with a problem in his family. I kept trying to get him to relax and relate to me as he usually does, but I didn't get far even in getting him to open up about the problem. I guess I should have just let him be. He really was in a one-seater that night." Perhaps Pierre's personality was germane after all. The dreamer had tried to en-ter her boyfriend's space, had been generous, loving, and anx-ious, but she just didn't understand the unusual circumstances that made it impossible for him to accommodate her this night.

Sometimes dreamers describe their dream cars in ways they bridge to their own bodies, their partner's bodies, to projects they are involved with, or to a particular aspect of their own or someone else's personalities. As we saw in the chapter on set-tings, cars can also describe one's way of getting around in the world, in which case, who is in the driver's seat becomes an issue. A businessman, whose new venture was collapsing, dreamt of a broken-down car that he kept futiley trying to jump start. Another businessman dreamt of a car that he was speeding in while trying to catch up to another car. He began to realize he was taking unreasonable risks, and that he was running out of gas; his competitiveness was getting the better of him. An-thony, a biochemist, dreamt of a Volvo, the type of high-quality car that he loves, even though it costs a lot to keep up. He said this with such feeling that he laughed as he recognized how well his description fit his wife.

PITFALLS TO AVOID

When Vera, another member of the study group, told a dream in which someone was wearing high heels, she described high heels as dressy shoes. Clearly, the question "What are high heels?" would not suffice. I coached the interviewer to ask, "What are high heels *like*?" Vera told us that the ones in the dream were black and very shiny, with four-inch heels and a very slim look. The interviewer smiled and said, "Oh, they sound nice." This was an unfortunate comment, because Vera had not yet let us know how she felt about high heels. Now that the interviewer had let it be known that she liked such shoes, and might very well wear them, Vera was inhibited in expressing any negative feelings she might have. Vera was silent. Was she being polite and withholding her thoughts? Another member of the group intervened, "Vera, strike that comment from the record. What do you really think about black, shiny high heels?" Vera then said that they are "shoes women wear to trivialize themselves, to buy into the male system of female weakness." Had the first interviewer not slipped in her opinion, we might have asked, "What kind of woman wears these shoes?" but this was now hard for Vera to say for fear of hurting the feelings of the interviewer who liked such shoes. From this example, you can see how difficult, yet how important, it is to keep your opinions to yourself when you are in the role of interviewer.

It takes a while, especially in working with objects, to learn to spot which aspects of an image are likely to be the most fruitful for bridging purposes. For instance, a woman dreamed that she was given her grandmother's precious and cherished gold bracelet by her mother. A novice interviewer asked, "What is gold?" This question was a tangential one, at least at this point. First, we should focus on eliciting a fuller description of the bracelet from the dreamer, so we can get a better feel for what the dreamer feels about the bracelet and which aspects of it are the most important to her. We could ask her to describe it more fully or simply ask her what makes the bracelet so special, which is a more interesting question for the dreamer to answer; it should elicit a richer response. Instead of asking her to give us a generic description of a bracelet, it seems more to the point to ask, "Why would your mom give you such a bracelet?" and then "What does it feel like to receive such a bracelet?" When posed, these questions quickly led the dreamer to tell us that she had always loved this particular bracelet of her grandmother's, that since childhood it had seemed so pretty and magical. Her mother's passing it on to her in the dream seemed like a very special confirmation and recognition of the dreamer's worth as a person and as a woman. Because the bracelet existed in waking life just as it appeared in the dream and because the dreamer did not emphasize its gold material, but rather its specialness and its lineage, asking about the characteristics of gold is just a bit off target.

Gold seems to trigger the projections of many novice interviewers who, assuming that gold should have especially intense meanings in dreams, charge past any number of characteristics of the image and focus on the gold. A woman who dreamt of a voice that said, "Putting gold glitter on does not hide the rest of yourself," was disoriented by the question "What is gold?" when her attention was caught up in glitter that is gold, not in gold the element. It would be better to ask, "What is glitter? When do humans wear it and why?" Then we could ask, "What is gold glitter like?" and discover the more specific nature of the glitter. As you practice working with a dream partner, you will get a feel for this through trial and error.

THE FRUITS OF
SUCCESSFUL BRIDGES

Wentworth had this dream:

> **My foot is calloused very badly;** it is almost rotten. I am
> surprised that it hurts a little, but not really that much. I
> can feel my foot underneath all these callouses, and it is
> sore but functional. But it is also very limited by the
> callouses, and this really concerns me. I am trying to
> show my brother, Martin, my callouses and the sore
> foot underneath. I want him to see it, and I want to
> voice my concern and pain. At first, he doesn't even
> notice. I try again. Finally, he notices, and says it proba-
> bly doesn't hurt. Besides, he says, it isn't hurting my
> performance at all. I tell him otherwise. He smiles and
> tells me to stop kidding. I am frustrated that nobody
> appreciates the callouses and the limits they are putting
> on me. I am surprised that I can even function *at all* with
> them.   (**CALLOUSES**)

Wentworth defined a callous as a hardening of the skin that is
produced by some rubbing or rough treatment. A callous covers over the vulnerable area and protects it, but it also reduces
the feeling in the area covered. The callouses in his dream had
not done their job perfectly, as the skin underneath was sore and
almost rotten. And because they affected his foot, his ability to
get around in the world was limited. Wentworth bridged this
description to the way he has covered up his inner pain so that
he wouldn't feel it or show it too much. "I am surprised how
little it hurt, given how bad my foot really is." His younger
brother, Martin, judges the world by external performances and
led Wentworth to think of the Martin in his dream as the part of
himself that thinks that as long as he is performing at a high
level, then everything must be fine. But Wentworth saw that his

calloused attitudes toward his own pain, as well as his inability
to feel and to relate to others, were limiting his entire life. The
problem Wentworth faced was getting the Martin within himself to appreciate the importance of the callouses and of the pain
underneath them.

Recently, I received a special letter from Tamalpa, who had
just read my first book on dreams and had incubated a dream
asking, "How do I *really* feel about my father?" She dreamt
about a television in a bathroom, but could make no sense of the
dream and thought her incubation effort had failed. So she incubated the same question the next night and woke up with the
song "I met him on a Sunday" in her head. That day she
worked on the dream with a therapist, who decided for her
which image was most significant. He chose badly, and they got
nowhere. After her session, she came home to find the song in
her head had become "*You* met him on a Sunday." Because she
had just read that songs can be valuable clues to dreams and can
act as meaningful dream responses in themselves, Tamalpa paid
attention. Then she got it—Sunday was the night of the first
incubated dream. She had met her dad, but failed to recognize
him. She went back to the dream, and this time she carefully
interviewed herself about the image the therapist had found significant. A dead end. Next she chose the most intriguing image
of the few in the dream: the TV. Here is what she wrote to me
about her interview:

> What's a TV? It's something that shows you movies or
> stories: things that look real, but they're not. Bingo!
> (Or "Aha! as you say in your book.) Two-dimensional
> life. You can only watch; you can't interact with a TV. If
> that isn't a perfect description of my father, I don't
> know what is. I had wondered why the TV was in my
> dream, because I hate watching TV (I only watch it
> when I'm sick and feel too horrible to do anything else).
> Hate isn't even a strong enough word. TVs just keep

spewing out their garbage whether you're listening or not. If you miss something, it's gone. You can't get it to repeat things. And the people in movies and TV shows are never quite right for the parts they're playing. They're too perfectly made up, plastic.

It's no wonder I have such an aversion to TV; my entire childhood and adolescence was like a TV program, not real life. God, what a revelation that was! I felt like bursting out laughing, I suddenly felt so wonderful. The only good thing about a TV is that you can turn it off. I suddenly knew that I didn't have to be controlled by my father's expectations. I could just turn him off. Wow!

Phew! I was exhausted, but aren't dreams clever?

Tamalpa could then easily see how the other dream elements fell into place once she had bridged the TV. Sometimes one must explore every image before the metaphor of the dream becomes clear. But if you are lucky (and open and careful), understanding one image will pull a whole dream out of the hat.

OF ARCHWAYS, DOVES, AND CROSSES

Let me tell you how Agatha described and bridged the image of a glowing archway in her dream before telling you the dream. Then, as you read the dream carefully and slowly, line by line, see how much of it makes sense to you.

INTERVIEWER. Could you describe the archway you see in the dream?

AGATHA. It is glowing and incredibly beautiful. It is pale, a calming color, and filled with a warm, glowing, golden light. It beckons gently, is very seduc-

tive, but is not the good it seems to be. It seduces
people, promising them warmth and magic, but
anyone who enters into this arch will be absorbed
and never come out the other side. The promise of
everything you ever want or need is a mirage.

I. What is like this in your life? Where is the glowing,
seductive, warm arch that promises magic, but is a
mirage that is not good, that absorbs those who fall
for its promise?

A. In my last relationship, I was absorbed. I had hoped
he would be my magic archway to a warm, gentle
world. Since we broke up, I feel a huge loss of the
magic, of the man who promises all. I fear I'll never
know the magic.

Now the dream:

I am wandering with a group of people in a sort of wasteland setting. I feel that I am leading the group. I earn
this leadership position by "saving" those who listen to
me, as described in the following sequence:

We come upon an archway. It is a beautiful, pale,
calming color, filled with a warm, glowing, golden
light. It beckons gently, but also feels extremely seductive and not the good it seems to be. I can "see" that if
people go through the arch, they will not emerge from
the other side. They will be absorbed. I tell people this,
and they believe me and are thankful to have been
saved.

A few days later, we are more lost and desperate, and
come on the same archway. It looks bigger, and the
light flows more profusely. It continues to glow seduc-
tively. The people are tired. We are wandering in a
tundra—snowy, ice-covered fields with very little veg-
etation. It is a depressing and hopeless-feeling setting.

The warmth from the glow feels so good. I beg people not to go through the arch, but some do anyway. I keep peering around the arch to confirm they are not coming out the other side. They are disappearing, just as I had expected.

Suddenly, I (not the me in the dream, but me the observer) hear the voice of a man: "Just a few more to put under and we can get a move on. Don't worry, it won't be long now and we can go home." I can see two men behind the scenes, putting into action the mechanisms that lure the people who are holding out to enter the archway.

Suddenly, one of the people with me cries out: "Look! My favorite place! Santa Fe!" A bright red image of a brick building has appeared on the edge of the road. It looks very real, not dreamlike, but it is sort of "set in" (like a framed picture on a wall), and you know it is not real. It sticks out like a sore thumb in an otherwise bland tundra. This same person breaks down in tears and reaches out toward the image, crying out apologies that he cannot resist. He turns and runs through the archway, and he, too, never comes out the other side.   (GLOWING ARCHWAY)

Agatha had commented on a photocopy of the dream account that this dream did not seem to answer her incubation question, "What happened between Alan and me? Please clarify how I felt and what I did along the way, and how he felt and showed his feelings."

The setting for this dream is a wasteland. The dreamer and her people are wandering lost and desperate on a snowy, ice-covered tundra. Our interview revealed how accurate a picture this was of how Agatha felt in her life now and had felt for a long time. The seductive, promising archway crystallized the needy, addictive relationship Agatha had to the hope of warmth and happiness. She saw how, in her emotional wasteland state, she had been vulnerable to men who seemed to hold the promise of the glowing magic and love, which she craved so badly that, like some of the people in the dream, she could not resist even when she knew the relationship was a destructive one. The fact that she was saving some people in the dream because she understood the manipulative mechanisms of the archway showed that she was beginning to find the insight and strength to save herself from her childlike craving for the magical world of peace and bliss.

Yet not all the people can resist, even when they have been warned. The man who cries out his apologies because he cannot resist is cause for concern. What is Santa Fe like? Agatha knows a specific couple who lives there, who "seem disproportionately fortunate and happy." Santa Fe has always seemed to Agatha a place of warm, soft colors, where people live peaceful, artistic lives. She described the man who succumbed to this lure as an addictive person who just couldn't resist the promise, even when he knew it was false. She bridged him to herself, to Alan, to the man she had dated before him, and to most of the men in her life. Maybe her incubation worked after all.

I spoke with Agatha as I was preparing this presentation of her dream, and she told me that in the several years since she worked on it, she has regularly thought of it and reread it. She said the images have grown even more meaningful for her and have helped her recognize and deal with glowing archways when she sees them and when she works with her craving for them in therapy. This dream is another good example of how one group member's dream can raise universal issues meaningful to everyone. Who is not addicted to the promise of eternal warmth, peace, and happiness? How many times has our good judgment failed us because we were blinded by our wretched need to believe in the false promises of those who sell snake oil? Agatha hoped that a relationship would bring her happiness; others believe achievement, money, a new geographical location, good food, alcohol, drugs, a new body, or a new dress.

Louis, who is deeply involved in the New Age transpersonal psychology movement, had an unusually insightful dream:

> **I reach to the top shelf** for a pretty clay heart lectern-music stand. It is in perfect condition, and I like it very much, but I am disappointed that it is unglazed.
>
> Then there is a tiny little basket with a dove, wings outstretched on it, and a salt cellar, which is not so good for salt, because it is woven like a basket. Maybe I could use it for something else.
>
> What shall I do with these tiny things? They are too small to be of practical use; they are symbols. I wish I had something of actual use. (SYMBOLS)

Louis described symbols as meaningful representations of anything. In the dream, these symbols were lovely and beautiful, like those that he worked with in his New Age career, but they were impractical. He didn't want merely the symbols of love and nurturing, he wanted the things themselves. Was he out of touch with the real world?

It is easy to use theory and symbols as a refuge from painful feelings. If we attach our feelings to theoretical structures, we can love them, and we will be safe from the messy things that can happen when we relate intimately to other human beings. This not only cripples the life of the lover of "greater things" but it also makes him a terrible dream interviewer. Beware the interviewer who knows what your dream images mean thanks to his superior, spiritual insight into symbols. For many people, that "insight" has become a destructive addition.

Religious symbols are perhaps the most vulnerable to mis-interpretation. Many of us have read treatises on what the symbol of the cross means and what it means in dreams.[1] But how could such common interpretations as "the cross represents man's creativity, eternal rebirth, and spiritual union" benefit the dreamer who once told me that the cross is a symbol of martyr-dom and immediately bridged this to her self-destructive mar-tyrdom, which had wreaked havoc in her life? The dream had artfully put the cross in a context that would have made no sense had we insisted on any other interpretation than her own.

No matter what the dream object, try to resist the urge to run to a book that will describe or interpret it for you; first give the dreamer a chance to discover and tell you what he knows. The dreamer can reach any depth or height of meaning described by the experts if he avoids intrusions and learns to focus on his own completely adequate resources of information regarding his own dream images.

HELP KEY

- ☐ *If a dreamer has trouble giving an adequately specific description of an object,* ask, "What is unique about a Y?" or "What distinguishes Y's from all other similar objects?"

- ☐ *To facilitate the dreamer's expression of value judgments in a description,* ask, "What sort of person would use such a machine (or wear such a coat, or drive such a car)?" Actually this question can effectively be asked concerning any dream element. "What sort of person would live in such a place (want to be with such a person, have such a feeling response, do such a thing)?"

□

CHAPTER
EIGHT

FEELINGS IN DREAMS

We have worked with feelings in every dream so far in this book.[1] As should be obvious by now, the basic building block of the dream interview—the description—must include the dreamer's feelings about the subject described or it often will be quite useless. Most dreams masterfully provide the dreamer with experiences of subtle or intense feeling that influence everything in the dream. Feelings are the tune to which are set the specific lyrics of the dream. A careful exploration of the feelings in a dream is absolutely indispensable to a good interview.

Most dreams are easy or difficult to understand neither because they are long or short nor because of their complexity. Their relative ease or difficulty is determined, in great measure, by the dreamer's ability to feel her own feelings both in daily life and in relation to the dream. A skilled interviewer has a variety of questions and strategies for making it as easy as possible for the dreamer to sense and express her feelings, for dreamers get better at identifying and expressing their feelings as they experience working with their dreams in a safe and encouraging environment. Most people in our culture have learned to repress and deny feelings better than they have learned to recognize and express them. Although our choice of spouse, work, lifestyle, and how we treat all other people in our lives is determined by our feelings, many people still pretend that having feelings is an optional life activity.

Given our culture's fear and suspicion of feeling, many dreamers are concerned that admitting to feelings is a sign of weakness. Worse yet, some people really don't know what they are feeling at any given moment and are honestly incapable of naming their feelings. In these situations, it helps to encourage the dreamer to describe the physical sensations in her body; this will eventually lead the dreamer to a recognition of her feelings. Some men worry that if they "break down" and cry, they will be seen as feminine, because they grew up being told that feelings are feminine and that only weak men cry.[2] It takes patience and reassurance to do good dream work with such people. I remember telling a gentleman of Japanese descent that it wasn't true that samurai don't cry. Real samurai are brave and not afraid to feel the pain that brings tears to one's eyes. With this new perspective, he was able to let himself feel his pain, and then he could feel the love and intimacy he had also been blocking. Generally, the act of crying opens the door to the dreamer's awareness of surprisingly specific feelings and thoughts that can be crucial to the understanding of a dream.

An interviewer who explores the dreamer's feelings during the interview itself will be in a position to ease the dreamer's occasional discomfort, and facilitate a freer flow of feelings. Many people do not record the feelings they experience in a dream nearly as completely as they do the actions. The most frequent feelings omitted in the recording and the telling of the dream are usually ones at the very end of it. I often ask, "How did you feel just then, at the last moment of the dream?" before beginning the interview proper. When the dreamer has just finished telling her dream, she has built herself up, via the plot development, to reexperience the feelings which accompany the last moment, and I like to catch the dreamer while she's on a roll.

Let's review the basic cue-card questions related to feelings:

20. *How do you feel at this moment in the dream?*
21. *Tell me more about this feeling.*
22. *Tell me about a time (or the last time) you felt this way.*
23. *Does this feeling of* (recapitulate the description) *remind you of anything in your current life?*

As is true of the cue-card questions in general, not all the questions will be necessary for all dreams, their order may vary, and a number of additional questions may be required. Part of the enjoyment of learning this method is the pleasure of learning how to create your own supplementary questions and knowing when and how to employ them with another dreamer or, indeed, with yourself.

The most frequent challenge to interviewers is that of helping a dreamer who only touches on her feelings very gingerly to find the courage and confidence to explore them more fully. Following is a list of questions that come in handy in many interviews. I consider them to be essential help keys, and so present them early in the chapter.

HELP KEY

□ *When a dreamer holds back her feelings,* try one of these strategies.

   1. Ask, "Could you amplify the volume of that feeling and describe it so we can get a better look at it?"

   2. Ask, "How about really exaggerating what you feel so we can see better what the feeling is like? Go ahead, really ham it up."

   3. Try, "You say the dream is a bit sad. What is the saddest part?" Asking this and staying with the question until the dreamer can answer you will usually precipitate a much greater awareness and admission of the sadness and, often, tears as well.

   4. If the dreamer is fighting back tears, try, "If your tears had words, what would they say?"

◻ *If the dreamer is having difficulty identifying and describing a feeling,* try some of these methods.

1. Try the Gestalt technique of asking the dreamer to pretend he is the character or the object that expresses the feeling in the dream. Then ask her what it feels like to be that image and to answer your questions from that perspective.

2. Try guessing the opposite feeling to evoke the dreamer's need to do better than your terrible guess.

3. Reassure the dreamer that you know how hard it can be to find words for some feelings, but to take her time and give it a try; she can always amend and correct this first description later.

4. As a last resort, you could try to accurately guess and name what the dreamer is feeling. This can give the dreamer a feeling of being supported and assisted. The risk is that the dreamer may settle for your word, which might not be colored in exactly the same way as a word she might have chosen, and she will not have done the work of examining her feelings closely enough to be able to identify them with words. But as long as you have confidence that the dreamer will correct you if you miss the mark, this is the best thing to do in cases where your other efforts have failed.

◻ *If the dreamer is anxious that the dream may be saying something upsetting,* as soon as you note this ask, "Are you sure you really feel like working with this dream right now? We don't have to." If this question elicits a clear willingness to proceed, ask, "What do you fear the dream might be saying?" and "What is the absolutely worst thing this dream could mean?" A discussion of the likelihood of the dreamer's fears being realized—and of the dreamer's options if they are—usually reduces the dreamer's anxiety considerably. The worst possible scenario is usually not as bad as all that, and even if it is awful, keeping one's head in the sand will only make things worse.

▣ *If the dreamer seems distracted, irritable, or bored,* ask, "How do you think this interview is going?" "Do you think we are barking up the wrong tree?" or "Do you think we've done enough for now?" Dreamers who look bored are sometimes just anxious, and when in a group for the first time telling a dream, they are worried that they are boring their listeners—who are usually so interested in the proceedings that they would never guess the dreamer is feeling that way! Asking about this and clarifying the situation generally does the trick.

▣ *When the dreamer is too busy figuring out what her dream means to reenter it and describe the images,* you could say something like "Feel, don't think and try to figure out where the dream fits into your life. Fit yourself into the dream, then the parallels to your life will come to you with little effort and greater accuracy."

▣ *If the dreamer would be embarrassed to admit to a particular feeling in the dream,* you might suggest another, more acceptable word for it. For example, many men have a hard time admitting to being afraid. An interviewer once asked a man who described being chased along a cliff by a wolf if he felt afraid. The dreamer said, "No. I knew the dream was a symbol." If you feel you must suggest a label for a feeling because the dreamer has hit a dead end, the use of less-threatening words such as "Does that make you feel anxious (uncomfortable, in danger)?" will usually start the dreamer on the road to examining the feeling. Later you may be able to elicit or suggest a more accurate description.

OTHER HINTS

Humor

If you or the dreamer begin to work too hard at the interview and forget the pleasure of solving the mystery of the dream, the interview will slow down to a painful, torturous crawl. A little humor about the bizarreness of the images or about your own bewilderment as to what to do next can release the pressure and reanimate the discussion. Sometimes clowning around a bit can clear a pathway for the dreamer to express feelings that she may fear would make her look silly. If she thinks she could take the risk without looking nearly as silly as you, she might take it. Of course, clowning can be hurtful, offensive, and distracting if employed insensitively.

Withholding

You may also feel stalled if the dreamer is secretly withholding important feelings and other information. Fifteen years ago, I led a group I'll never forget. It was impossible for me not to fall asleep, nearly or actually, while leading this group of four mental health professionals. I tried napping in the day before seeing them; I even drank caffeinated coffee, which I usually avoid because it has a very wiring effect on me. But it was to no avail. Finally, in our third session I brought up the problem, and noted that all the dreams we had so far dealt with were difficult, and each dreamer seemed to be very quick to bridge almost exclusively to matters concerning work only. Almost in unison, the students replied that they were not prepared to discuss their personal material in a group setting. They had come just to learn the method, so they felt they could confine themselves to the ways in which the dreams related to their work issues! Once I had convinced them that deciding in advance what they were willing to bridge to required a level of withholding that made my job a torture as well as impossible, they changed their policies, and suddenly I could stay engaged and awake.

In a few instances where dreamers are especially defensive and withholding, and in many where the dreamer is being regularly oppositional, I have found that throwing up my hands and admitting defeat has been effective. The dreamer then has a chance to offer to help you—or lose her interviewer. I have been amazed at the sudden insights, descriptions, and bridges such a challenge can trigger. When I had a daily radio show on dreams, I discovered that I could take advantage of those maddening weather reports. When a caller refused to reflect on a feeling to see if it evoked any bridges to his waking life, I said I was sorry, but it looked like I couldn't help him with this one, "but hold on for the weather report and we'll return to see if you've been able to see any parallels on your own." This challenge often motivated callers to stop resisting and start feeling.

THE FUNCTION OF FEELINGS IN DREAMS

Feeling as a Vital Key to Any Dream Image

Without knowing how she feels about an image, a dreamer will be helpless to understand it. As we have seen, how the dreamer feels about Zubin Mehta, or a lion, or the emerald green python/rhinoceros snake, makes all the difference in the way the dreamer bridges and understands both the image and the dream that contains it. Many of the questions we ask in the descriptive phase are really aimed at eliciting feelings that are as specific as possible through focusing the dreamer's attention on the concrete image as she experiences it in waking life, as well as in the dream. The word *like* in the questions "What is X like?" and "What is a Y like?" is crucial. By taking advantage of the dreamer's propensity to relate to her dream concretely, feelings—in the form of opinions, attitudes, and value judgments—are quickly drawn out with a minimum degree of the defensiveness that tends to be triggered as soon as the dreamer starts wondering what the dream might mean on the level of metaphor.

I was writing this chapter, when Beatrice brought a dream to a group session. In the dream she was wearing a black dress. Her definition of black dresses was that they were black, worn by women for dress-up occasions, and were considered basics. When she told us what black dresses were *like,* this elicited how she felt about such dresses: "They are very feminine. I love them. They are sensual and womanly. I saw a famous writer who is in her fifties in one lately. She looked *great.* She looked very centered. Black dresses make a woman look sure and sexual, but not in a coy way. The women who wear them are not playing games, but are straightforward and confident. It's not that silly caricature of sexuality."

In the dream, Beatrice was dressed up in a black dress, and she looked beautiful. This is the same woman who had the dream of the Bohemian Grove in Chapter 4 and who, in waking life, had decided that she could never be beautiful because she clearly did not fit her brother's rigid definition of female beauty. You can see how much Beatrice's feelings about black dresses add to our ability and her own to appreciate what being in a black dress means to her. Imagine how different it would have been if she had told us that she found black dresses dull and unimaginative and that black is a color she has never liked!

The Crystallization of Familiar Feelings

Often when people are seriously depressed, or heading for a nervous breakdown, their dreams are set in very barren, lonely, isolated, and otherwise dismal environments, and the plots regularly involve feelings of isolation and helplessness. Typically the dreamer does not come up with any way to cope with these situations by the time the dream ends. These dreams are valuable warning signs that the dreamer had better seek the services of a good psychologist or psychiatrist to help her deal with the pain in her life. Tess presented such a dream:

> **I am in a vast, lonely, empty place** that seems like a surrealist painting. It is as if I am in a picture that is quite flat. Now it seems that the place is also a plane. It is large and I am alone. There is nothing else. No people, no sound. I have one child's shoe. **(ONE SHOE)**

Tess recognized the feelings in the dream easily. "This frightens me. It is a good visual picture of my feelings," she said. She described the details of the shoe in the dream and noted that she had a pair of shoes like the one child's shoe in the dream. She hoped that having only one shoe suggested that she had only one-half of what was available. But she also said that she feels like a child with only one shoe, and she always has. Her mother was emotionally absent and her father was an alcoholic. She never felt secure or well cared for. The bleakness of Tess's dream and her focusing on "the positive," as she called it, of the missing shoe suggested that she should waste no time in finding a good therapist to help pull her back into the real world of feeling and action. This was not going to be easy for Tess, as another dream from that session suggested. She dreamt that she felt like a clam, tightly closed. She said of clams that you have to steam them to open them up. She awoke from the clam dream tense and with clenched teeth, feeling cold. Would she look for and find a therapist who would have the skill and finesse to steam, rather than pry her open?

The Recognition of Repressed Feelings

Because most of us have the habit of ignoring, reinterpreting, forgetting, projecting, and in other ways repressing uncomfortable feelings, and since dreams show us how we really are and what we really think, it is no surprise that many of our dreams help us to recognize feelings we have swept under the rug.

Aileen, whose life was going pretty well, and whose dreams did not suggest severe problems in coping with life as Tess's did, nevertheless tended to minimize the depth of her conflicts. One night she dreamt:

> **Liz says that I'm really depressed,** at least in the morning. I seem to perk up at noon. I'm surprised. She says to check my notes and I may notice it. I realize that Liz must have lost her baby because she's not pregnant.
>
> (LIZ)

INTERVIEWER. Who is Liz?
AILEEN. She is my cousin, and she is a counselor.
I. What is she like?
A. She leads a full life and has lots of fun. I admire her for her work and her way of living. She is pregnant in waking life, but not in the dream. I would trust her perceptions.
I. Is there anyone in your life or a part of yourself that is not pregnant and, like your cousin, has fun and lives a full life, whose perceptions you would trust?
A. That's how I see you.
I. What is Liz telling you?
A. That I'm really depressed?

I. Are you?

A. It's not that bad!

I. How do you respond in the dream?

A. I am surprised. Liz says to check my notes, and maybe I'll notice it.

I. What notes do you keep?

A. In my dream journal, I keep day notes and dream notes!

I. Why don't you look through them.

Aileen had a number of dreams that tried to get this message through to her. She finally had one that convinced her to get into therapy, which has benefited her greatly.

Crystal had a dream that, like Aileen's, contained a surprise. She lay in bed masturbating while a woman at the foot of the bed watched. When she had become quite aroused she told the woman she was ready now and to go get Crystal's husband. Suddenly, the woman tore off her skirt to reveal a big penis, threw up her arms and said, "Not on your life. My name is REVENGE!" (Woman with Penis)

Crystal, who was not sexually aroused by women as far as she knew, was astonished. In exploring the dream, she said that her sex life with her husband was not good, that she was far more interested in sex than he, and that she had trouble trusting that he would come through if she took him up on a sexual pass. But what was this woman doing in her dream? Crystal described her as big and determined. Women with penises, she thought, would be strong, powerful, aggressive women.

I asked Crystal if revenge might have anything to do with the fact that recently she had been the one who was too tired for sex when the issue came up, even though she experienced herself as the sex-starved, neglected wife? Crystal had had a very rigid Christian upbringing, and until this dream she had not been able to recognize that she wanted revenge on her husband for all the times he had turned her down. This dream helped her begin to accept the reality of repressed feelings that had led to some puzzling types of behavior. It also helped her to see that she was not a helpless victim, but that her responses were perpetuating a vicious circle of disappointing sex, in which both she and her husband played a part.

Josie, who was an artist working at home, dreamt that she and her husband and friends were having a fine time swimming when her husband had to leave, as did the other people, who were mostly her husband's colleagues from his work. Josie felt left out of the action; they all had to go somewhere, and she was not included. Josie understood her dream to be pointing out that she felt left out of the world of those who committed themselves to daily work that included an esprit de corps, a real working camaraderie that her husband and his colleagues shared. She said that as she reexperienced the sadness she felt in the dream, she was amazed to discover that she envied her husband a job she had thought of as a terrible infringement on his freedom. She decided to take a part-time job to feel part of a team. (Abandoned Swimming)

Amber had a dream that, like a carrot at the end of a stick, induced her to reconsider the way she led her life:

> **I am running in a big public race.** I arrive a couple of minutes late, but that is okay—there are thousands of us running. I am running with another woman. We talk as we run, and this makes the run more fun and keeps me going. To my great surprise, I place fifth in this huge race. My name is placed up on the board with the top five who placed. I have done really well. I didn't even know I had a chance! Wow! Next time, I'll start on time. I would have been here on time if I had known that I was in the running.
> (UNEXPECTED FIFTH-PLACE PRIZE)

Amber thoroughly enjoyed this dream and was delightfully surprised by the outcome. She described the setting as a big race, open to all, and lots of fun. She informed us aliens that humans run these races to give themselves a goal to work toward while they develop their fitness. Amber bridged the sport of running in races to life, in that "both take training and discipline, but almost anybody can do it to some extent. It feels good, makes you healthier, and gives you a goal." Her arriving late reminded her of her tendency to be too laid-back and to put things off. Asked how it feels to arrive late to the race, Amber said, "It didn't bother me. I didn't think it was important. I wasn't really competing." Amber could describe the woman only as a good running partner. A running partner she described as someone with whom you can talk, who sets the pace, who keeps you going, keeps you propelled, and keeps you from thinking how difficult it is. Amber said that she and her partner were each running at her own pace, she was engrossed in talking to her partner, "and my concentration was on our running rhythm; that was my world." She bridged this feeling and action to the way she and her husband had opted out of life in the fast lane and had created an environment that allowed them to go at their own pace. Amber thought a female running partner conveyed a better sense of a running partner because her husband, in waking-life running, goes at a faster pace and doesn't like to talk as much as her women partners. Her bridge to her husband and to that part of herself that is her own "pacer" was based on the feelings involved.

We asked her what it is like to place fifth in a race on earth, and we were told that this signifies that the runner has done very well in a big race and that she should be very proud. Asked how she felt in the dream, Amber said, "It felt great! I never expected that I would be that good. And getting the recognition of having my name written on the board felt very gratifying, especially considering how little effort I put into competing. It showed that I was one of the winners. The fact that I placed gave me the impression that I could easily do better without extreme training if I just got to the next race on time."

How many times in her life had Amber arrived late for a race because she thought she didn't have a chance of doing well? After a week's reflection, Amber said that many times she had not "gone for it" because she thought she didn't have a chance. She said, "I've always told myself that I'm simply not the competitive sort." That attitude had for a long time camouflaged unrecognized feelings of inadequacy for Amber. Who says you can't learn through pleasure as well as pain?

Recognizing the Dynamics and Patterns of Feelings

Most dreams offer the dreamer the chance to understand better not only what she feels, but also why she feels what she feels. Dreams will often show how certain feelings were born and how different life situations evoke those feelings, as well as how those feelings entrap or liberate the dreamer. Cecilia brought such a dream to one of our groups:

> **I am walking uphill.** Despite the exercise, I feel very cold. I crouch beside some shrubbery for shelter. Then Rudy is there. He's not wearing a shirt and I huddle against him to get warm. I am wearing many rings. Most of them seem to have large stones like amethyst and aventurine and the ring that my parents gave me is also there. I rearrange the rings, trying them out on different fingers to get the best effect of color and pattern. Rudy and I are then in a house, he still has his shirt off. I mention that he has lost weight, and he says yes, and that he has forty pounds more to lose. At this point, the scene is a bedroom. Later it is a kitchen. I am unsure how I feel about Rudy sexually, and the feeling is unresolved at the end.   **(THE MAN WITH NO SHIRT)**

Cecilia told us that she felt very sad while typing up her

dream and feared being labeled a pariah in the group for being associated with "this filth." You will see what she meant by this as we look at the highlights from the interview.

INTERVIEWER. What did you feel like walking uphill and feeling very cold?

CECILIA. I felt lonely and vulnerable. I feel that way a lot in my life.

I. Who is Rudy?

C. He is the ex-husband of an ex-friend.

I. What is he like?

C. We never got along. He and his wife looked like the Walton family, but in fact, there was incest in the family.

I. What is his personality like?

C. Miserable. He is moody, temperamental, and sulky like my dad, who sexually abused me. And like my dad, Rudy is unpredictable: affable and sociable one moment and weirdly hurt and withdrawn the next.

I. How do you feel talking about this with us?

C. It is very painful, and it feels like a big risk, but I want to do it. I have to learn to talk about it.

I. Okay. So Rudy is like your dad in that he looks like a solid Walton family man, but he is an abuser, he's moody, temperamental, and sulky. He can be affable one minute, then hurt and withdrawn the next. Does he remind you of anyone else who is? [I repeat the recapitulation.]

C. Well, actually, that sounds like my boyfriend, except for the sexual abuse.

I. In the dream, you are feeling cold, lonely, and vulnerable when you crouch beside some shrubbery and find Rudy. Does your boyfriend provide you shelter from these feelings?

C. Well, he's Mr. Unavailable, but he has been healing for me in the past.

I. How do you feel about his not wearing a shirt?

C. A little uncomfortable. It is tacky. There is the hovering possibility of sex. Once I greeted my dad with my shirt off. He scolded me. I was ten or so.

I. Tell us about each of your rings.

C. I like the amethyst a lot. I bought it for myself when I turned forty. The aventurine is supposed to be balancing and connecting, and I need balance and I need to be better connected to my feelings. The ring my parents gave me for my thirty-fifth birthday is a ruby. I used to wear it on my wedding ring finger. I guess I still felt married to my family. . . . I took it off when my sister rejected me because I wanted to talk about the unspeakable incest in our family. My removing it was a symbol for rejecting my family's influence and a decision to take care of the wounded little girl in me.

I. In the dream you are wearing the ring again.

C. Yes, and I'm with a man like my father again, for warmth even if it is uncomfortable.

I. How does it feel to be rearranging the rings?

C. It feels like a distraction from what is really going on.

I. What is the house like that you and Rudy are in?

C. It is his tract home in the dream. It is like one I grew up in, but it is a little bit nicer, at least it is warm.

I. How do you feel about Rudy's weight loss?

C. I want to congratulate him; he looks better than he used to, but he's still not too attractive.

I. What is the difference between a bedroom and a kitchen, the two places where you are with him?

C. A bedroom suggests sex to me, and a kitchen, nurturance. Those are the two issues I'm dealing with regarding men, all right.

I. When the dream ends, you are unsure how you feel about Rudy.

C. Yes. He offers warmth and some closeness, but I don't like him, nor do I find him attractive, although he is better than he used to be, the way my boyfriend is better than my father was. At least his tract house has warmth. But the fact remains that Rudy is a person essentially like my dad, and it looks like my boyfriend may be too.

I. What do you think about your relationship with your boyfriend as you look at this dream?

C. He's not a great possibility, but I've been telling myself that this is better than nothing. Maybe it is not.

I. How are you feeling now about working on this dream with us?

C. Tired, but glad I've done it. I feel supported, not rejected. But I still feel very embarrassed. I am going to join a group for incest victims to learn to talk about this and to deal with it.

Remembering Forgotten Feelings

There are times when remembering feelings we had under certain conditions could save us from repeating serious mistakes. Sandra's dream did just this.

I am standing, facing my old boyfriend, James. As I look at him he looks so warm and sweet and welcoming. I am attracted to him all over again. As I start to approach him, various big farm implements like rakes and shovels and pitchforks come whirling, flying out of his head. I know that if I get close to him I will be horribly injured by these things that are flying out of his head, so I back away. As I do, he starts looking sweet again and promising love and warmth. The farm implements are gone. He looks so dear that I approach him again. Again, as I approach, the implements come flying out of his head and I step back. This cycle repeats itself several more times.   **(FARM IMPLEMENTS)**

As we began to discuss the dream, Sandra told me that she had been quite hurt by this guy, and had broken up with him almost a year ago. After she carefully described the seductive sweetness of her ex-boyfriend and her feelings while approaching him, as well as her feelings of needing to pull away to protect herself, she said she had long ago recognized that he was no good for her. Then I asked her if there might not be some waking situation that might have reanimated her liking of him and triggered this dream that reminded her of the destructive cycle they participated in. Only then did Sandra think it might be relevant to tell me that the boyfriend in the dream, whom she had not seen for a year, had just telephoned her and asked her if they could meet. This dream led Sandra to think seriously about the likelihood of her still being vulnerable to his seductive warmth and destructive ways.

Have you ever dreamt of doing something you used to love to do, but have let slip out of your life, such as a sport, an art, a pleasurable pastime, or even something like regular walks in the park? In my first book, *Living Your Dreams,* I described how my dreams about my beloved ice skating haunted me for years, while I ignored my impulses to skate. When I finally took my dreams to heart and got back to skating (with the generous encouragement of my partner, Bob Castle), I appreciated that the feelings I have when I skate fill all of my life with courage, discipline, enthusiasm, and a passionate love for the sense and expression of beauty.

A number of my clients have had similarly rejuvenating experiences when, having been taunted by their dreams with the memory of how great it felt to do this or that, they drop all their excuses and go out and do at least a little of it.

Discovering New Feelings

Diana, whose dreams about her con-man, Mafia-like husband we considered in Chapters 2 and 3, had come a long way in getting to know herself better when she dreamt:

> **I am a goddess,** but I fear seeing myself in the fullness of my grace, wisdom, and power. A voice says, "You can have all this."   **(A GODDESS)**

Asked "What was the fear like?" Diana said it had to do with the fact that moral Catholics should not be proud. According to some Jungians, to confuse oneself with a goddess is to risk psychological inflation. Asked what the personality of the goddess was, Diana said, "She was not inflated. She really did have these qualities, and her heart was good." In the dream, Diana was looking at and experiencing for the first time what it was like to feel like a goddess, and it felt solid and healthy. At the same time, she was feeling the impact of beliefs that kept her from admitting these feelings to her daily experience of herself. Diana thought that she should take the dream voice more seriously than the fearful voices from her childhood.

Pairing the Recognition of Denied Feelings with Their Antidote

In my dream column for *New Realities* magazine, I described Gina's dream, which is the clearest example I have come across of a dream in which the dreamer sees clearly—perhaps for the first time—a problematic feeling or attitude and, in the same dream, a vision of what must be done about it.

> **Rick Bauer and I are** getting romantically involved. [Gina told our dream group that Rick is a soap opera star who is very loving, strong, with a chest and character like granite, who wants to do good in the world and who is very good to women.] Rick has a wonderful, consistently loving energy. He is constantly hugging me—giving me what I need. I love being so consistently loved.
>
> At one point, I run into Cassie, who has just been jilted by a man she loved. The guy was Phillip [also from the soap opera, whom she described as a gorgeous, swashbuckling type who used women for sex]. I hug Cassie and commiserate with her pain, having been jilted myself by that type of guy. I tell her that it is a good thing that this man has dumped her. He really isn't very nice. She should find someone like Rick who will really love her and be there for her.[3]
>
> (MR. WRONG)

Gina described the men she has always liked as being like Phillip, the swashbuckling and dashing type. Asked to define dashing, she said, "exciting, unavailable . . ." Upon hearing herself say that the very men she wanted were the unavailable ones, Gina told us that she, like Cassie, had grown up with a need to go after men who were unavailable, like their fathers, and always felt insecure and lonely. It was dawning on Gina that the antidote to her pain and loneliness was in part to find a man who had it in his present (rather than potential) character to be warm and loving, like Rick.

THE IMPORTANCE OF
INTERVIEW-RELATED FEELINGS

How does the dreamer feel as she presents her dream and as she works on it by herself, with one interviewer, or in a group of interviewers? A failure to monitor and deal with these feelings can sabotage the chances for a successful dream interview. Sometimes a dreamer will habitually apologize for her dream before presenting it. She may say it is just a fragment, confused, dull and boring, or not as interesting as the others she has heard in the group. Just a few words of reassurance and encouragement usually put the dreamer at ease. If this happens again, the interviewer might point it out to the dreamer and ask if she would like to talk about her need to apologize for her dream. If there are more-experienced dreamers in the room, they can usually share similar feelings they had when they started working with their dreams. Once, a member who was new to one of my groups told one of her dreams for the first time and worked very well and courageously with it. To our surprise, she apologized that it turned out to be about such a mundane topic as her relationship to her boyfriend. It seems she thought we would have preferred that she engage us with a dream about "something more important, something spiritual." We reassured her that we could think of nothing more important or more spiritual than her looking honestly at the dynamics of her relationship with love. She soon saw that most dreams do indeed deal with our relationships to love and work, just as Freud said. But she also saw that these issues had no boundaries to contain them in any one area of life or level of consciousness.

As the interview proceeds, being alert to signals that the dreamer may be feeling anxious, argumentative, overly compliant, impatient, or secretive can allow you to ask the dreamer how she is feeling as she discusses the dream with you. Airing half-realized feelings will allow the dreamer to proceed more easily. If the dreamer is keeping secrets about issues the dream touches on or about critical feelings she is having about the interviewer, it is important to clarify this. It is not necessary that any secrets be divulged, but it is important to establish that secrets are being kept so that the dream partners can decide if there is a possibility of conducting a fruitful interview under these conditions.

A dreamer works hard during an interview. She travels through the times and feelings of her life at high speeds and juxtaposes feelings and attitudes in new and startling ways. If the dreamer seems to become overloaded with the number of excursions and insights triggered by the interview, ask her if she has had enough for the time being. Dreamers can become refractory if they work on too many dreams in one sitting and can become so in the space of one interview about a long dream. Dreamers are regularly astounded at how much there is in one dream. If the issues are particularly sensitive ones, I think it is better to do less rather than more. Let the dreamer reflect on a manageable part of her dream for a while and see how she deals with it. Taking the exploration beyond the dreamer's overload point will only lead to a glassy-eyed stare. In some cases, the dreamer will feel threatened and put up defenses for a while, often by being unable to recall her dreams for a short time afterward.

If the feelings that come up in a dream or in a dream interview seem to overload or overwhelm the dreamer quickly, it is time to suggest that the dreamer enter psychotherapy. Dreams offer invaluable insights, but if the dreamer cannot tolerate them or if she is unable to integrate them into her life, then she needs a therapist who will assist her in the sometimes hugely challenging task of incorporating new insights.

□

**CHAPTER
NINE**

ACTION IN DREAMS

Novice students often have a tendency not to see the forest for the trees. They get so engrossed in having the dreamers describe and bridge the settings, people, objects, and feelings in the dream that they lose sight of the immediate action context of the image, as well as of the larger context of the plot of the entire dream. This is where the regular practice of dream diagraming and dream outlining will develop the skills of keeping the larger picture in mind. Strange as well as prosaic dream action will usually yield descriptions that, when recapitulated and bridged, metaphorically elucidate the dreamer's waking conflict, pain, and/or accomplishment. The following five questions from the cue card will also remind the interviewer not to overlook the major dream actions:

24. *Describe the major action or event in this scene.*
25. *Does this action* (recapitulate the description) *remind you of any situation in your life?*
26. *How so?*
27. *How would you describe the central plot of this dream?*
28. *Does this plot* (recapitulate the description) *remind you of anything?*

It is after question 24, asking the dreamer to describe the action, that you may need to employ the sort of follow-up questions only an alien would think to ask. By asking if a given action is typical for humans or what it suggests about humans who do such a thing, you will quickly be able to elicit the descriptive adjectives and value judgments necessary for a good description, which in turn is usually necessary for a solid bridge.

To maintain the Martian state of mind, it is important not to succumb to your need to appear well informed and intuitively attuned to the meaning of the dream.

> Yoshimichi Yamashiti, head of Japanese operations for Arthur D. Little, has a theory about the executive's role in creative processes that yield great ideas. "The manager must learn to be stupid." Personal authority must be set aside, and homage paid to the ideas of the workers, whose working knowledge and insight can lead to breakthrough products and processes.[1]

The interviewer, like the manager, must learn to be stupid, and set aside authority. The concrete descriptions made by the non-interpreting mind of the dreamer are like the ideas of the workers, and it is this working knowledge of the dream elements that produces the bridges and insights that lead to emotional and creative breakthroughs in the life of the dreamer.

In Beverly's dream, which follows, the major actions, some of which we explored in the interview, are underlined:

> I am walking down the street near work with Stan. He had his arm around me in his usual enveloping, affectionate way, and I am trying to keep in step.
>
> Across the street I see Tim McFeeny and his stepbrother on the roof of a house. I point him out to Stan and wonder aloud what he's doing. He's such a ne'er-do-well that I can't imagine he's working very hard. On the other hand, if he is working, it is probably a school project.
>
> I disengage from Stan and go into the house to see what's going on. I assume Tim is working with Derrick Wilshire . . . or perhaps the feeling is as if Derrick

were supervising. But it turns out that it is actually Dad and his new wife, Toni, who are in charge. They are laying charges of dynamite throughout the house.

The students are to stand in a doorway when the charge is detonated so they will be relatively safe as the walls and ceilings collapse. I am Marge now. I stand in the doorway wondering if I actually want to be there. I am, after all, only visiting, and a doorway doesn't seem that safe, but the demolition is already under way. I'm glad there are enough sheltered places to include me.

The charge is barely audible, and only a little rumbling in the building is heard. Some of the students think it didn't work, but I tell them it takes time for the crumbling to happen even though the supports have been blown up. I feel as if the foundations are now gone, and this house is very precarious, yet it is still standing. I wonder if it will hurt if the floor collapses. Because this is a school project, it has been made as safe as it can be, but the project itself is dangerous, so there may be injuries. This is a class in real-life situations, after all.

Toni is as cheerful and energetic as always. Dad and some of the students are going downstairs either to set more charges or seek shelter in other parts of the building. I want to go downstairs too, but feel the building is too unsafe for me to risk moving away from the door frame. (The implied action here: I stay in the door frame because I am afraid to risk moving away from it.)

Dad then emerges from below, and as I see him, I have that usual feeling that all will be fine now.

(DEMOLITION)

As you may have noticed, major actions can include realizations and feelings if they seem to be an integral part of the action. We do not use hard-and-fast rules about exactly what constitutes a major action because this is an exercise in recognizing important, often affect-laden dream actions; it is not an exercise in grammar.

If we were to outline this dream as in step 3 of the dream interview method (Chapter 2), this is how it would look:

ACTION	FEELING
1. Walking down the street with Stan.	1. Cared for and enveloped.
2. Trying to keep in step.	2. Need to keep in step.
3. I disengage and investigate house.	3. Letting go and curiosity.
4. Dad and Toni lay dynamite in house.	4. Interest.
5. I stand in doorway for protection.	5. Anxious, do I want to be there?
6. The demolition is under way.	6. Bracing myself, here we go!
7. Only a little rumbling is heard.	7. Surprise, some relief.
8. I correct students' understanding and misinterpretation that the demolition effort did not work and tell them it takes time.	8. Clarity.

9. Dad and students go downstairs to seek shelter or set more charges.	9. *Desire to go with them.*
10. I stay in door frame.	10. *Too fearful to move.*
11. Dad emerges from below.	11. *Reassured that the project will work out.*

The actions and feelings of the first paragraph were easy to bridge once Beverly had described Stan: "He is the great daddy at work, he fixes things, loves women, and surrounds them with affection just like Dad. He can't take compliments; he feels unworthy to receive, so he must give—again, like Dad. For a long time I have been basking in his affection, trying to be his good girl and to keep in step."

Tim McFeeny was a childhood neighbor, a child of one of two families who swapped spouses. He always acted as if he didn't care about things and had cut himself off from his feelings so that he couldn't tell what—if anything—he wanted out of life. Thus he became a ne'er-do-well. Beverly, who worked in a job far below her intelligence and many talents, felt at times like a Tim whose passions were not free to guide him to something he might want to do with his life. Beverly said that her work on disengaging from too dependent a relationship with her father reminded her of a sort of school project. If Derrick Wilshire was in charge, things would work out. He could adequately supervise Tim because Derrick was the kind of person who got the job done.

It turns out that it is Dad and Toni who have created this Derrick-like atmosphere of good supervision. It is they who are laying the dynamite throughout the house. Beverly bridges this action to the fact that her dad had recently married Toni, and now they were moving to a town a few hours away and would be selling the former family home in the town where Beverly lived. She bridged her anxiety for her safety during the demolition to her anxiety about this momentous shift in her life. The old family structure was indeed being demolished, for the better she thought, but she was still liable to be hurt in the process. Beverly identified Marge as the part of herself that was increasingly willing to take risks and could observe the tumult of her life with an eye toward learning from it. From this perspective, Beverly reminds herself that she is only a visitor in this house. She is glad for the shelter that her work with her dreams and her therapy provide during the demolition.

Telling the students that such demolitions take time, she thought, was her way of telling the same thing to herself when she worries that things aren't working. Then the house is partly demolished but still standing, and her dad disappears. This reminded Beverly of her feelings of insecurity as things were changing and of her dad's regular trips down south to his future home. But in the last scene he reemerges, and she is reassured that the project will work out after all. The plot of this dream, for all of the attendant anxiety, showed that what began as a disengagement from a relationship where she was compliantly trying to keep in step, carried with it a fair amount of fear, but the context was one of learning under well-supervised conditions. Beverly had not lost her dad or her well-being, but an old structure of a former family system that had left much to be desired.

DREAMLETS

Sometimes the action of short dreams or dream fragments is enough to give the dreamer a powerful message. The woman who dreamt of a huge, lead steamroller flattening her husband recognized the effects of her "black moods" on a husband who was overwhelmed by her heavy, continuous anger. The woman who dreamt that her father was pouring concrete all over her body said she has a constant sense of being rigidly encased in a stiff body. She saw the dream connecting this to her response to her father's sexual abuse; even as an adult she felt stiff, rigid, and unable to enjoy her own body. She was bulimic and also insisted on vomiting after having sex. The same woman dreamt:

> **A vampire sucks my blood.** I protest. He says, "You have to let me. You and I made a bargain."
>
> (VAMPIRE)

The vampire reminded her of her father and of other men she has known who seem like him. The bargain mentioned invited her to begin to look at what she was getting or hoping to get in exchange for letting the vampires suck her life blood.

The man who dreamt of stealing his best friend's car immediately saw the parallel to his desires to have an affair with his best friend's wife. The horrendous guilt he felt in the dream about the car gave him pause.

When Charles dreamt of starting college again, feeling hopeful and determined to do it right this time, he thought of the fact that he was starting a new job and had a new chance to do well after having sabotaged himself in his last job.

Thomas awoke with a start after having dreamt that he had missed the first week of his new job. He thought this might have something to do with his having found an excuse not to go with his wife to their first therapy session the week before.

WHEN STRANGE THINGS HAPPEN IN DREAMS

The apparently bizarre and silly things that happen in dreams will usually make perfect sense if you elicit a good description of the action. Mimi dreamt the following scene in the midst of a long dream:

> **I am on a date** with this man who is bald, not physically attractive, but whom I love deeply. As we leave my apartment, I realize that I have forgotten to wear my shoes and I haven't brought any with me. I also realize that I had intended to call someone about what happened earlier in the dream, but I had forgotten.
>
> (BAREFOOT DATE)

Mimi commented that in the dream she was a little spaced out, forgetting things like this. She also felt that while she was with this man she was hiding in some way: "There was a sense here of losing myself in the midst of this relationship." Mimi's dream action of forgetting basic and important things when she was with a man she loved was reminiscent of her pattern of getting scattered whenever she let herself fall in love. The strange man in the dream had some surprising and telling resemblances to her husband, whom Mimi did not love deeply, but with whom she felt she had a nice friendship. The dream seemed to suggest that perhaps her fear of losing herself, of getting scattered when in love, was blinding her to the possibility of sharing the love she longed for with her husband.

Samantha had an odd dream:

> **My father is in his last illness,** almost gone. I am taking care of him in my home, when another person important in my life also becomes ill and I need to take care of that person too. I forget all about my father until I realize that I need to call an ambulance for the second person and will have to tell the ambulance/police that I have a several-day-dead person in the house.
>
> (THE NEGLECTED DEATH)

Samantha's husband had had a serious heart attack soon after her father died. She was so concerned about her husband, that she did not mourn her father until a year or so later, when her mom died and she returned to the family home to settle the family affairs. Samantha had indeed neglected her father's death and her psychological house would not be free of his dead body until she buried him with the necessary mourning.

MAKING DECISIONS IN DREAMS

Decision making is a very important category of dream action. After hearing a dream, or after reading your notes on your own dream, ask yourself if a decision was made, and if so, whether the action that followed the decision was of a positive or troublesome nature. Poor decisions tend to be followed by bad consequences and good decisions by happy ones, although the imagery must often be bridged before this is evident. When no decision is made in a situation that demands one, the dream usually lays out the dynamics of a poorly understood conflict in the dreamer's life. Sometimes the dream decision is simply to reject one or more options without designating a solution. This is usually one of the steps along the way in a dream series helping the dreamer to clarify, narrow, and later choose his options.

Francesca brought in a series of dreams that demonstrate a number of these phases in decision making. In the first dream, she makes a decision she is not happy about. She had incubated a dream asking whether or not she should go back to work with Leo, her former boss, who was starting a new company and had offered her a senior executive position.

> **I was in an office.** There was a group of men talking with Leo about new ventures. One of the men looked at me as if to say, "You're going to spoil this for us." I

ignored his look and said, "You know we will incur big insurance expenses if we take this venture." Leo said this was no problem, just buy it.

I walked into the next office and Herb followed me. Leo said he had planned to give me the office next to his, but someone else had taken it. My office opened onto the space where the clerical staff worked and was not very nice.

All of a sudden Alivia and Simpson were there asking me if I were going to work there. I told them that I had worked out a schedule so that I could. But I was confused about it. Then I was outside. A woman and a little girl were next to me. A man was there. He was being nice to the woman. I wanted to warn her not to trust him, but I was afraid to say anything out loud or the man would hurt me. There were a lot of trees that had shed white flakes. I began picking them up and throwing them at the man and woman. They laughed and started throwing also. My mom was there and she joined us. We took pictures until all our film was used up.   (**WORKING FOR LEO AGAIN**)

The opening discussion in the office with Leo and the other men reminded Francesca of how her boss tends to take unwise risks and plunge prematurely into things. She is aware of not wanting to be there and the men also are aware of this. Leo's following her into her office shows how he wants Francesca's approval in the dream as well as in waking life.

Francesca's office is not what it was supposed to be, just as Leo's promises about the great job offer might not be entirely fulfilled. Alivia and Simpson appear. They are close colleagues who have actively discouraged Francesca from going back to work for Leo. After being reminded of their position, she is confused about her decision to take the job.

Francesca thought the woman and little girl might be a picture of herself and her daughter, or of the little girl within Francesca. She described the man: "Like a man on *Unsolved Mysteries* who murders women for money and leaves." He was being nice, but Francesca knew what he was really like. He reminded her of Leo, who takes great advantage of her. The man also reminded her a little bit of her father. In the dream Francesca decided not to tell the woman not to trust him because she was afraid that if she said anything out loud, the man would hurt her. This, of course, reminded Francesca of her father's sexual abuse and the fearful silence she kept. Might this fear of being hurt be what was now keeping her from saying no to Leo's job offer? Was her indecision a reflection of this fear? Was her relationship with Leo recreating similar dynamics?

After a week's reflection, Francesca thought that the laughter and the throwing of the white flakes was a picture of her tendency to cover up, camouflage, and distract. Her mother's appearance at this moment, after the decision not to warn but to cover up, is crucial. Francesca falls into the negative, depressed, and angry pattern of feelings that surround her mother, who in her own life never spoke out about what was going on in the family. Luckily, they take pictures so we can see what has happened in the dream. (Photos, video recordings, and tape recordings that the dreamer takes during the dream usually turn out to be a reference to recalling and recording the dream so that it can later be understood.) Before this interview, Francesca had had no idea that her crippling indecision about this job was related to her troubled relationship to her father. Her dreams were showing her the many parallels between her relationships with the two men.

About a month after the dream of Leo, Francesca worked with a dream in which she was looking at the deeper levels of this relationship. She was much happier with the decision she made in this dream:

My husband, Shep, and I are renting a car for a vacation trip. In the rental office, I see Tholy and Schief on bar stools, smoking. I don't like them and ignore them. Then I realize that there must be a good reason they are in my dream so I decide to talk to them. Maybe they have a message for me.

When I say hi to Tholy, I see that he is really Ted. Ted says that he likes me but that I hurt him very much by not having thanked him for some information he sent me. He is in tears as he tells me, "I am as intelligent as you but I did my work in a different way. You did yours in a beautiful way, I did not." He's referring to how he stabbed people in the back. He's sad and sorry he's such a bad guy. I am what he would have liked to be.

Tholy and Schief, who is now Howie, walk over to me. I am uncomfortable; they are smirking with that ha-we've-got-you look.

A man asks me to dance. I want to dance in a different way. But he holds me with my back to his front and it gets sexy. I refuse to have another dance with him, it is too sexy. I tell Lindi, "NO MORE!"

(THE SEXUAL DANCE)

All this action takes place in the context of renting a vehicle for a trip with her husband, Shep. Francesca described her husband as a very closed person from whom she is legally and financially separated, but with whom she sleeps every night until she decides whether or not to divorce him. He will not talk about their relationship. She feels he uses her for a warm body at night, and she is often filled with anger and rage at his closedness. Perhaps this dream is exploring their trip together, their rental vehicle, their rental relationship.

Tholy is described as "warm but untrustworthy." He is a coworker who spreads rumors and is out for himself underneath the friendliness. He's lazy, has low self-esteem, and always needs to pump himself up. Schief, like Tholy, is untrustworthy. He's a hard worker, but he always has a hidden agenda, hides his feelings, and uses people.

Francesca said the bar stools and the smoking made her think of places where people hide out from life. To her surprise, the recapitulations of these descriptions reminded Francesca of her father, in some ways of her husband, and of her important boyfriends before him.

Tholy turns into Ted. Ted is "really sleazy. He would stab his mother in the back if it were useful to him. He is an alcoholic; he lies, cheats, and is terribly incompetent." Ted's tears and regrets seem an image of what Francesca's father might have felt had he ever recognized what a mess he had made of his life. Francesca had cherished a very compartmentalized picture of her father even after years of therapy. She saw his incestuous behavior as only one aspect of a man who was an alcoholic, but also a genius and, at times, a kind and thoughtful father. The dream revelation, that the distasteful Tholy was in reality the sleazy, back-stabbing Ted, suggested that her dad was more profoundly unsavory than she had let herself recognize. In unpacking the bridge between Ted and her father, Francesca added that the night before the dream she had reread a horoscope her father had written for her by hand just before he died. She cherished it as one of his acts of kindness. She didn't want to lose her image of having had a good father who was a genius and loved her even if another part of him had done horrible things. This was very sad.

Schief has turned into Howie. Howie "is like Tholy, incompetent, not a hard worker, a comedian like Dad." Regarding their action, Francesca comments, "they approach me smiling in the way the villain smiles before the attack. It reminds me painfully of my father. And the unknown man who insists on making the dance sexual—that is my father."

Francesca described Lindi as a gregarious, outgoing woman

who is her own person. She was abused by her first husband, got rid of him, and never remarried again. Francesca proclaimed the decision not to engage in the sexual dance any more to this woman who had succeeded in stopping the cycle of abuse and in making a life of her own. Francesca made a decision in this dream that she was not able to make in her dream about Leo, only one month before. Because such insight usually comes to us in dreams well before we are capable of it in waking life, Francesca still had a lot of work to do. But already this dream had shown her patterns that, in less violent versions, she had repeated in several relationships to men who shared traits similar to her closed, alcoholic, manipulative, untrustworthy father, who she saw as having wasted his genius and his life.

A month after this dream, Francesca had a dream in which she made a decision and this time took positive action:

> **I am walking through my rental house.** It is very messy, and the doors have been left unlocked. I have apparently lent the house to some people who partied here and left the place a mess. I am upset to see this. The upstairs, where the bedrooms are, is even messier than the downstairs.
>
> Back at my family home, Charneth and another woman go to the rental house to clean it up. My mother laughs saying that Charneth is so slow they'll never get that cleanup done. Later, Charneth and the woman return for a break after having cleaned up the bedrooms. I apologize for not having done it myself, but I was just so tired. I am glad they have begun the job so well.
>
> In a different house owned by a woman who is very together, I sit on a couch between two men who are arguing. I try to keep them apart with my hands because it is my job, and because as they argue, they turn

into horrible monsters with hairy faces and fangs. At this point I think this must be a movie. One of the men looks like the actor Michael Douglas. My job is to hold them apart so they don't destroy each other. I decide that I am tired of this job and of the arguing and go into the next room and lie down on another couch.

A small baby is walking around by herself. It is strange that no one cares for her.

The back door is open and I see the woman who owns the house sitting on the porch getting some fresh air. She wants to take me for a ride in her new van. We get into the van and I say, "Oh, you sold your truck!" She does not respond, but tells me she has to practice her backward driving. She is very excited about having discovered this way of driving. She says she used to go in the other direction (forward), but that meant she had to go around and around Asbury High School. Now if she drove backward, against the one-way sign on this almost always empty short street right by her house, things worked much better. "It's so much easier to get where you want to go by driving backward!"

(THE ARGUMENT)

In the dream "The Sexual Dance" Francesca was renting a car for a trip with her husband. In this dream, she is visiting a rental house she used to own, but has sold in waking life to finance a year off from work away from Leo. When I heard this, I thought of, but did not comment on, the possible parallels between the rental house and Francesca's relationship with Shep, her husband from whom she is separated.

Francesca described this house as being for sale in the dream, and she wanted it to look as nice as possible. She was upset that it had been left such a mess. The unlocked doors meant that "People can come in and steal things and vandalize it." Francesca bridged this to her feelings about having started (at my suggestion) couples therapy the night she had this dream. She liked the psychologist, but had the feeling that, like the house, she looked strong and fine on the outside, but felt very messy on the inside. Wanting the relationship to look as good as possible and feeling it was now unlocked and open to intrusion also reminded her of opening her relationship to a therapist. The bedrooms are the messiest part of the house. Francesca bridged to how she hates the lonely, tense nights in bed with her husband. This was the most painful, messiest part of their relationship.

Francesca described Charneth as a cousin who "is indeed very slow in getting things done, but has the strength and determination to be there for you if you really need help. She is certainly not wishy-washy, as I am. And she does get a lot of work done on the bedroom floor of the house. My mother's critical prediction that she'll never get it done does not seem likely to be fulfilled." Upon recapitulation, Francesca said that her past therapy, her dream work, and the beginning of couples therapy have made a good start on cleaning up her house, but added, "I feel so slow. I am forty-five. When am I going to get through it all? I do criticize myself the way Mom criticizes Charneth. I often think I'll never finish cleaning up this mess." In the dream, Francesca was too exhausted to do the cleanup herself. Now she thought that she could and had, in fact, called on the part of herself that is strong and determined, if not speedy, to get the work done. She had no sense of who the other woman was in the dream, but perhaps she was an image of the dreamer who can do the cleanup with Charneth's help.

No sooner had it become clear that the house was getting cleaned up, than Francesca finds herself in the house of a woman who is "peaceful, all-together, and mellow. Her presence is wonderful and shows in the way she looks, walks, and talks. She is the woman I would like to be." One of the arguing men looks like Michael Douglas whom Francesca described as "a nice guy, very caring, who is too self-critical. He has said his acting on *The Streets of San Francisco* TV show was not good. He focuses too much on technique and doesn't realize how well he communicates and comes across to his viewers. He is warm and intelligent." Francesca bridged him to herself and the other man to her husband. She said that they both turn into monsters when they fight. Francesca hates to argue because she has so much stored-up rage. She has felt that her job was to keep herself and her husband apart so they would not destroy each other. Isn't it interesting that on the very night of her first couples therapy session, Francesca dreams that she is tired of this job and goes to lie down on a couch in another room of this fine woman's house? That night, after the therapy session, Francesca and her husband got into another fight. She said that she was just so tired of arguing, getting criticized, and trying to hold her temper that she simply withdrew to a bubble bath.

So far in the dream Francesca has started to clean up her house and quit her job as the one who keeps the arguers apart. But what to do now? Will the two monsters kill each other? What will become of Francesca on a couch in a room by herself? What needs to be done now?

In the next scene, Francesca sees a small baby walking by herself and finds it strange that no one cares for her. Here is a good example of how important it is not to take things for granted. Conventional wisdom often interprets a baby as a new and positive potential, or new life in the dreamer. While this is sometimes the case, listen to the surprising description Francesca gave of this particular baby:

FRANCESCA. It is a little girl.
INTERVIEWER. What is she like?
F. She is a shrunken woman who is so small as to be a baby.
I. And how old would you say that she is?

F. [Long pause.]

I. Normal age? [A noncommittal prompt.]

F. Yes normal age. [She laughs with recognition after saying this.] She is my age!

I. And no one cares for her.

F. No one is caring for the part of me that feels like a lonely, vulnerable little girl.

You can see how much we would have lost had we interpreted the baby as simply some wonderful but neglected new growth in Francesca.

Through the back door, her more private, less obvious access, Francesca sees the delightful owner of this house taking in some fresh air. (This is something that Francesca always does in waking life to relax and reflect.) The owner has bought a shiny new van. She has sold her old pickup. Asked to define and describe pickups, Francesca said, "They are uncomfortable vehicles with a flat bed in back and a cab that keeps you from the driver. There's only room for one or at most two and for carrying a lot of junk in the back." I asked her what the one referred to in her dream is like.

F. It was all beat-up. Most of my life I have felt beat-up and confined and cutoff living in the old way.

I. So this lady who has such presence, whom you would like to be, has sold the beat-up truck and bought a van. How is a van different from a truck, and this van from that truck?

F. A van is more open, you can talk to the driver. There is more room for other people, you can have a whole group. With a van, you have room for more people in your life. This van is shiny and new, and very nice. It has not been through so much, not tarnished. It is fresh and neat and very comfortable. In my life, I want a fresh start like this.

We are told that next the lady wants to show Francesca how she has learned and must now practice this wonderful new way of driving backward against the flow of traffic on a one-way street. Now, to an earthling this might well sound like a very bad idea. But being of another planet, we ask, "What is a one-way street?" "A street on which traffic is allowed to flow only in one direction. In this case, that caused problems; it kept the lady driving round and round Asbury High School, which was not where she wanted to go."

I. What is this place like?

F. Well, I don't know of such a place. Asbury is the name of a middle school near my house where my daughter used to play soccer. When we went to the games, I would sit in the stands and marvel at the beauty of the place and wonder what it would be like to have a house there from which to see the beautiful surrounding mountains.

I. And what is high school like for human beings?

F. It is supposed to be lots of fun. While you learn, you have friends and date and go to proms and all that. But for me, it was terrible. My father was jealous and would not let me date anyone. For me, it was just a chore of studying and very lonely.

I. So it is in driving forward that the owner of the house would go round and round this high school, right? [Francesca nods in agreement.] Have you in driving forward, trying to get where you want to go, been hung up going round this sort of pretty-looking, but lonely, place where life is a chore of studies?

F. My work life has been like that. I have driven myself in one way, forward, in part to escape my past.

I. Is it dangerous for this lady to drive backward down the one-way street?

F. Not in this case. It is a short street and there is almost never any traffic on it. And besides, she could always go forward when needed.

I. The lady has found that driving backward gets her where she wants to go much more quickly, and she needs to practice this?

F. Right, and she is very excited and happy to tell me about it.

I. Is there any way that driving backward would make it easier to get where you want to go.

F. I guess I still have to work with unfinished business in my past, because even though I thought I had done that, my dreams make it clear that old feelings are still messing up my current adult life.

DEATH AND SUICIDE

The different categories of dream actions are innumerable. The questions and strategies you have already encountered and have yet to read about in this book will equip you to handle almost any action you care to explore in a dream. There is, however, the question of what to do when confronted with death and suicide motifs, which come up frequently enough and are of such importance that they deserve special attention.

Many people worry that the death of someone in a dream means that this dream person, or someone close to the dreamer, will die. While reasonable people have given detailed accounts of such experiences, the most credible ones are rare, and perhaps because of the unpredictable occurrence of the experience, these accounts have yet to be confirmed scientifically. As Stanley Krippner, one of the foremost researchers in the field, states, "The jury is still out on the phenomenon of psychic dreaming."[2] In the meantime, I must say that all the dreams of someone's death that I have heard in my practice and at our dream center have, on exploration, been meaningful to the dreamers on the metaphorical, rather than the literal level.

In Liam's dream, his aunt Ruth died and he felt very sad. He described Ruth as a woman who challenges him, yet respects him. I asked, "What would you lose if the Ruth who challenges you, yet respects you, were to die?" "I would lose someone who believes in me, who loves my practical work and my intellect," said Liam with tears in his eyes. He bridged to having lost the Ruth within him the last few weeks and especially the day preceding the dream, when he had been very discouraged and pessimistic about doing well on his medical board exams. If Liam had followed some purveyors of conventional wisdom and interpreted this dream as a necessary and good thing, a prerequisite to the rebirth of something better in his personality, he would have failed to appreciate the importance of Ruth in his psychological economy. If Liam had taken this as a literal dream, he would have worried needlessly about his aunt, who was fine, and he would have missed a chance to recognize the importance of not letting the Ruth within him die. By attending to how he felt about Ruth's death in the dream and to how he described Ruth, Liam was able to find the answer that had most relevance to his waking life. (Aunt Ruth's Death)

When working with your own dreams or with those of a friend, colleague or client, it is of the utmost importance that you recognize the possible signs of potentially suicidal feelings, which will often make their first appearance in dreams.

Some dreams wave big red flags:

> **Two puppies were in a cage** on top of fire embers. I waited almost too long to get them out, and they were very listless. I was enormously sad inside. I said to myself, "I don't want to live like this anymore."
>
> **(PUPPIES)**

The dreamer bridged the vulnerable, neglected, listless puppies to herself, and in unpacking the bridge described how she had once, over a decade ago, attempted to kill herself by taking pills and hiding herself in a closet so she would not be found. Having confirmed that the dreamer was feeling sad, not glad at having discovered the puppies just in time, it was time to insist that the dreamer talk about her feelings about not wanting to live any longer. Because I do not practice psychotherapy, I also insisted that she begin psychotherapy immediately. Had I been this woman's therapist, I would have focused all my attention on her suicidal thoughts for at least the next few sessions.

When a person kills himself in a dream or kills others, it is wise to fish about for possible suicidal thoughts. While such dreams can be about seriously self-destructive attitudes and behaviors such as using drugs, or being drawn into a masochistic relationship, they are often an expression of suicidal thinking and should be examined closely. When I have any suspicion at all, I ask directly if the dreamer has had any thoughts of killing himself lately and invite him to tell me about it.

Robert Litman gives some very practical advice in his article "The Dream in the Suicidal Situation."[3] He cites dreams of being trapped and struggling with few resources, dreams of death and dead people, and violent dreams destructive to the dreamer and to others in the dream as common components in the dreams of suicidal patients. I strongly encourage not only therapists but also anyone else interested in dreams to read Litman's article carefully.

Not all dreams with these themes signal suicidal problems, but dreams of the death of the dreamer almost always indicate a problem that threatens the well-being of the individual. Once I dreamt that I was watching two Nazis killing Jews, one at a time. It was vivid and horrendous. When I couldn't stand it any longer, and another one came up for his turn, I pushed him out of the way and took his place. The two Nazi's decided to kill me quickly in recognition of my good intentions, but just as the poison from their needles entered my shoulders, I said to myself, "Damn, this was stupid! There must have been another, better way to try to save the Jews." I had just realized that my sacrifice wasn't going to save any Jews in the long run, despite its valor. I described Jews as those who for centuries have honored learning and preserved this learning, who have refused to give into the fashions of culture and for that very reason have been repressed and killed off, and who have had little power to protect themselves in many cultures.

I first bridged the Jews to the way I see dreams, which have been repressed and unappreciated in Nazi-like cultures that deny feelings and hold up as a hero the man who feels nothing but the need to succeed and do his duty for the authorities. At the time of this dream, I was working much too hard, "killing myself," trying to launch the Association for the Study of Dreams with inadequate assistance. What I was doing was stupid. If the association were to do any long-lasting good for the reputation and study of this much-defamed field, I had better learn how to be a more effective delegator. My husband and friends had all been commenting on the change in my personality from a rather cheerful one to that of a dreary type-A workaholic. As I reflected on the dream I saw how it signaled a longer-term self-destructive pattern of hurling myself into hopeless situations, believing that I was honor-bound to try to save others even if it cost me my life. I was finally beginning to see that I should use my brains, not just my valor. (Saving the Jews)

Litman notes that when a person's suicide plan has matured, the final decision to actually execute it is often indicated by peaceful dreams of taking leave. I have seen this sort of dream take the form of a dreamer's exiting from a stressful situation and entering an extremely peaceful state without having resolved or understood anything about the stressful state. I have heard people with such dreams tell me that they left the stress and merged into a huge, peaceful, black darkness, or entered a meditative state of pure nothingness where everything was calm. These dreamers sometimes try to convince themselves, and me, that they have found a higher level of consciousness and have transcended the problems of their unenlightened ego. But if I can persuade them to explore their feelings just a bit, we often find some suicidal thinking and uncover a secret plan.

Even in people who have not progressed beyond being tempted by the possibility of escape by suicide, we hear dreams that are warning signs, in which the dreamer is struggling, say, walking a difficult, precipitous path, when he "nearly goes over the edge" or sees, "over there to the side, a beautiful, quiet, peaceful meadow." Dreams like these, and dreams in which the dreamer is battling against overwhelming forces can, like suicide attempts, be an appeal for help. The important thing to remember is that unless you are a professional trained in suicide prevention, you are not the best person available to the dreamer. The best thing you can do if you know a dreamer of such dreams is to refer him to an experienced professional.

X-RATED DREAMS

Sexual dreams can be among the most pleasant or the most unpleasant in our dream repertoire. People often ask me how they can have great sex in their dreams. You can greatly increase your chances of having one of those straightforward, delightful, oneiric orgasms by denying yourself sexual satisfaction for extended periods of time while awake. If this method does not appeal, you could try preoccupying yourself with sexual matters: read books on erotica and sexual technique, and practice a lot. This second approach will usually lead to dreams which help you examine your sexual hang-ups, although the dreams may not necessarily include sexual imagery.

Some overtly sexual dreams actually teach the dreamer how to improve his or her responsiveness or technique. If you incubate a dream asking for insights into and ways out of your inhibitions, don't be surprised if you overcome a certain shyness and have a richly rewarding sexual encounter in the dream or the morning after with your partner. A number of my male clients have told me dreams in which they are making love to their wives and are really enjoying foreplay for the first time. In these cases, the dreams are not telling the husbands something they don't already know, or that their wives haven't already told them, but the dream experiences can spur the dreamer past his reticence, reluctance, or laziness to practice a more exciting level of sexuality and romance. Women, too, sometimes have graphic dreams in which they are engaging in sexual activities that they are too inhibited to try while waking. If the dreamer wants to, she can use these pleasurable dream experiences to nudge her into becoming a freer, better, and more satisfied lover.

A common dream is that of finding yourself making love to someone other than your waking partner or partners. You might be having dream sex with a boy from high school, a co-worker, an employee, a neighbor, a movie star, or an opera singer. In order to understand these dreams, ask yourself, "What is making love, or having sex? Why do humans do it?" Then describe how the lovemaking felt in the dream. Did things go well? Were there interruptions or other problems? Does this remind you of any feelings or circumstances in your waking life in or out of the sexual arena? Give a good description of your dream lover, both as he is or was in waking life and how he is in your dream. Be ruthlessly honest and ask yourself if the personality traits and/or behavior of your dream partner remind you of anyone in your life. Usually, but not always, your dream lover will highlight unrecognized or underappreciated characteristics in your current partner, and may even point out a pattern of traits common to many of the partners you have known.

This is welcome news if your dream lover is romantic and manifests qualities you like. For example, your dream man or woman might be someone you find especially exciting and trustworthy. As you describe him or her you may recall how much your dream lover is like your husband or wife. The dream figure could help you to appreciate your spouse at a time when you have lost sight of his more exciting qualities. If your dream of wonderful sex with dream lover X reminds you of X himself, or of another man you know who is like him, then you have a chance to explore your attraction to this sort of man. What does it say about the state of your current sexual relationship that you dream vividly of such a man? Is something important missing in your waking love relationship? What can you do about it? Talk with your partner? Get into therapy? Make a change?

Many people worry about dreams in which they make love with a person of the same sex (if they are heterosexual) or of the opposite sex (if they are homosexual). These are not abnormal dreams and can mean many different things. Ask yourself the same questions suggested above about the act of sex and about the particular partner, including the dream partner's sex. Most humans have some attraction to both sexes, but most of us know what our primary sexual orientation is without the help of our dreams. The answer to such dreams usually lies elsewhere. Louisa, a heterosexual New York journalist in her mid-forties dreamt:

> **I am making love to Stephania,** a correspondent from Rome who is a Lesbian. She is very loving and accepting of me and my body. Even though I recognize she is another woman, I feel quite comfortable with her. But I don't feel very turned on. I say to myself, "It is like making love to someone of the same sex."
>
> (SEX WITH STEPHANIA)

Our interview did not take long:

GAYLE. Why do humans make love?

LOUISA. To share intimacy, for the best of emotional and physical feelings. Sometimes out of habit, sometimes just for physical release.

G. Okay. What was it like to make love to Stephania?

L. Well, it was nice. She was kind and pleasant, but I've got to say, it lacked a certain romantic, sexual zing.

G. What is Stephania like?

L. She is a top-rate journalist, and very successful. She is bright, fun, interesting, sort of like a cousin or a sister to me. I feel accepted by her. In the dream she didn't mind that I'm ten pounds overweight. I'm not particularly attracted to her, though, as far as I know.

G. So, is there anyone in your life, or any part of yourself that is bright, successful, top-rate, interesting, and fun like a cousin or a sister with whom you are intimate, but with whom you miss the romantic zing?

L. I hate to say it, but my boyfriend who is also a foreign correspondent for our paper, has seemed to me more like a supportive sibling than a romantic partner of late. He is really nice, but . . . well, the male-female tension is missing. It's more like making love to someone of the same sex—which, for me, just isn't as exciting.

Louisa found it easy to see the gist of her dream, but she wasn't happy to have to face the fact of her dissatisfaction with a relationship which was a very good one in so many other ways. Although she dreaded discussing the problem with her boyfriend, she knew that she'd better deal with the issue sooner rather than later. Her work with the dream forced her to stop pretending that the problem would go away on its own.

It is crucial that you pay very close attention to the quality of the feelings you have while making love in a dream. Jean Marie, a wildly successful writer from Los Angeles was shocked to recall a dream in which she was having sex with a man and feeling that she would do anything at all to win his approval and love. In her waking life, Jean Marie is a powerful, independent professional who likes being in control of her relationships with men. But in the dream she saw an often hidden part of herself, so profoundly needy that it made her feel that she was reduced to a desperate wretch begging for love through sex. She didn't like the feelings in the dream, but she explored them and realized that there was indeed an undercurrent of these same feelings in a number of her sexual relationships. She began to admit to her deep need for approval from men, and to see how it sometimes led her into somewhat masochistic relationships.

If you dream of making love to your daytime partner and experience feelings of anger, hurt, jealousy, disgust, or unexpected warmth or love, carefully look into the possibility that these feelings, unbeknownst to you, may be playing an important part in how you two get along. If you and your partner work with each other's dreams, remember that your dream of the sexy bombshell at work is almost never about the feelings you already know you have about her. The dream will more likely be about that kind of woman in general, another woman like her, or about that part of your wife or girlfriend who is like her or whom you treat the way you treat the bombshell in the dream. It all depends on how you describe and bridge to your dream lover and to the quality of sex you have with her.

I cannot leave this section without commenting on a frequently whispered question: Will my dreams give me away if I am having a secret affair? The answer is that they probably will if you share your dreams with a good interviewer. Since we dream about the issues of greatest concern to us, it is likely that a fair number of your dreams will deal with either the problems attached to having an affair or with the quality of the relationship itself. More than once, TV and radio talk show and lecture hosts have asked me to work with their dreams in front of their audiences. I always decline the proposal because you never know what a dream will reveal. While I can easily protect an audience member who proffers an incriminating dream by immediately generalizing about such dreams or by using various distracting comments, with a host who wants to control the interview and find out what his dream means, things can get a bit uncomfortable. Once, a very assertive radio host persisted in asking me to work with his dream in spite of my warnings, so I insisted that we first discuss the dream during the news break to make sure he wanted to go public with the material. The host, whose name was Lex, told me the following dream while the news and weather report aired:

> **I was on a very nice pleasure boat** in the Mediterranean Sea near Monaco. Marilyn Monroe and I were making love when she suddenly jumped off the ship and pretended to be drowning and in need of immediate rescue. I was very angry because she knew how to swim and was in no danger at all. She was just trying to manipulate me into leaving the ship.
>
> (MARILYN OVERBOARD)

Quickly, before we had to go on air again, I asked a few questions:

GAYLE. What is it like to be on a pleasure boat near Monaco?

LEX. It's the easy life. Comfortable, warm, luxurious.

G. What was Marilyn like in life and in the dream?

L. In life she was absolutely the sexiest thing ever, but in the dream she was just as manipulative and dishonest as she was sexy.

G. What was she up to in the dream?

L. She was faking being in trouble in order to get me to rescue her and leave the boat where I was having a good time.

G. So, is there anywhere in your life where there is a woman who is the sexiest thing ever, but who is faking the need to be rescued in a manipulative effort to

get you to leave your comfortable, warm, luxurious
ship?

L. My God—I have been having an affair with a sexy
woman who has been doing just that sort of thing,
and I have nearly fallen for it! And my relationship
with my wife is warm, comfy, and luxurious. Well, I
guess we can forget telling that dream on the air!

THE INTERVIEWER'S COMPASS

The dramatic structure of a dream, of what happens in what
order, and how each part relates to the overall plot, acts as a
directional compass for the interviewer. The thrust of the plot
will help you design questions that keep you on course and will
let you know when you have wandered off in the wrong direction. For example, if the dreamer has just described his best
friend in glowing terms, but you note that in the dream the
friend is slipping sedatives into the dreamer's orange juice, you
will know that there remain some negative qualities about this
friend that have yet to be described.

Keeping in mind the overall plot of the dream will also help
you avoid one of the most common and seductive pitfalls of
dream interpretation: Interpreting one image or one part of
a dream in isolation, without regard to its role in the whole
dream. Suppose we had worked only on the part of Francesca's
dream "The Argument" in which she was being shown how
to drive backward. Had we not worked with the qualities of the
woman driver, the reasons for her driving like this, and the description of Asbury High School within the context of the
whole dream, it would have been very easy to misinterpret this
dream.

Here is a dream that Kathryn presented during our first session. She had read my book *Living Your Dreams* and brought

with her a copy of the dream interview she had conducted with herself in her journal. A month before the dream, Kathryn had bought a set of "Animal Medicine" cards, which describe the characteristics and lessons to be learned from each animal on a card. She took my warnings not to rely on external symbol systems only half-heartedly, and Kathryn consulted her cards for the meanings of the animals in her dream. To demonstrate the problems that arise when one does not describe the dream images for oneself and when one does not fully consider the context of the dream, I shall show you the dream as well as Kathryn's carefully recorded notes before we look to see what came out of the interview.

Kathryn incubated this dream asking, "Why don't I feel motivated? Why do I feel stuck?" She dreamt:

> **I am viewing the house where** I grew up from above. It is winter and there is snow on the ground. I see an antelope that is caught between the house and an evergreen tree. He has long, dark antlers and he is tossing his head in an attempt to use them to free himself.
>
> I see wolves and foxes moving away from the house across the snow, sort of migrating to another place. I have some concern that the wolves will eat the foxes, though I don't have any reason to think they will.
>
> I am in the woods with someone and we are running the path the animals have run ahead of us. It is snowy here and I notice two shiny yellow vinyl sleeping pads partially frozen in the snow.
>
> I see a polar bear behind me in the opening to the woods and I tell whomever I am with that we'd better get a move on or the bear will get us. He is coming our way. Somehow I have become invisible and am able to duck behind some bushes as the polar bear approaches. I notice that I am able to walk on the ground here be-

cause there is no snow. My feet make no noise as they touch the ground. Whoever was with me is gone. I am alone here.   (MY TOTEM ANIMALS)

Commentary. I bought a set of animal cards a month ago because I was attracted to them from the first time I saw them. They are a personal growth tool, and I have used them frequently since I bought them. The American Indians used animal medicines to empower them and assist them in life. Each of the animals in the deck is described according to the lesson that animal has to teach.

I understood upon awakening that I needed to understand what each of the different animals meant by looking to my animal medicine book. Each of the animals has a lesson and each lesson is summed up by one word that is the essence of what the animal represents.

Foxes are my own personal medicine, my "animal within." Lately, as I've played with the deck, I have pulled the fox over and over again. It is the animal dearest to my heart, but I don't understand what it is trying to say to me. The card gives *camouflage* as the key word for the fox.

Wolves are the "teachers," this much I know from reading my book.

Antelope represents "action," and the fact that he was stuck in my dream is right to the point of my life. I feel stuck, unable to break free, unable to act.

What is snow? Ah! Frozen water! My life feels frozen. What is the house of your childhood? Where I grew up. Where my beliefs and attitudes and expectations about life were formed. I lived there until I was thirteen.

What is an evergreen tree? The only one that doesn't

look dead in the winter. It always looks the same. It's green, fragrant, and alive looking.

What is the action in the dream? I am viewing the scene from above. I see the snowy landscape, my old house, and the antelope caught between the house and the evergreen tree. I identify with him. Then I see the foxes and wolves migrating away from the house.

Then I am running through the woods with the understanding that the animals have come through here ahead of me and whoever is with me. I see the two sleeping pads. I see the polar bear and hide in the bushes. I feel invisible.

What is a migration? The movement of a large group of animals away from a place where they will die if they remain, to a warmer environment that will support them and keep them alive.

What are the woods? A quiet place in nature, the home of trees. Refuge, a sanctuary.

What is a polar bear? This was the one animal in my dream whose significance I didn't know. I was surprised and somewhat amused to find that the key word for bear is, "introspection." How perfect!

What are sleeping pads? They are shiny yellow vinyl and highly visible in the snow. They are waterproof because they are vinyl. It seems they were left by someone.

Kathryn put a lot of effort into her commentary and described a few of the images according to how she saw them. Unfortunately, by looking up what the animals were supposed to mean according to the system these cards claimed to represent, she forfeited her chance to give and to examine her own descriptions. By the time we worked with the dream, it was hard to tell what she believed about an animal, and what she had read she should believe. One thing was clear: Kathryn could not see how the animals as defined by the cards fit into any sort of coherent plot. And most important, she had no idea why the dream should end with her hiding, being invisible, inaudible, and all alone. She had been so engrossed in the magic of her animals that she could not see their roles in the larger drama.

Instead of looking at the specifics of the interview, let's look at the structure of the dream and see what it suggests. The dreamer is viewing her childhood house. She may be looking into a life issue, via the dream, that had its beginnings in her childhood. It is winter; the snow reminds the dreamer of the frozen quality of her life. The animals are migrating "away from a place where they will die if they remain, to a warmer environment that will support them and keep them alive." According to the plot, the antelope is stuck and will die if it does not migrate away from this cold, wintry house of the dreamer's childhood. Kathryn described antelopes as sweet, swift, and graceful, but dumb, having no teeth, and easy prey. It is stuck between the house and an evergreen tree, which the dreamer described as the only tree that always looks green and alive. Kathryn identified with the antelope's vulnerability, its sweetness and grace, and the fact that it was stuck. She also said that in her family, and now in adulthood, she feels a great pressure always to look good and alive. Somehow then, she must be stuck in her life, unable to get away from her frozen childhood emotional home to a warmer, more supportive environment, because she is stuck in her need to look good and not show pain or discomfort in her life.

The wolves and the foxes know it is time to leave this cold childhood environment and they are on their way. *Before* the dream, because of her reading, Kathryn thought of wolves as teachers, and in the interview described them as romantic, beautiful, wild dogs that can be vicious. The key word for foxes was *camouflage,* which she looked up *after* the dream. She abandoned this "meaning" after she heard herself describe foxes as pretty, crafty, agile, and creative. These teacher wolves and crafty creative foxes were the parts of herself that knew how to get away, but the antelope in her was stuck and would die if it couldn't get out from behind the evergreen tree.

The sleeping pads were partially frozen; the people who slept on them had each slept on a separate, insulated, waterproof pad. This seemed to allude to some of the qualities of the dreamer's present relationship with her boyfriend, but she was reticent about discussing it in detail at this point.

Kathryn described a polar bear as hugely powerful, big, and fuzzy and as living in cold environments year round. She went on to say that polar bears are mellow, laid-back, and cute, until they find cause to unleash their wild power. At this point, Kathryn saw the parallels to her boyfriend, who she at first insisted was a very mellow, extremely laid-back sort of fellow, but with whom she felt she must be careful, look good, and act right because she did not want to trigger what she supposed were deep reservoirs of anger underneath a very cool personality style. Then she began to make sense of why in the dream she was hiding from the polar bear and why the real Kathryn had to be invisible and inaudible to avoid a clash with him. No wonder she felt all alone in this cold world. Now, the opening scene tells us that the entire action of the dream has to do with Kathryn's childhood, but up until now she had not shown any tendency to bridge any images or feelings to aspects of her childhood. Because Kathryn was new to serious dream work and because she was shocked enough to see how much of herself she was hiding from a boyfriend who she preferred to see as a teddy bear rather than as a polar bear, I thought it best to leave until her next session the question of whether there was anyone else in her life who seemed like a cute, fuzzy, powerful, and threatening polar bear from whom she hid much of herself.

As Stern and Boss have so eloquently shown, a respect for the integrity of the dream can save the dreamer from both slight and significant misinterpretations.[4] When a dreamer takes a particular action in a dream, the feelings and events that follow in the next scene are often the result of that action. They also serve the crucial function of further describing and evaluating that action. For example, in one dream, the dreamer is offered a car that has a seat that won't let him reach the brake. The roof of the car is falling down. He buys the bargain car hoping that a few repairs will make it drivable. We must know if the next scene suggests that his hope is realistic. If the next scene shows the dreamer discovering even more serious problems after the purchase or if he discovers that the salesman has charged his credit card for ten times the original price, then the dreamer's hope begins to look naive and unfounded. He would then bridge not to somewhere in his life where he has made a good deal, but to a situation in which he *thought* he had made a good deal and may be ignoring the evidence of his mistake because his unrealistic optimism is blinding him to the obvious.

When a dreamer has been able to provide good descriptions and bridges to the major images and feelings in a dream, a summary of the plot should help to elucidate the unbridged sections, and all the pieces of the dream should fall into place. Any parts that do not seem to fit either have been inadequately explored or indicate that the bridges already made may be inaccurate.

A good interviewer should always be ready to change directions at any point if new information suggests that he has been barking up the wrong tree. A dreamer who is resisting looking at a particular problem area in his life may consistently and defensively bridge to anything but that area and mislead both himself and his interviewer. Eventually, if each part of the dream is explored, these false or weak bridges will collapse because they will not fit into the context of the dream plot. As the dream fails to "come together," many dreamers, eager to see how the puzzle fits, will let down enough of their defenses to admit feelings that will build solid bridges and yield meaningful interpretations of the dream.

Scene Changes

The often discontinuous and surprising scene changes in dreams have contributed to the widespread belief that dreams are meaningless products of indigestion or the random firing of neurons in the brain.[5] As we have seen, on careful investigation these scene changes make sense when considered within the context of the dream. They express transitions in attitude or mood, shifts in the perspective of a particular problem, the developmental history of a problem, developments in the dreamer's progress with an issue, and outcomes already realized or likely to be realized resulting from the actions and attitudes portrayed in the preceding scene or scenes.

Commenting on the nature of scene changes in dreams, Jung noted, "The irrational sequence is to be understood as a *causal* sequence."[6] This can be seen in scene shifts like the ones in Francesca's dream "The Argument." One could say that because Francesca has started to clean up the mess in her life, especially where it concerns her marriage, she realizes she does not have to continue keeping the arguers apart from each other. One result of her refusing to do that job any longer is her recognition of the part of herself that is like a lonely little girl for whom no one cares. This recognition allows her to see, contact, and learn from a part of herself, becoming as flexible as the owner of the house, who refuses to obey the troublesome one-way sign. One scene leads to the other and actually makes the next scene possible.

Last Scenes

"Very often the end of a dream can teach one something; at the end something has usually happened to the figures that appeared on the stage, so that the situation at the beginning and the events between are quite explicable."[7] As Jung noted, sometimes the whole dream seems to lead up to a central fact that is revealed at the very end of the dream. In Kathryn's dream "My Totem Animals," the fact that she is alone in a harsh, cold environment at the end of the dream must be recognized if she is ever to break free of her entanglement there. If she goes on denying this statement of feeling and fact regarding her loneliness, she will continue to hide herself and keep up the evergreen facade.

HELP KEY

◘ *When you are confused by a dream after having explored a number of its images and feel lost,* refer to the dramatic structure, summarize it, and simply repeat it to the dreamer. This might trigger the dreamer's ability to bridge, and at the very least it will underline the important reference points of the dream.

◘ *When you find the action of a dream to be rather prosaic and uninteresting,* make your curiosity burn. Remind yourself that this may be an important clue to the meaning of the dream, and for all you know as an alien, this could be described in very unpredictable and unexpected terms by your dreamer. Even when you are interviewing yourself, you will often be surprised by the way you describe the most common dream actions.

CHAPTER TEN

INTERMEDIATE STRATEGIES TO IMPROVE YOUR INTERVIEWING TECHNIQUE

After you have worked with several dreams, you will be ready to incorporate a few more skills that will help you elicit richer descriptions, bridges, and summaries from yourself and from your dream partners. This chapter provides you with suggestions and ideas that will improve your basic dream skills.

DESCRIPTIONS

When our students first start using the dream interview method, they are usually delighted with the specific and often surprising descriptions they obtain by pretending to come from another planet. They feel a new respect for the uniqueness of their own and their partners' dreams. Yet, in the midst of their new excitement over the efficacy of asking naive questions, there arise moments when they relapse into old habits of injecting their preconceived notions into the dream interview. Students sometimes feel that certain images, or categories of images, are exempt from idiosyncratic interpretations. Louie, a Jungian analyst who was learning the interview method, asked a dreamer good questions about various images. But when he got to the injured right arm of the uncle in the dream, he reverted to quoting Jung's statement: "The right arm is always the symbol of power."[1] Had she been asked, the dreamer might have come up with the exact same description of a right arm, but wouldn't it have been better for the dreamer if she had been given the chance to do it for herself? And what if she had used slightly different words? Her words would have been the best ones to recapitulate to her. And what if she were left-handed, or if her uncle had been? What if she had thought of "sitting at the right hand of God" or of a "right-hand man?"

One of the most seductive traps is the belief that while most symbolic systems are arbitrary or inaccurate, you have access to one that is based on a trustworthy authority or on your own experience and is, therefore, reliable. Freud fell into this one when he wrote:

> In the case of symbolic dream-interpretation the key to the symbolization is arbitrarily chosen by the inter-preter; whereas in our cases of verbal disguise the keys are generally known and laid down by firmly estab-lished linguistic usage. If one has the right idea at one's disposal at the right moment, one can solve [apparently senseless] dreams . . . wholly or in part even indepen-dently of information from the dreamer.[2]

Jung believed that certain universal dream images, or arche-types, could only be interpreted by someone with specialized knowledge in mythology, astrology, the history of religions, folklore, alchemy, and so on. Freud, too, believed that

> as a rule the technique of interpreting according to the dreamer's free associations leaves us in the lurch when we come to the symbolic elements in the dream-content. . . . [In such cases we must] adopt a combined technique, which on the one hand rests on the dream-er's associations and on the other hand fills the gaps from the interpreter's knowledge of symbols.[3]

The danger of such attitudes is, of course, that the interpreter may force any dream and any dreamer into a preconceived the-ory that may be too limited to recognize experiences and in-sights that are not included in its system. Remembering that your beliefs about the meaning of certain symbols may not be shared by your dreamer will allow both of you to make important discoveries. Remembering that you yourself might describe a dream image in surprising ways to someone from another planet will allow you to break out of symbolic systems, which may have been limiting your ability to understand your own dreams.

It is easy to fall into the trap of filling in the gaps that appear when the dreamer has very few associations to an element in a dream.[4] But before rushing in with what you think is relevant to the image, ask the dreamer a few of the questions described in the chapter on that element. The dreamer can almost always tell you what you need to know, if you know how to ask the right questions.

For example, suppose that your partner dreams about a snake and tells you only that snakes are frightening creatures that slither. If you then tell the dreamer that in mythology, snakes represent a rite of initiation, or that they are phallic symbols, you have short-circuited the dreamer's chances for discovering much about the snake in her dream. If instead, you ask about what the dream snake was like and what such snakes are like in general, the dreamer will be free to create her own description and find her own meaning.[5] General symbolic systems tend to overlook the crucial differences between boa constrictors, rattlers, and garter snakes. If there are profound, deep, or spiritual meanings in the dreamer's experience of the dream or in her experience of working with the dream, they will eventually come from the dreamer as she explores her own imagery.

It is good to remember how very concretely a dreamer thinks and perceives while dreaming and while discussing a dream. If you recapitulate a description by saying, "Does *that* remind you of anything?" or "How do you feel about *that*?" the dreamer may well roll her eyes and become disoriented. "How do I feel about what?" she may ask even though she has just given you a description of the thing your word *that* refers to. Say your dreamer has given you a sparse, feelingless description of pigs, "I don't know any pigs, I've never seen one except in pictures, I guess they are friendly and agile." Let your next question incorporate some of her description: "So pigs are friendly and agile, tell me more about their personalities." One of my clients responded to this question by saying "Pigs are indiscriminately trusting creatures, ingenuous, happy, friendly animals." This fuller description led the dreamer to recognize that the pig that was about to be sacrificed in her dream was much like the unsuspicious, carefree, happy part of herself that she was sacrificing to her workaholism. When asking for a fuller description of a dream action, instead of "How do you feel about *that*?" try "How did you feel as you saw the bear falling off the cliff?" and your dreamer will be more readily able to respond.

Sometimes, while the dreamer is describing an image, she will become excited as new aspects of the image come to mind. At this moment, the interviewer may also become excited by her delight that the dreamer is catching on or by her own desire to ask the next question suggested by the description. It is important not to interrupt the dreamer while she is in the process of finding new descriptions, discovering new associations, and making new connections. In our classes we say, "Don't interrupt or corral the dreamer while she is on a roll." Often the last line of the dreamer's excited description is the most telling. In a small study group, one of the dreamers was describing horses as "animals used for recreation, magnificent animals, full of power and strength," when an interviewer interrupted. We motioned her to wait. The dreamer continued, "Horses are agile," and the interviewer looked like she was about to burst with an insight. We motioned her to be calm. The dreamer continued, "And horses have the ability to carry a heavy load, they are work animals." At this point the dreamer started to cry, saying that the injured horse in her dream could no longer carry a load. She saw the horse as an image of herself and of her inability to withstand the stress of a career because of her unhealed emotional wounds. Had the interviewer interrupted with her hunches related to the dreamer's description of horses as recreational animals, she would have missed the more relevant associations to the horse as a work animal.

The fact that dreamers are so concrete in their thinking is a great advantage because it keeps them close to the dream and to fresh perceptions. When a dreamer tries to figure out what an image means and gives you interpretations before she gives you a good description, reassure her that there will be plenty of time for interpretation, but for now she should stay inside the reality of the dream and not worry about what it might mean. When I said this to a neurologist new to dream work, she said, "Oh, thank you. I feel more relaxed already." It is only from standing inside the dream that the dreamer can focus clearly on the dream experience and be relatively free of anxiety about what the dream might mean. The more you can encourage the dreamer to be concrete in the description phase, the better. Resist pointing out to the dreamer that this or that image reminds you of another one of her dreams. This usually takes the dreamer out of the current dream, disorients her, and causes her to shift into a different emotional dream environment. Even if you have noted a relevant connection, this short-cut effort to enhance the dreamer's associations, and perhaps demonstrate your perceptivity, is not worth the disorientation it causes. If you wait until this dream is worked through, you will have better grounds and a more receptive dreamer for your comparisons to other dreams.

If you have to corral the dreamer because her descriptions are becoming dull or tangential, it may be useful to reassure her that you do not expect her to monitor herself about the relevance of her descriptions. That is your job to do as best you can; you might well discover that you have prematurely corralled her, but if so, either of you can always return to the interrupted description.

Interviewers often ask if it is important to invite the dreamer to describe the physical appearance of a dream image. As a general rule (but with a number of exceptions), such descriptions are almost always useful if the physical appearance in the dream is in some way unusual or unlike the expected appearance. The dream modifications usually have metaphorical significance that can be discovered by asking how the unusual feature modifies the image. For example, Angela dreamt of a red-haired John Kennedy. She described Kennedy as an exciting man of power and intelligence, with whom she was flattered to be invited to share a table, but who had a very unhealthy and underdeveloped attitude toward women. When asked what redheaded men are like, she said they are very unusual and very intense. When asked how red hair would modify Kennedy, she said it would make him even more unusual and intense: very, very special. Upon hearing the recapitulation of her description she bridged easily to her admired, intelligent, but chauvinistic father.

When a dreamer presents an image of an unknown person, the physical appearance becomes a major source of description. Kirstin dreamt of walking through the woods with her brother; they were trying to find their way home. Because Kirstin has no brother, we asked her to tell us what a brother is. She told us that a brother is a good companion who understands you and who is not competitive the way a sister would be. When she then described the dream brother's physical appearance, she said that he was "tall and handsome . . . sort of like my husband!" Kirstin recognized that in the dream she was dealing with the supportive, brotherlike aspect of her husband that she needed to rediscover if they were to find their way home to happier times in their marriage.

Remember that the descriptive words you elicit from the dreamer (or from yourself) are the precisely ground lens that will make it possible for the dreamer to see the metaphoric quality of the dream clearly. It is generally through words that the dreamer is able to bridge the dream experience to waking-life situations. We ask the dreamer to translate her dream experience into her own descriptive words and then to see if these words remind her of anything in her waking life. We do not impose another layer of meaning onto the dreamer's words and concepts, if at all possible. Such impositions can be misleading and are almost always unnecessary. Psychological concepts, even when they are accurate and helpful in understanding human patterns of development and behavior, are expressed in stereotyped terminology, which can distract the dreamer from focusing on her private experience and force her to think instead in abstract theoretical terms about herself. As Fromm and French note, the language of dreams "has a precision *which we lose* when we try to translate it into a . . . technical language."[6]

For example, if a man dreams that his youngest sister's daughter is ill, it would be premature to conclude that the imaginary daughter represents an unknown woman or a feminine factor, or the anima of the dreamer. Wouldn't it be better to explore what the dreamer's youngest sister is like, what she reminds him of and then explore what he feels about that sister's dream daughter *before* we ask the dreamer to see if the ill daughter reminds him of a part of himself or of something else? And if the dreamer identifies with the daughter, he will have a much more specific sense of her after these descriptions than he will ever have of his abstract "feminine factor."[7] We encourage our students to avoid the use of psychological terms as much as possible while working with dreams and to focus instead on the valuable and more potent words that come from the dreamer's mouth.

BRIDGES

It is amazingly easy to unwittingly "lead the witness" when you ask for a bridge. If you believe that a particular image or action refers to a specific person in the dreamer's life or to a part of the dreamer, you must be careful to phrase your bridge question in a way that leaves the dreamer room to go in her own

direction. Asking if the description reminds the dreamer of anything, anyone, or any part of herself is preferable to asking if it
reminds her of only any*one* in her life. In practice, however, such
a question is a bit wordy and can be abbreviated especially once
the dreamer is accustomed to the interview process and has
confidence that you are not attached to a particular level of
meaning. You will be able to edit out your leading words and
inflections fairly easily if you keep a lookout for your need to
appear wise, intuitive, and well informed. If you can return to
an attitude of curiosity and base your recapitulations and
bridges on the facts of the dream and the dreamer's descriptions, you will find it relatively easy to phrase helpful and productive questions.

Both the dreamer and the interviewer can cooperate to pre-
determine a bridge by assuming that the present bridge will
work out the same way as did bridges to one or more similar
images in other dreams. This is where working with dreams in a
series can cause trouble. If the dreamer has made an inaccurate
or stereotyped interpretation of a dream character once, he may
fail to reexamine the character when it reappears a second and
third time and so continue to misinterpret it over and over. It is
tempting to assume that the dreamer will tend to use the same
images to express the same things, even if the dream contexts
are not exactly the same. We have found that dreamers will
sometimes moderately and even drastically alter their use of
similar dream images. As we saw in Chapter 5, Adrianne's
dream "Woody Allen" at first seemed to fit her frequent dream
images of her husband, but in this instance, it actually described
her better. So, while working with dreams in series allows you
to corroborate and link together insights, be careful to treat each
dream on its own terms before you look at it as a part of a series.

In my experience, although it is very rare, a dreamer will
occasionally bridge to a waking situation that gives a sort of
"reversal" interpretation to the dream. As we have seen, much
of ancient dream interpretation included reversals, as did Freud

in his work. Such interpretations seemed highly arbitrary to Jung and Boss, as they do to me. However, consider the case of a client who dreamt three times that her husband had an affair with another woman on the very nights following days in which she was tempted to have an affair herself. In each dream, the dreamer sobs with terrible hurt and in the dream itself is surprised to realize how important it is to her to have a monogamous marriage. Now she has lost something she undervalued while she had it. In each interview, the dreamer bridged to the "golden rule" and felt her dream was giving her a taste of what it would feel like if the tables were turned and her husband had an affair. The dreams had the effect of firming her resolve to keep her marriage vows. Then, after reviewing her dreams of the last few years, she noticed that in several her husband refused to make love to her and had sex with another woman. These dreams helped her see that in fact she *did* feel her husband was "unfaithful" to her, in that he seemed more interested in her body (the other woman) than in her entire person. Her sense of being emotionally left out of their sexual encounters was highlighted when she found herself attracted to other men who seemed to promise a more meaningful intimacy. If I had helped the dreamer to focus more intently on the major action and feeling of the dream, that she felt betrayed by a husband who was having easy sex with another woman, we might have broken through her more-comfortable golden rule interpretation sooner. This case has taught me to distrust even the dreamer's reversal interpretations and to keep the door open for surprising interpretive revisions.

When the dreamer makes a bridge that is so general as to be unwieldy, such as "Well that reminds me of my life," you can usually elicit a more specific response by gently asking, "Does it remind you of any particular part of your life?"

If a dream character or object is difficult to bridge early in the dream, waiting until it has appeared in later scenes will give the dreamer a chance to enlarge its description and increase the likelihood of a solid bridge. Generally speaking, if you are patient and encourage the dreamer to move on to the next image each time she gets stuck trying to make a bridge, by the end of the dream, you will have gathered enough information to establish at least a few good bridges.

Be careful to pose your bridging questions from the dreamer's perspective or on the level at which the dreamer would most likely be aware of the issue while waking. For example, suppose your dreamer has just described X, a person she despises for her rigid, critical ways. If you ask the dreamer whether this rigid critical person reminds her of anyone or anything, she may well say that the description fits X and that's it. If, however, you have asked what factors in X's life led her to become this way, you can ask, "You say X became rigid and critical because she felt inferior and dealt with these feelings the way her mother did with her inferiority feelings. Does this remind you of anyone who grew up feeling inferior like her mom and who used a rigid critical attitude to cope?" Because the dreamer may be only dimly aware of her rigidity and criticalness, you will do best to start from a point that is more familiar to her. Dreams are usually ahead of the dreamer and contain surprises that the dreamer will appreciate only in a step-by-step approach. The breakthrough insight is, by definition, new to the dreamer, so bridging is usually a question of taking things one step at a time, until a series of bridges or insights come together to deliver a punch line. In formulating your questions, ask yourself, "How is the dreamer likely to see this problem while awake? From the symptom, rather than the cause?" and work from there.

SUMMARIES

In summarizing the dream, whether or not you have been able to elicit a bridge for all the images, you have the opportunity to review the facts of the dream. See if you have left out any important elements that could cause you to revise the hypotheses formed from the bridges made during the interview. Double-check weak bridges by getting a little more description and give the dreamer enough time to see how all the pieces fit or do not fit together. Point out any facts of dream imagery, action, feeling, or association that don't seem to fit with bridges the dreamer has made and ask for clarification. Notice if your theoretical bias is intruding and forcing the facts to fit together in a certain way. If so, you might want to confess this to your dreamer, so that she will be forearmed to take your suggestive summary with a grain of salt. She might then be able to join you in examining your reasoning to see if it does or does not fit the evidence of the dream and the dream interview.

Every part of the dream counts and forms an important clue to the understanding of the whole dream. By interpreting only one part of a dream, you can miss out on vital information that should be an integral part of the understanding of the whole dream. While Freud and others believed that any apparent coherence of the manifest dream was due to disguising subconscious "secondary revision,"[8] Jung and many others have insisted dreams are revelatory and are associatively coherent on the manifest level. A surgeon named Malcom incubated a dream on what he should do about his long and wretched marriage. He had the following dream, the second part of which was as important as the first:

> **I am swimming, saving a guy** on my back in the ocean. I get to shore where an operating room nurse or assistant awaits. The man has a melanoma tumor the size of a grapefruit on his back.

It did not take Malcom long to bridge to this part of the dream saying that this is how he feels about his married self, that he is drowning and dying with his wife who is like a deadly, vicious tumor on his back. In the second part of the dream:

I see that the tumor goes deep and if the man is to survive, it must be removed. Even some good skin around
the edges must go because the tumor is deep. I explain
to the assistant who wanted just to whack it off that we
need special instruments and more research in order to
perform the delicate operation.

(DELICATE OPERATION)

As Malcom described how the assistant wanted to just
whack it off, he bridged to his desire to get out of his marriage
quickly after so much pain. The depth of the tumor led him to
think that his marriage was more life threatening than he had
realized and more deeply entrenched. The fact that some good
skin would have to go made him think of how he would lose
not only the comforts of marriage, like a sense of home, but that
he would lose a good deal of his wealth and future income in a
huge legal battle. He said that his dream need of special instruments and more research brought to mind this unwelcome association: if he were to survive the stress of what would be a
hellish divorce with any hope of seeing much of his beloved
children, he would have to act carefully and employ sophisticated legal procedures to protect his children's finances from his
wife's fury and irresponsibility. You can see that each part of
this dream served to inform the dreamer; had any part been ignored, the story would have been incomplete. As always, when
working with an incubated dream, or with any dream for that
matter, it is good not to assume that the dream will answer a
question or serve a particular function, like compensation or
confirmation. Waiting to see what the dream has to say for itself
will discourage summaries that force the dream to fit a given
expectation and will encourage summaries that respect the facts
of the dream and the experience of the dreamer.[9]

During the summary, the dream outline will help you keep
in mind the dramatic structure of the dream. For example,
Mariko incubated a dream asking if she should apply to a par-

ticular school to study psychology. She dreamt that she was being shown an apartment in a part of town she had always thought elegant and far more sophisticated and wealthy than the one she grew up in. As the realtor took her through the apartment, she was disappointed that there was only one small window in the dark living room. The two bedrooms were small, but the kitchen was well equipped, with a large and fancy refrigerator that had a lot of storage space. She thought that she would always have something to eat in this apartment. The refrigerator, with all its special compartments and state-of-the-art features reminded Mariko of the professional school she was thinking of attending. At the end of the dream, Mariko is going over the apartment in her mind and worries that it has only two bedrooms, when she actually needs three. (Small Apartment)

The structure of this dream develops from the dreamer's liking the elegant apartment house, to finding the living room dark and constricted in its view, to noting two small bedrooms that remind her of a friend's apartment with inadequate space. Then Mariko is pleased by the refrigerator, which is fancy and will assure her food to eat and which is like her school. But the dream ends with her worrying, although not quite realizing, that the apartment is too small for her. Mariko was very anxious to start her professional training, and the school she had in mind looked elegant and promised financial security. But her concerns that it was too narrowly focused and too rigid surfaced in the single window, the darkness, and the inadequate space. Structurally, the dream described an attractive but ultimately inadequate apartment.

In the summary the dreamer needed to be reminded of each aspect of the dream, because she tended to focus only on the elegant surroundings and the big refrigerator. In the next chapter, we shall discuss the matter of dream structure in more detail.

Occasionally, a dream shows the dreamer relatively content in a situation that appears unacceptable to the dreamer in waking life as she reviews the dream in the summary. Sarah dreamt that she was left with the responsibility to take care of the estate and dog of an absent, wealthy gentleman. In the dream she felt overloaded with work and puzzled. In waking, however, she was irritated that all this had been dumped on her. Then she dreamt that she was a secretary of a group of artists. The head man, a very gentle painter, tells her that he is sorry about all the paperwork and bookkeeping she has to do. Sarah says she doesn't mind at all, as she likes to be around art and the pay is good. Sarah bridged both the absent gentleman and the gentle artist to her husband. The work of a secretary she bridged to her mother/wife role of taking care of everyone's dirty work while they go off and do their work and art. It was in the summary that she was struck with the realization that she does indeed mind doing the family's dirty work and that no amount of money is worth completely losing the opportunity to live one's own life. Sarah saw how she sets herself up for such a position in her family by insisting that she likes her role and by failing to arrange a more comfortable distribution of duties within the family.

Finally, remember that a dreamer works hard during an interview and experiences new feelings and thoughts that can be threatening and can often leave the dreamer fatigued. If the dreamer seems to be resisting looking at parts of the dream, you must decide whether to encourage her to look once again or whether to end the interview for the time being. I often ask the dreamer what she would like to do. Pushing the dreamer can cause her to become defensive and oppositional. Better to leave her a bit puzzled about the dream than to have her think you are pushing her where she does not want to go. If you notice that your dreamer is becoming resistant or is just plain tired, it is sometimes best just to note that fact and then say something like "Shall we stop for now? You have done a lot of work this evening." You can suggest that the dreamer reflect on the dream during the next few days or write out a summary at home, and if the dreamer is not too resistant, the dream will often fall into place.

ADVANCED METHODS FOR EXPERIENCED INTERVIEWERS

> Every interpretation of a dream is a psychological state-
> ment about certain of its contents. This is not without
> danger, as the dreamer, like most people, usually dis-
> plays an astonishing sensitiveness to critical remarks,
> not only if they are wrong, but even more if they are
> right. . . .
>
> An extraordinary amount of tact is required not to
> violate [the dreamer's] self-respect unnecessarily.[1]

This counsel from Jung points to the great advantage of helping
the dreamer to make his own interpretation. The better you get
at interviewing, the more careful you will be to be sure your
invitations to bridge are not interpretations in disguise. As you
gain expertise in dream work, you will appreciate how many
surprises may lie waiting in the simplest of dreams. If you remind yourself and tell the dreamer that on simply hearing a
dream you have no way of knowing what the dream means, the
dreamer will be spared the anxiety of wondering what you
know that he does not, and you will be relieved of the role of
sorcerer.[2] As Jung wrote, "It is therapeutically very important
for the doctor to admit his lack of understanding . . . for nothing
is more unbearable to the patient than to be always understood."[3] Admitting your confusion during the interview can
take the pressure off you and can reinforce for the dreamer a
sense of shared responsibility and adventure in the interpretation of the dream.

As you become more fluent in your ability to ask questions,
be sure to pace them and phrase them in such a way that the

interview does not become an inquisition. Leads like "Describe a motor boat" and "Describe how a meat grinder works" can sound like orders and demands, especially if they are paced too quickly. Keeping a conversational tone and asking "What are motor boats like?" and "Do you know how a meat grinder works?" will put the dreamer in a more relaxed and productive state of mind. Asking the dreamer to explain certain givens in a dream will frustrate or bore him and often lead him to feel pressured. When the dreamer says, "Suddenly, I was on top of an elephant," asking him how he got there will get you nowhere. If you are not sure if a particular dream event is a given, you can ask, "*Do you know* how the starlet got into your bedroom?" The dreamer can then easily say no, if the starlet's appearance was a given in the dream.

Keeping up the momentum of the interview takes practice. While it is necessary to allow pauses for reflection on the part of both the interviewer and the dreamer, as interviewer you should generally aim at staying in a "close tango" position following your partner and not lag behind while deciding what step to execute next. During the interview, the dreamer's feelings fluctuate in intensity as he describes, bridges, and summarizes various dream elements. The dreamer will be most ready to make a good bridge or grasp a sound insight when he is at one of his peaks of emotional intensity. For example, say the dreamer has been excitedly describing the terrible plight of gorillas in the wild who are killed by poachers, and then starts to lose the intensity of feeling as he wanders off to descriptions of their eating habits. The best time to ask for a bridge may have been missed, and it will be necessary to ask him to tell you more about the plight of gorillas, so that he can recapture the intensity of his feelings and more easily bridge to an area in his waking life where he may be only vaguely aware of such feelings. The timing of your questions in relation to the dreamer's peaks and valleys of emotional intensity will never be perfect, but should improve with practice if you pay attention.

As in sports, where unnecessary movements are weeded out as the athlete's skills become more refined, dream interviewers learn over time to use as few words as necessary to accomplish their goals. Extra words take up valuable time, slow the pace of the interview, and can distract both the interviewer and the dreamer. Asking "Well, let's see, I was wondering if you could tell me what George is like" is both less efficient and less engaging than asking "What is George like?" Asking "What I'd like you to do is tell me about how you felt on arriving on this strange planet" is not as effective as asking "What is this planet like?" and then "What does it feel like to be on such a planet?" Keep in mind that questions that begin with phrases like "Now, let's see here," "May I ask you about," and "I get the sense that" create unnecessary and distracting shifts of tone, which could be avoided by asking questions more directly without introductory references to yourself. Remember, the dreamer is the "star" of the interview; the interviewer plays a facilitating, supporting role.

When you are at a loss as to what question to ask next, ask yourself: "What am I most curious to know at this point in the interview?" Then work backward to find the type of question or questions that are likely to elicit the answers you need. For example, if you want to know why the dreamer chose the second of three dresses offered her, you would need to ask first for a description of each dress and see what the dreamer bridges each one to. Then the dreamer should be able to tell you why she chose the second dress and what that means to her. If you want to know why the dreamer's mother-in-law set fire to the dreamer's home, asking the dreamer directly will get you nowhere. But asking why a person might set fire to a house will get you going in the right direction.

High-Level Interview Strategies

Here are a few strategies to keep in mind as you work with another dreamer. The attitudes they encourage will probably overflow into your private work with your own dreams.

- *Commiserating* with the dreamer, or letting the dreamer know that you appreciate his feelings even if you cannot know them exactly, can give the dreamer the comfort and courage to continue.

- *Schmoozing* with the dreamer consists of repeating, sometimes more than once, the dreamer's descriptions and expressions of feeling. This repetition can be done after the recapitulation, while the dreamer is reflecting on a possible bridge, or during a pause in a summary. While schmoozing, you may rephrase the descriptions slightly to keep things interesting. The aim is to help the dreamer to let his descriptions "sink in" as he warms up to what he has said and to his feelings related to the dream. You might repeat the action of the dream as well as the descriptions. As you retell part of the dream story, you can reanimate it for the dreamer. This strategy may sound dull and repetitive, but if done with feeling, it often allows the dreamer to make new bridges and move beyond impasses in the interview.

- *Jazzing up* the dreamer entails encouraging him to amplify the dream feelings by tactfully teasing him into a more lively account of the dream or of a description. This is extremely important if the dreamer seems distanced from his feelings about the dream. If you cannot get the dreamer to recognize his feelings about an image or a scene, you will get nowhere in the interview. You can stand on your head, ask the most artful questions, but if the dreamer cannot or will not engage his feelings, there is no hope. However, don't give up until you have explored every image and made at least one summary, even if there have been no bridges. At the eleventh hour, you may succeed in jazzing up the dreamer through humor or by focusing on a particular image.

One of our dream group members, Sophie, had great difficulty allowing herself to be aware of her feelings both when dreaming and when awake. She automatically intellectualized and formulated analyses of her experiences. Needless to say, her dreams are exceptionally hard to understand. Sophie dreamt of going to her mother's nursing home, where she saw a person wrapped up like a mummy and tied down to a table. She realized in the dream that her mother had been tied down like this once before and that it had somehow benefited her. Her mother looked healthy and uncharacteristically happy. In the interview, we asked her to reread the dream, but this time with feeling (she tended to tell her dreams as if they were financial reports). Having known her for a few months, we teased her to really let go with any emotion she could detect. But not much emotion surfaced. She described a mummy as usually a dead person, but she told us that this one was alive. We asked what it would feel like for a living person to be wrapped like a mummy and tied down, and Sophie responded, "Well, one would be totally controlled and tied down." We kept at it asking, "How does it feel to be totally controlled and tied down like a mummy?" Then Sophie said, "It is horrible, you have to give up control, can't express your feelings." To our surprise, Sophie could at last see a connection between the mummy and her mother's having to submit to the nursing home regime if she was to be happy. Learning to control her temper and follow the rules of the home had been a necessary rite of passage for her. Sophie saw this as a metaphor of her own work situation, where her refusal to cooperate with the university administrative system had cost her her job. Sophie, who had so much difficulty expressing her personal, intimate feelings, adamantly resisted controlling her oppositionalism at work. Feelings were a problem she had yet to learn to deal with. She saw the mummy wrapping as a temporary, disagreeable, but necessary rite of passage for her in her work environment. (Mother-Mummy)

☐ *Offering unfinished sentences* to the dreamer when he is having trouble finding words to describe a dream character, bridging, or linking scenes together will sometimes do the trick. For example, you could say to the dreamer, "In the dream, this stranger sells you a car that is too small and has a hole in the gas tank. That would suggest that this salesman is . . . ?" Or "A car that has a hole in the gas tank is . . ."

☐ *Damage control* is a strategy to use when you have said something you wish you hadn't. When you inadvertently add your own words from your own associations to a dreamer's description, or when you ask questions that are not germane or are inappropriate, retreat quickly by saying, "Oops! I take that back," "Strike that from the record," or "I wish I hadn't said that." Then recap from the last description or bridge made on the solid ground of the dreamer's words.

☐ *Stepping down* a question means breaking it up into its component parts and/or rephrasing it so that it is less daring, ambitious, or threatening. If you ask a question that elicits a confused or disoriented response from the dreamer, check to see if you have asked too complex a question without first having laid the groundwork by approaching one aspect of the question at a time.

For example, if you ask a dreamer how New York City is different from Ames, Iowa, he may give you a blank stare. But if you step down the question by breaking it up into its component parts and ask first what New York is like and then what Ames is like, the dreamer will be able to tell you the important differences between these two settings.

Suppose a dreamer has just described the Fred in her dream as a manipulative, untrustworthy sort of guy and then bridged him to her fiancé, whom she sees as a *little* bit like Fred. Let's say that the next element in the dream is an action: Fred takes all the dessert goodies at a dinner party. Instead of asking "How does your fiancé take all the dessert goodies at dinner parties," try "Why would Fred take all the dessert goodies?" "Is there anything wrong with his taking all the dessert? What?" and "What is it that made Fred into the sort of guy who would take all the dessert?" When you find a response that would not be too threatening, you can see if the dreamer is willing to verify the original bridge between Fred and her fiancé.

It is important to remember that many questions you ask carry with them potential risks and benefits, and you can't always guess how the dreamer will react. Some questions are worth the risk of disorienting or leading the dreamer, and others are not. If you find that one of your questions has had an undesirable effect, it is a relief to know that you can usually make amends without much trouble if you are alert to the dreamer's signals.

◻ *Challenging* the dreamer to take a more active role in exploring his dream is necessary if the dreamer is especially passive and seems to be waiting for you to ask just the right question so that *you* can figure out what his dream means. Saying things like "I can ask questions, but only you can make the connections" or "Only you know how the feelings in the dream relate to your life. All I can do is encourage you to discover those feelings and connections" will sometimes get the dreamer to sit up rather than sit back and wait for you to do his work. It also helps if you monitor yourself and note how you may be cooperating with the dreamer's expectation that interpretation is your job and that you are totally competent and in control. Telling the dreamer, for example, that you are only the midwife, while he is like an expectant mother who has to make the greatest effort, usually gets the point across.

☐ *Underlining* consists of emphasizing important parts of a dream that you have reason to suspect the dreamer will minimize or deny as he reflects on the dream in the coming weeks; it can be an immense help to the dreamer.

Carlin worked on a dream that led her to describe a figure who reminded her of her boyfriend, Derrek, as a very charismatic egoist who needs to take over the attention of any group he enters. This often results in her feeling totally eclipsed, outshined, overwhelmed, and invaded by Derrek, who takes up her space. Carlin said she felt guilty about this response; clearly, she thought she should not feel this way. The interviewer underlined by pointing out how the dream character's inappropriate invasion of the dreamer's space reminded her of how Derrek does something similar. The interviewer then asked if anyone else has ever commented on this characteristic of Derrek's. Carlin thought a moment, then said, "Well, now looking at it a bit more objectively, his roommate says he always feels outshined by him, and his sister said so, too. In fact, she told me it has taken most of her life to get over it." This sort of emphasis of the more slippery insights in a dream helps the dreamer to keep them in her awareness.

VERY ACTIVE INTERVIEW TECHNIQUES

Only after our students have mastered the basic, intermediate, and advanced strategies do we suggest they use the following techniques, which are designed to be used when all less-intrusive methods have failed or when time is short and the interviewer is skilled.

▣ *Suggesting descriptive words* to a dreamer struggling with a description is fraught with the problems of putting words into the dreamer's mouth that either don't fit or that might discourage the dreamer from finding his own more precise words. But if the strategies we have already discussed—such as guessing the absurd or the opposite—fail, you might try guessing the obvious or the likely, and if the dreamer accepts your word, ask the dreamer if he has a better word to describe his image. If the dreamer says no to your guess, don't guess again, but take advantage of his awareness that your word was wrong and ask, "If it is not like this, then what *is* it like?"

▣ *Suggesting interpretive hypotheses* is another last-resort strategy. If you are working with dreams in therapy and have little time to work on the dream or if you are working with a dreamer who knows this method and trusts that you do not believe your hypotheses should be taken on faith, then you may find that occasionally suggesting a posible working hypothesis regarding a bridge or regarding the linking of some or all the bridges of the dream may save time. The problem, of course, is that the dreamer will have lost the opportunity to make the discovery for himself. But in some cases, the dreamer may not be able to grasp the metaphor of his descriptions before too long a period of weeks or months. The way you phrase your hypotheses can make a difference. I have heard students say, "It seems that your dream is showing you . . ." It would be less intrusive to say something like "You have said that you are using discipline now in your waking life to teach yourself how to write. You said that the guide in your dream is Mongolian and that Mongolians are very disciplined people. Your Mongolian guide tells you that your hands can fly. Do you think this dream might have something to do with your writing and your need for discipline?"

Even if your hypothesis is based on a careful examination of the structure of the dream and the dreamer's descriptions and bridges, it still may be quite incorrect. Ask the dreamer to assist you by letting you know what he thinks about your hypothesis and how he thinks it should be modified. You could, of course, offer him several hypotheses on which to reflect in the next few days.

▣   *Distraction,* which one avoids in most dream work, can be a very handy tool when used purposely. When a dreamer shifts into a grinding, effortful mode of trying to figure out the dream, you will get few lively, emotional, unguarded descriptions. To relieve the tension and shift the dreamer into a more relaxed, spontaneous mode, you could move on to another image and return to the difficult one later. Or if the whole scene or dream is difficult, you could tell a joke, get some refreshments, or tell a story about another tangen- tially related dream you once heard. This lets the dreamer get off the hot seat and often allows him to come back to the dream with a fresh, more comfortable attitude. Obviously, this technique can be quickly overused, but when it is em- ployed skillfully, it works wonders. In couple and group work one can distract by addressing the listeners and thus give the dreamer a moment of rest.

▣   *Noting and commenting on the dreamer's style in the interview* may become necessary if the dreamer is particularly resistant, oppositional, overly accepting, nit-picking, critical, or pla- cating. Frequently, the dreamer will be unaware of such styles and may be working on a dream that explores them. If the dreamer is unable to discuss problematic behavior in one of these areas, his dream work will be slow and ardu- ous. Such people often need individual or group therapy to keep these stylistic obstacles from sabotaging their dream work and their relationships.

RESISTANCE

Resistance is a way we have of warding off feelings, thoughts, or fantasies that, if let into awareness, we fear would cause discomfort and pain. We all resist knowing how we really feel and think about some things. Dreams are one of the best tools we have for getting through the barriers we set up that keep us from seeing our lives more objectively. Many of the strategies we have discussed are designed to help the dreamer overcome resistance and become more open to new insights that, once allowed into awareness, lose much of their threatening character. However helpful insight is, it can be very challenging and painful. Walter Bonime, a sensitive New York analyst, has said the resistance against change is understandable when you consider that when someone suggests that you change, "it's like pointing a gun at you and saying, 'stop being you.'"[4]

Our resistance to insight rises when we are anxious and lowers when we feel safe from criticism and public exposure. This is why interviewers must pay close attention to their styles and to creating a sense of safety for their dreamers. It is important to remember the cautions we have already mentioned regarding the recapitulation of negative descriptions. If you leave out the most offensive adjectives describing an image, the dreamer will be freer to bridge it to himself or to a loved one. In summarizing, the same precautions should usually be followed. For example a man's dream may help him realize for the first time that his idealized father was actually an emotionally limited, controlling, rigid, inadequate parent. The dream character is usually represented as a very unsavory character easily associated with the father. The dreamer will use very harsh words to describe the dream character and to describe his own father, even though he has grown up idealizing him. If you use his harshest words in your summary, the dreamer may hear his own words with guilt and need to defend his father from *your* criticisms. If you recapitulate and summarize gently, the dreamer will usually fill in the rest at his own pace.

If a dreamer avoids even mentioning the possibility of an obvious bridge, that may signal a high level of resistance. One dreamer who described at length a dream snake as fleshy, rigid, with a triangular head that was crawling up her leg had not one single sexual association to the snake. The group was very patient and kept asking for more descriptions. The dreamer's husband had originally been holding the snake up for her to admire, it was very big, and the dreamer was afraid of it. The fact that the dreamer did not even note the possible sexual connotations signaled her discomfort with the issue. She suggested that the dream had to do with her spiritual training and concerns. When she finally said, "I'll bet you think this has to do with sex," the group broke out laughing. But we hurt the dreamer's feelings by doing this. In the end, the sexual issue with her husband was only part of the story; an affair of the heart, which he had experienced a while back, had wounded the dreamer's willingness to trust her husband on the most initimate levels.

Often dreams take up the issue of the dreamer's resistance more or less directly. Dreams in which the dreamer runs or flies away from pursuers or conflict can sometimes indicate that the dreamer is resisting insight. The same could be said for dreams in which the dreamer tries to lock all the windows and doors to keep intruders out. Dreams in which the dreamer confronts conflict, or seeks out the source or cause of problems suggest a willingness do the same in waking life.

Julie was in therapy while she was studying dreams with me and had the following dream:

> **I look in the mirror** and see myself in a boring brown outfit with Ivy League loafers that are not at all elegant.

I don't have the right clothes to wear to my therapy session. I don't want to go, anyway.

Next I'm driving to therapy and I'm very late. I feel I should call or be on time. But I don't want to go, anyway. I don't want to show my ugly self, though I've been thinking that I didn't want to go because it is too expensive and takes too much time. Now I realize that this was just an excuse as were my thoughts that my therapist is not very good.

Next, I'm running from my therapist and run behind the cloakroom and hide in a tiny, dark toilet closet. I pull the toilet paper to make the therapist think I am going to the bathroom so she won't intrude. She calls my name three times. I hope the coat-check lady will keep her out. (CLOAKROOM TOILET)

Julie described a coat-check lady as a desperate victim-type who must really need this boring job. Julie bridged saying, "I do that with my therapist. I talk and talk about my boring daily trials and use them as a smoke screen while I just pretend to be dealing with serious private emotional business, as in the toilet scene." This dream touches vividly on almost all the most popular excuses people use to resist psychotherapeutic exploration. It is unusual for a dreamer to reflect in a dream and recognize her own self-deceptions so clearly and honestly. Julie seemed on the way to making a change in her willingness to use therapy for growth.

For over a decade, Julie had been married to a man she never loved, but whom she married on the rebound from a man for whom she continued to pine. She brought dream after dream to the study group about her inertia and her "mistaken" marriage. She refused to go into couples therapy and was not sure if she would enter individual therapy or even stay in her dream group. One day she brought in this dream:

I am in a haunted house at night. I'm in the girls' locker room and a man—a teacher, adviser, friend—comes in. He is warning everyone that the murderer is coming!

I look down the hall and see the murderer silhouetted as he slowly walks toward the bathroom. He's a Hulk-Frankenstein, but more intelligent and muscular. I look toward the bathroom stalls and see a girl hiding in one of them. I know the murderer will be able to see her and may be stimulated by her shadow to rape her.

The murderer comes in. He knows exactly where she is. He turns and stands facing her stall. The girl is now me. I know he knows I'm here, so no sense pretending. I decide to act normal and come out and pretend I don't know he's a murderer. I act as if he's just the anesthesiologist he's pretending to be. I come out trying to be happy and light, talking a lot.

He is supposed to draw blood gases from me. He's sticking me repeatedly because he doesn't know how to do this, while I keep talking—jabbering—keeping the subject light—trying to go along with it. All the while I am trying to figure out a way to get out of this situation.

I wake up several times, return to the same scene and finally wake and get out of bed.

(MURDERER)

Julie dealt with the murderer in the dream exactly as she dealt with conflict and uncomfortable situations in her waking life— with lots of talk, trying to keep things light, and pretending she doesn't know there is any problem. She pretends to herself as well as to those around her. In her dream, she is unable to figure a way out other than stalling. After the murderer draws her blood, she expects he will do his foul deed. Julie said that she pretends that her husband is only a dulling, anesthetizing partner, but she fears he is murdering her life spirit. She also said that she is murdering herself by staying with him. But as in the dream, she feels stuck.

At one of our workshops for advanced students, we asked the students to list the ways they have found most helpful to reduce resistance in their dreamers. Here are their recommendations:

- ☐ Create a safe, nonjudgmental, confidential environment.
- ☐ Have compassion and respect for the vulnerability of the dreamer.
- ☐ Keep your curiosity and humor available.
- ☐ Make the anxiety explicit and ask, for example, "What would be the worst or most embarrassing thing this dream could mean?"
- ☐ Bracket the dreamer's fearful interpretations, keep them in mind as possible leads, and treat them as part of the associative material, as Jung suggested.[5]
- ☐ Ask the dreamer if he wants to continue to explore the dream and let him off the hook if he does not.
- ☐ Tell the dreamer that he is not alone with the problem in his dream, that you or others you know have had to deal with it as well.
- ☐ Tell the dreamer that you have worked with a lot of your own dreams that were painful to explore, but that the insights you gained were well worth it.
- ☐ Predict the occurrence of embarrassing dream motifs to a new group member or new dream student, so that when he has one he will be more comfortable bringing it up.
- ☐ Let the resistant dreamer's frustration with his difficulty in making bridges motivate him to break through his resistance. Don't try to save him.
- ☐ Ask the dreamer, "How do you feel as we talk about this dream?"

THE DREAM'S DRAMATIC
STRUCTURE

It is easy to teach interviewers to underline and point out to the dreamer the problem stated in a dream with comments like "So you want to get through the door into the train, but you can't because you have too much luggage in your arms." Interviewers also learn quickly how to spot and underline any "surprise points" in a dream by saying something like "In the dream you are surprised to find a dead body in your house" or "You are surprised to discover that the real identity of the queen in the dream is your mother." By incorporating the statement of the dream problem and any surprise points into partial summaries, the interviewer reminds the dreamer of the essential components or dream's dramatic structure, which can be meaningfully bridged to the dreamer's waking life.

However, it is much more difficult to teach interviewers to appreciate the whole structural context of the dream. For most interviewers and dreamers, the importance of always bearing in mind the dramatic structure of a dream is not evident. As we have seen, dream dictionary books from almost every culture generally treat images in isolation, with little or no consideration for the context of the dream plot or the feelings associated with it. Freud even believed that any apparent cohesion in the dream story was due to the disguising function of the unconscious censor and secondary revision. He made it an "essential rule invariably to leave out of account the ostensible continuity of the dream as being of suspect origin" and to treat dream images and actions by association and symbolic substitution with little regard to their sequence or structural context.[6] Ignoring the structural integrity of the manifest dream removes a number of checks and balances against wild hypothesizing and interpretation. Allowing yourself to plunder a dream only for the "important" or "relevant" parts makes it much easier to use the text of the dream not to discover but to prove a point. And the dreamer always loses when we do that.

Jung, on the other hand, insisted that not only the images but also their order and role in the development of the dream revealed meaningful relationships to the dreamer.[7] After a dreamer sees how a particular dream character is much like his present and past law partner, as well as his brother, we must know what this character is like in the dream, what he is doing, and the effect his presence or actions have on the development or outcome of the dream before we can understand the meaning of his appearance.

In the 1960s, Fromm and French worked to counter psychoanalysts' tendencies to disregard the importance of the dream's structure by encouraging analysts to make the reasoning behind their intuitive inferences explicit and to take into account the manifest structure of the whole dream. They wrote that the most frequent reason why analysts do not always agree on the interpretation of a dream is that they often base their conclusions "only on one small part of the evidence," and each analyst may choose a different part of it.

Fromm and French concentrated on parts of the dream, one at a time, choosing the most accessible imagery first, then, step-by-step, tried to integrate it into the whole.[8] They were still using heavy doses of Freudian interpretive presuppositions and valuing their intuition over the dreamer's ability to furnish important bridges, but they were an important force that encouraged psychoanalysts to consider the dream and the associative material as a whole. They went so far as to train themselves "to be sensitive to gaps and discrepancies in the evidence so that, when we find a discrepancy, we try to discover the reason for it."[9] They insisted that these gaps and discrepancies are "the best clues for discovering relationships that . . . [we] had not suspected."[10] In the interview process, the interviewer is constantly on the lookout for gaps and discrepancies in the dreamer's descriptions and bridges, and he uses questions to explore them and their relation to the dream's structure, to the associative material, and to the dreamer's life situation.

KRAMER'S DREAM
TRANSLATION METHOD

Dr. Milton Kramer, Medical Director of the Sleep Disorders Center of Bethesda Oak Hospital in Cincinnati, has developed a method for extracting a great deal of information about the dreamer from the written account of a dream.[11] Knowing only the dreamer's age and sex, and using only a copy of the dream text without any of the dreamer's associations or personal history, Kramer examines the structure of the dream and adds what he thinks would be the most likely associations to draw a metaphorical translation of the dream. Indeed, he calls his method "dream translation" and suggests that meticulous attention to the text of the manifest dream can suggest possible leads to the current conflicts or concerns of the patient. Kramer certainly recognizes that the dreamer's associations and a knowledge of his history and current situation are needed to verify or correct hypotheses made on the basis of the dream text alone. He also recognizes that the dreamer's associations and life context allow the interpreter to make specific what must often be left as general interpretive statements without the personal and associative material. But Kramer masterfully demonstrates that much can be learned from the dream text and that, used carefully, the structure of the dream can keep the dreamer and the interpreter close to the facts of the dream and discourage interpretations that disregard or contradict it. Kramer points out that dream translation could be useful in the early stages and in times of impasse in psychotherapy, as well as in supervision of therapists-in-training, when it is not easy to get access to the patient's associations.

Because Kramer's method depends in large part on a careful

analysis of the structural context of the images and feelings in the dream, practicing this method sharpens the interviewer's (and the dreamer's) appreciation of the directional importance of dramatic structure. After an interviewer has elicited a good description and bridge of a dream character, for instance, he must find out how the character acts and what he does in the dream, as well as what effect his presence and actions have on the development or result of the plot, before the meaning of the character can be known.

Jan dreamt of Charles de Gaulle. She described him as a tall, proud, sometimes arrogant and reactionary man who stood up bravely to huge powers and discovered that he reminds her of her boyfriend and her father. It makes all the difference to the interpretation of the dream to know whether she dreamt that de Gaulle was acting brave and proud, or stubborn and arrogant, and whether he was rescuing the dreamer from the Nazis or from a domineering gorilla she bridged to her current boyfriend. What if de Gaulle were barring her entrance to the University of Paris because he thought her French had been too corrupted by borrowed American words? And what about the rest of the dream plot? Without making consistent references to the structural framework of the dream, it is easy to wander off into the "wild blue yonder," as Kramer puts it. Practicing Kramer's dream translation will sharpen skills that come in handy when you are interviewing a dreamer and have the luxury of eliciting abundant and focused descriptions, associations, and bridges.

In examining the dream account, Kramer assumes that the issues treated in dreams bear a continuous rather than a compensatory relationship to the subjective waking life of the dreamer—to his waking concerns and personality styles. He bases this assumption on laboratory studies that demonstrate this continuity hypothesis. Thus if a man dreams that he is being crushed by a steamroller, we would guess that in his waking life he feels like this sort of thing is happening to him or that somehow he is steamrolling himself. We would certainly not jump to the conclusion that he is experiencing new heights of power and confidence. Even if the understanding of how he is allowing himself to be run over at work ultimately compensates his idealistic attitude that the meek will inherit the presidency of Ford Motor Company, such compensation relates to the effect of the interpretation, not to the metaphoric significance of the dream imagery.

Kramer also works with three interrelated hypotheses, which will be familiar to dream interviewers:

1. "The manifest dream report is strictly determined"; in other words, no image or feeling appears accidentally or by mistake, and they each carry meaning for the dreamer.
2. "The order of the elements in the manifest dream report is strictly determined" and, therefore, meaningful.
3. "The order or sequence of elements in the manifest dream report are causally related"; thus each scene builds on the last, and one scene seems to result in the action of the scene that follows it.[12]

Kramer outlines three different orientations a translator might take toward the dream as he guesses at its likely metaphorical meaning. One could see the images as expressing the dreamer's attitudes toward other people in his waking life, memory, and fantasy, thus interpreting on an objective, or interpersonal, level. One could interpret on the subjective, or intrapsychic, level. On a narcissistic level, one could interpret how the images reflect the dreamer's attitudes and concerns in relation to his self-esteem. Kramer adopts the interpersonal approach. For the purposes of teaching the interviewer about structure, I would suggest that we consider all three possibilities because we regularly see that dreamers bridge on all these levels.

Kramer leaves to the translator the choice of viewing the dream as simply reflecting the dreamer's concerns; reacting to the dreamer's concerns, functioning in problem-solving roles; or anticipating the dreamer's future goals. Again, dream interviewers would consider all three possibilities and would look to the text for clues, which may, of course, be inadequate to clarify the issue and which may require the dreamer's help to resolve.

Translators approach the dream as a metaphor, or an imagistic poem, and use their own associations to try to discover the metaphoric meaning. Kramer warns against using rigid symbolic substitution and encourages the translator to stick to the inherent meaningfulness of the dream image. An interviewer may find this difficult at first, having worked so hard to seek the dreamer's descriptions and bridges, not his own. But this exercise will help the interviewer think about the different associations the dreamer could have, which would change the course of the meaning of the dream. I am certainly not suggesting that you translate dreams for other dreamers, but certain translator skills will help you improve your interviewing skills.

As in interviewing, one starts at the beginning and follows the sequences of the dream. In his translations, Kramer often uses a psychoanalytic paradigm based on the Oedipal triangle, which considers any three-person situation as potentially reflecting the oedipal concerns of the dreamer. This paradigm is fundamentally sexual in orientation: same-sex pairs are believed to represent homosexual concerns; opposite-sex pairs, heterosexual concerns. Dream characters of the dreamer's approximate age and status would be seen as representations of siblings and would invite conjectures regarding, for example, sibling rivalry. This and other psychoanalytic presumptions are not necessary for the interviewer, who tries to see what he can without such theoretical formulations, although this openness will often mean that the translation raises as many questions as it answers. We employ this method, however, not to interpret the dream so much as to sketch out a skeletal framework for the dream and leave the dreamer to flesh out the dream and indicate its specific features and dynamic formulations.

Let's look at a dream text of a thirty-five-year-old woman and see what we can learn from it and what we will need to ask the dreamer:

> **Three women are getting released** from prison "with time served." They don't have to finish their sentences because of some trickery or cleverness on their parts. They are getting away with something. They are wearing bathing suits when they are released, and I wonder why.
>
> The woman with whom I am switching places is wearing a sarong the next time I look at her. I wonder what it will be like to look like such a different person, but when we switch it doesn't seem so odd.
>
> The prison is in the basement of a church, and there is a snack bar down there too, with menu items given names that don't tell you what you are getting. My husband was supposed to start work there on the day of my release/vacation, but now that's postponed.
>
> Carla [from *Cheers*] is one of the women released, and just before they make love, she tells her husband about all the men she laid in prison. I think she's cruel.
>
> In the parking lot of the church we are going to take the skis out of the ski rack on the car, but we have to be careful not to make it look easy or criminals will steal them later. (**SWITCHING PLACES**)

The dream opens with the release from prison of three women. Inserting my guess about the dreamer's likely association to prisons, I would guess that the women are moving out of a place of confinement into greater freedom. This could represent the dreamer's release from an imprisoning relationship with family or spouse or even work, but the impersonal description of the prison suggests to me that this more likely represents the dreamer's release from imprisoning, rigid attitudes into a freer way of being in the world.

There are two women in the dream besides the dreamer: the one in the sarong and Carla. The dreamer turns into the third woman. The women gain an apparently legal release through cleverness or trickery. They get out "with time served," which means that somehow they have managed to get out before serving their entire sentences. We will have to ask the dreamer how she feels about this, but for now I will guess that she is not highly disapproving, because there is no suggestion that the women are dangerous criminals and there is as yet no competitive or negative description of them. Is the dreamer angry or jealous that the three are getting away with something? Or is the dreamer pleased? Bathing suits seem inappropriate garb for leaving prison. The dreamer does not describe the suits as either pretty or sexy or vulgar; she just wonders why the women are thus attired. We will have to ask the dreamer to describe bathing suits to know if she likes them, wears them, and what she thinks of the particular dream suits on the dream women. The dreamer probably thinks the women are inappropriately exposed.

Because scenes are often causally related, it could be that the women managed to get out by wearing bathing suits, or by exposing themselves. If so, has the dreamer used self-exposure to get out of her prison? Has this exposure been an expression of her cleverness or has it been a ruse, an unauthentic form of trickery? We will have to ask the dreamer to clarify whether the women used cleverness and/or trickery to get out.

The dreamer switches places with the woman in the sarong. We know that this woman looks different from the dreamer and that switching places seems to mean switching bodies. After the switch, the dreamer writes that it doesn't seem so odd. What is this woman like? Her differentness and her sarong are all we have to go on. How does the dreamer feel about sarongs? What sort of people wear them? If I had to make my best guess (and that is what Kramer says to do), I would bet the dreamer thinks sarongs are worn by feminine, graceful women. She might think such women oppressed, but since the woman has been released from prison through her cleverness or trickery, I would bet on the more positive association. It seems as if the dreamer is trying on a new, more flowing, graceful, perhaps exotic way of being and finding it not as odd as she might have thought while she was still a prisoner of a more confining, rigid way of life. Because the dreamer exchanges body and probably, to some extent, identity with the woman in the sarong, a subjective interpretation seems most likely.

The fact that the prison is in the basement of a church may be a visual and architectural metaphor for the dreamer's belief or recognition, in the dream at least, that what seems like a place of spiritual community sits on top of—or is, at its base—a prison. The dreamer must tell us what *sort* of prison. Is it an emotional or a spiritual prison? Or both? How so? We can conjecture that the dreamer sees organized religion as a spiritual and emotional prison. The church could represent the dreamer's actual religious history, family history, or her general attitude toward the way people should relate to each other as well as to God and to meaning.

She seems to be bothered that the prison snack bar menu doesn't tell you what you are getting. Were the item names trendy? For example, was a hamburger listed as a Father Thomas special? Did the dreamer enter or grow up in a church or a lifestyle that was like a prison and that did not clearly indicate what it had to offer? Does the dreamer like snack bars? I suspect that the dreamer might say snack bars don't offer complete meals and that her nourishment in her life's prisonlike environment was both insubstantial and trendy. The dreamer's husband had planned to work in the snack bar. Why? Perhaps to be close to the dreamer. Has the husband been drawn toward the prison system of thought or belief or behavior by the dreamer?

Suddenly we learn that the dreamer's release as the sarong-clad woman may be only a vacation and, therefore, temporary. The husband's involvement with the prison snack bar is only postponed, not canceled. Is the dreamer's movement to this freer, more graceful mode of being only temporary? It is clear that the husband's life changes dramatically according to the dreamer's relative freedom and imprisonment.

In the next scene Carla, a character in a television show called *Cheers,* is cruel to her husband. I have no idea what sort of person Carla portrays in the show, which I have never seen. Even if I knew her character, my impression of her might have little to do with the dreamer's. Because Carla is tormenting her husband, just before making love, with her many prison escapades, we might well suspect that Carla feels some good amount of hostility toward her husband and needs for some unknown reason to put him down or to make him jealous. A description of Carla's character would probably tell us why the dreamer thinks Carla would act in this way. I think it likely that Carla and her husband are a picture of the dreamer and her husband because of the emphasis of the couple relationship that begins in the previous scene.

So far, according to my general hypothesis, based on my best guesses about the dreamer's possible associations, the dreamer, her sarong-self, her husband, and her Carla-self have been released from a religious, or rule-oriented, world that is, at its base, a prison that dispenses only trendy or fast food. The dreamer tries on her more graceful, pretty self and, at the same time, lets out her Carla-like hostility to her husband.

In the last scene, the dreamer talks of "we," who may be herself and the women, but because the last two scenes were of husbands, I would guess that "we" refers to herself and her husband. They are in the church parking lot, so they have not left the prison-church's field of influence. They are going to liberate their skis and presumably use them somewhere where there is snow, away from the parking lot. Because the theme of release is repeated, and there is no sign to the contrary, I would guess that the dreamer likes to ski or likes the idea of skiing, which she may think of as a free, powerful kind of earth-flight. Skiing would, in all probability, take her out of the church's parking lot and sphere of influence, but apparently the car that bears the skis (whose car is it?) is to be left in the lot. So the dreamer and her husband, if indeed these two are the "we," may get away for a while, but it seems that they will be back after what may be only a vacation, rather than a release.

The dreamer and her companion(s) feel they must make it look like it is difficult to take the skis out of the rack even though it is easy, so criminals won't steal the skis later when they are kept there in the future. Who are the criminals? What does the dreamer think of this possible theft and the ruse of making something like liberating skis look hard when it is easy? Is the dreamer pretending to her rigid, confining, religious self that breaking out of her controlled world to be free and go skiing is hard when, deep down, she knows it is easy? Does she hide from herself the knowledge that it is easy because she fears the church people would steal even her temporary means of release? Are the church people the criminals of the parking lot? Maybe, maybe not, but if I had to guess, I would say they were.

After thus examining the dream, I have its structure clearly in mind and have identified particular dreamer responses that are vital to the understanding of the dream. If the dreamer's interpretation contradicts the basic structure of the dream action, I will notice it quickly. Dreamers regularly try to interpret their dreams by ignoring uncomfortable facts in the imagery. If the dreamer were to overlook the fact that the release from prison and the release of the skis both seem to be only temporary, the interviewer who had a good grasp of the dream's structure would be less likely to make the same mistake.

After I formulated in my mind this analysis of "Switching Places," we interviewed the dreamer, Amber, and she spent a few days reviewing the tape of the session. She transcribed parts of the taped interview so she could study them more closely. Here is a summary of how the interview and Amber's review compared with my structural analysis and associative conjectures, about which she knew nothing.

Amber did feel that she was moving out of a prisonlike attitude toward herself and the world. She described a prison as a place of rigid rules and no freedom where one must conform and do what one is told. This reminded her of her job and then of a general attitude toward life in which she often felt a prisoner of her family and of her former religious group. Amber grew up driven to work very hard and to follow a constricting set of rules. This was reinforced by her living three years in an ashram.

Describing bathing suits as "the most revealing thing you can wear in public and still be in the realm of the acceptable," Amber said that it was by revealing herself in her dream study group and in her Alcoholics Anonymous group that she has begun to break free of the rigid constraints she has kept on herself. In fact, she told us that she's so modest that she hates to wear bathing suits and avoided doing so even when she was twenty and had a great figure. She said that the bathing suits in the dream were "normal" and that the women were perhaps wearing them because they did not want to wear the dull, gray, ugly prison garb anymore. Amber was not sure whether the women had used trickery or cleverness or both to get out early, but she was happy for them and enjoyed the idea that they were getting away with something.

According to Amber, sarongs are "pretty, soft, like a modest bathing suit for the South Seas, relaxed and very feminine." She described the woman wearing it as not yet in full adulthood, slightly hippie, free, and not tied down. Amber liked her, and felt fine in her body. She bridged to the young, but developing part of herself that is more relaxed in her body and freer in her feelings and attitudes. Her wondering how it would be to switch reminded Amber of her anxiety about changing her personality.

Amber bridged the prison in the church basement to her deep involvement with the New Age movement that included her ashram years. She entered the movement and the ashram thinking that she would learn to be freer and happier, but found instead a prison where freedom is cut off in a repressive, highly conformist atmosphere. Amber bridged the snack bar to the nonnutritious, fast-food, trendy attitudes she adopted in the counterculture, which did not produce real freedom and growth.

Amber's husband, Chet, had grown up in a highly repressive religious family. He had been attracted to Amber in part because she was in the counterculture and seemed free of many of the rigidities from which he wanted to free himself. Chet had wanted to join Amber in the counterculture. Amber said that he had found some real freedom recently since she had become freer and since Chet had become more involved with AA. Amber did not want to think that her release was only temporary and resisted looking closely at this point for the moment.

Amber described Carla as a very barbed, armored woman who puts people down and said that it would be awful to think that she was in any way like that. She could not bridge to anyone in her life and, after her review, concluded that her recent irritability with Chet, which often took the form of putting him down every time he put her down, could constitute a modest bridge. Upon further reflection, she came to think that perhaps her putting down of Chet was less justified than she thought and that her open hostility was part of her greater emotional freedom and honesty. She did not think that she had been cruel to Chet, and she did not put him down by comparing him to other men. We hoped that a later dream, or later waking insights, would clarify this matter.

Amber described skiing as a form of freedom, almost flying,

and thought it was silly to try to make it look hard to get the skis out of the rack. She thought the criminals who might steal her skis were the church-prisoners or that part of herself that still wanted to enforce rigid, imprisoning attitudes in the name of virtue. She said she played games with herself all the time, making what was easy look hard and trying, like the women in the bathing suits, to get away with something her internal authorities would disapprove of without making a clean break with their system. Upon reflection, Amber was struck with the realization that there was no snow near the church and thought that the dream was a picture of a first but incomplete step toward release. Amber could not identify the "we" in the last scene, and she thought "we" referred to herself and perhaps anyone she was in a relationship with. She said that she would not be free until she took her car, her motive force, out of the church parking lot and drove it into the mountains where she would find snow and be able to ski.

A number of my associative guesses were close to Amber's associations, but her work to find her own associations and the words she used were important to her discovery process and her willingness to take responsibility for the dream. Had the dream images been more idiosyncratic or had her associations been unusual, my guesses would have been far less helpful to me in the structural analysis, because she would have been using the images in ways I would have not foreseen. A comment derived from the structural analysis—"It looks like you are planning to bring the skis back to the parked car"—caused Amber to stop denying the temporary nature of her release and look at the implications of this dream fact. It would have been easy to be satisfied with her enthusiastic bridges to her sense of definitive emancipation from her old church-prison attitudes had we forgotten certain structural facts.

The structural analysis exercise of dream translation helped me focus my attention and could have shortened the time necessary to work on the dream. I could perhaps have asked just a few pivotal questions whose answers might have integrated well with my structural conjectures and led to an understanding of the dream, as long as I distinguished between my associative guesses and the actual dramatic structure of the dream. At any point, the interviewer must be ready to abandon or modify hypotheses based on his own associations when those of the dreamers are different. These discrepancies will be more pronounced, the more idiosyncratic the images and the dreamer's definitions and associations. But the structure of the dream must still be respected.

Because my work with clients is devoted exclusively to dream analysis, we usually have plenty of time for the dreamer to cover every step of the interview and thus maximize his discovery and learning processes. However, working with dreams in the context of a psychotherapy hour often requires that the therapist work quickly with the dream to leave time for other work in the session. While I do not in any way advocate telling the dreamer what the dream means based on structural and associative conjecture, asking a few well-aimed questions can greatly speed the interview process. Also, when time is short, the interviewer who has a solid grasp of the dream's dramatic structure can suggest that the dreamer ask himself a few specific questions when he later works on the dream alone.

I recommend that you practice dream translation in written form until you can grasp the essential structural features of a dream as you first hear and read it. This takes quite a bit of practice, but being able to keep the dream's framework in mind will help you organize and focus the interview as well as respect the facts of the dream.

□

**CHAPTER
TWELVE**

NIGHTMARES, RECURRING DREAMS, AND COMMON DREAM THEMES

Frightening dreams have been recorded by every culture since humankind learned to write. The villains in the dreams of ancient and medieval people were often demons, evil spirits, malicious or vengeful gods, church authorities, witches, vampires, and, no doubt, tax collectors, inquisitors, and other feared people and animals. Today our dream villains are Nazis; execution squads; thugs; white men, if you feel like the Mehinaku Indians of Brazil; black teenagers, if you fear them; communists or capitalists, depending on your politics; and bad guys and monsters from literature, television, and movies such as Frankenstein and Darth Vader. We even dream of evil machines that are beyond human control and of aliens from other planets who are out to do us in. And, of course, some of us still dream of nasty spirits, wicked stepmothers, and big bad wolves. People have always pictured their dream villains as fearful or evil creatures from myth, fable, religious beliefs, and social attitudes popular in their times. What bad dreams have had in common throughout time is a high level of anxiety and a serious threat to, or actual attack on, the emotional and physical well-being of the dreamer or someone dear to her. The tremendous difference between nightmares of the past and those of the last century is the meaning attributed to them by the majority of the population. Well into the eighteenth century, before the ideas of the Enlightenment had become widely accepted, most people believed that the demons in their dreams were real and that various waking rituals were necessary to ward off their power. By the twentieth century, thanks in large part to Freud, most people in developed countries have come to see their dream monsters as reflections of feelings and conflicts within themselves.[1]

Before continuing, we should distinguish among a variety of experiences generally referred to as nightmares. Dreams that develop a plot and fill you with so much anxiety or anger that you wake up from them are what researchers call nightmares. Dreams that replay traumatic events of your life, such as combat scenes, or catastrophic experiences, are called posttraumatic stress nightmares and are usually part of a posttraumatic stress disorder, which is sometimes delayed and sometimes chronic. Frightening, sad, angry, violent, or repulsive dreams with dramatic plots that do not jolt you awake are referred to simply as bad dreams. Nightmares and bad dreams occur during the rapid eye movement (REM) period of sleep, which occurs cyclically every ninety minutes throughout the night as we shift through stages two, three, and four in between REM periods. Each stage has its characteristic brain waves and physiological concomitants.[2] Our regular dreams also occur most often during these REM periods. Posttraumatic stress and other nightmares can occur outside of REM in stage two of sleep, if the condition is severe.

One of the most frightening sleep experiences is the night terror, which disrupts the transition from stage four to stage three sleep and may have a physiological cause.

NIGHT TERRORS

Night terrors are characterized by "cataclysmic panic" accompanied by bloodcurdling screams and disorientation on awakening.[3] Unlike REM dreams with their clear plot development, night terrors often leave people with memories of only short, vivid images of being crushed, strangled, horribly menaced by a "presence," or attacked. Many people awake from a terror having no recall of what has terrified them. Indeed, in one study, only 58 percent of those who had night terrors in the laboratory were able to recall any distinct content of the terror. This level of recall is characteristic for people awakened from stage three or four sleep.[4] Night terrors occur in the first third of the night, during arousals from stage four sleep and are most common in children between the ages of three and eight.

According to Ernest Hartmann, psychoanalyst and author of *The Nightmare,*

> there is a tendency for night terrors to run in families, and some children may have a genetic susceptibility to them. Night terrors can be considered a minor abnormality in the brain's sleep-wake mechanisms producing unusual arousals. However, in a susceptible child, there is no question but that environmental or emotional factors play a part.[5]

Researchers who studied adults with night terrors report "that the psychic content associated with the night terrors was coherent, psychodynamically organized, and related to the subject's REM anxiety dreams of the same night."[6] It is not known why some people do not grow out of their night terrors and continue to have them as adults. Hartmann suggests that some of these people may simply have a greater neurological susceptibility, while others may have a psychological predisposition that triggers an underlying physiological potential. He adds that "some adults with night terrors have been noted to have phobic or obsessional personalities. There is sometimes a sense that these people are unable or unwilling to notice or express strong feelings in the daytime; in them, the night terror episodes may express a kind of outbreak of repressed emotion."[7]

In cases where night terrors occur for the first time in adolescence or adulthood, they may be caused by various drugs, excessive alcohol, or they may be the first sign of temporal lobe epilepsy.[8] If you think you have night terrors, you might want to have a consultation with a specialist at one of the many sleep disorder clinics around the country (see the resources section for help locating one in your area).

I have never personally had a client or student who suffered from night terrors. However, whenever I lecture or talk about dreams on radio or television, at least one or two people tell me of their horrible nightmares that, on investigation, turn out to regularly occur in the first couple hours of sleep—especially when the dreamer is stressed and fatigued—and may really be night terrors. These people have been greatly relieved to learn that they are not crazy and that the condition may be due to physiological rather than psychological causes.

Hartmann writes that treatment for night terrors usually consists of taking the individual off any drugs that may exacerbate the condition and encouraging adequate sleep as well as stress reduction. In cases where sleepwalking accompanies the disorder, precautions should be taken to make the sleeping environment a safe one; sharp or breakable objects and windows should be a good distance away from the dreamer. Hartmann says that in some cases, therapy can be useful in reducing stress and providing a safe place for the night terror sufferer to examine frightening emotions of rage and anger.[9]

POSTTRAUMATIC STRESS DREAMS

Kramer, who has extensively studied the traumatic nightmares of Vietnam War combat veterans, has discovered that although the acute disturbance of these nightmares generally "improves with time . . . it can recur after a lengthy period of apparent remission."[10] By comparing the dreams and sleep patterns of combat veterans who had suffered only acute posttraumatic stress disorder with a group that suffered chronic delayed posttraumatic stress disorder (which includes the traumatic dreams) and with a group of noncombat veteran dreamers, Kramer found that the sleep patterns of both combat groups had been altered. Compared to the noncombat subjects, "both combat groups slept less, took longer to fall asleep, took longer to enter REM sleep, had more awakenings, and lighter sleep. . . . These descriptions suggest that once you [have] had combat experience and developed acute post traumatic stress disorder, you [have been] permanently altered. The possibility then that later in life you will develop [the chronic form of this disorder] is much greater."[11] Kramer notes that the combat group that was not suffering from the chronic form of the disorder was vulnerable to a reactivation of the disorder, which could be triggered by stress, such as a divorce.

Posttraumatic nightmares can occur in REM and stage two sleep, and may occur in other stages as well.[12] While most cases of this disorder resolve themselves within weeks or months after the traumatic event, especially if the individual is able to talk out her feelings soon after the incident, some people who experience particularly severe or long-term trauma or who are unusually vulnerable may be haunted by these nightmares for decades. Individual, group, and family psychotherapy, as well as behavioral deconditioning techniques have only occasionally been successful in the treatment of this disorder. Antidepressant and antipsychotic drugs, including lithium, have sometimes been found helpful,[13] and Hartmann suggests that there are others drugs now available that may alleviate the nightmares, but so far there is no reliable treatment for the chronic form of this disorder.[14] Lawrence Schoen, Milton Kramer, and Lois Kinney have shown that some forms of posttraumatic stress disorder, in which the nightmares arise mostly out of sleep stages other than REM may, like night terrors, be due to, or triggered by, disorders of the arousal mechanisms in the sleep cycle.[15]

NIGHTMARES, BAD DREAMS,
AND RECURRING DREAMS

Hartmann and his coworkers have conducted two extensive
studies of frequent nightmare sufferers who have had weekly
nightmares since childhood. He has found that this group has
personality characteristics that differ markedly from people
who have night terrors and from veterans with chronic posttraumatic nightmares. Hartmann describes the frequent nightmare sufferers he studied as unusually open, vulnerable, and
sensitive and as having thin emotional, identity (ego), turf, reality, and interpersonal boundaries. They tend to be artistic and
show certain schizoid patterns in psychological tests.[16] These
people seem to be overly trusting and relatively defenseless
from childhood onward.[17] They may benefit from psychotherapy, which helps them structure reality more firmly, cope with
the pain of extreme sensitivity in a rude world, and develop
their talents and interpersonal skills.[18] In contrast to some earlier
theories, Hartmann and his colleagues found that frequent
nightmare sufferers, who may make up as much as 1 percent of
the population, "are not persons with powerful hostilities, and
our impression from the interviews is that they are not persons
with an unusual number of fears. It rather appears that the ordinary fears, feelings of hopelessness, and rage of childhood,
which we probably all experience, 'get through' in these persons and enter into their dreams more than they do in most of
us."[19]

Hartmann describes several physiological causes of nightmares. If you suddenly begin to have frequent nightmares for the
first time in your life, check with your physician to see if any
drugs you are taking could be causing them. Certain drugs occasionally have this side effect including some used for hyperten-
sion and parkinsonism. And Hartmann cautions, "Nightmares
that become more frequent over a period of weeks, accompanied

by insomnia and daytime anxiety, may signal an impending psychotic condition that requires treatment."[20]

Nightmares are common among children between the ages of three and six and usually reflect fears of bodily harm and loss of loved ones in the child's life. It is not uncommon for a child to have a terrible nightmare following an especially severe scolding or punishment from parents. The monsters in these dreams may well graphically picture the child's image of his parents or the child's own forbidden, and therefore threatening, retaliatory aggression toward his punisher. *Gently* interviewing children about their dreams, if they are willing, can help them express their innermost feelings and can provide the parents with important information.

For most adults, nightmares are relatively rare, but extraordinarily valuable events. Nightmares and bad dreams show us that somewhere in our lives something is very painful or very wrong. If we can understand these dreams and locate the problem, of which we may be largely or entirely unaware while awake, we can often do something about it. Daytime events and feelings that trigger nightmares and bad dreams are usually linked to deep, perhaps lifelong fears, frustrations, resentments, and needs that are hot spots for the dreamer. These lifelong concerns have often been referred to as childhood fears and drives, but I prefer to think of them as basic human concerns for survival, love, self-esteem, and productivity or growth.

Nightmares and bad dreams sometimes spotlight the existence of an ignored problem, sometimes point to the sources of the problem, and sometimes point to the dreamer's questionable method of dealing with the problem. Some bad dreams show the dreamer how to make a breakthrough toward resolving the problem. Ignoring your nightmares and bad dreams is like ignoring the warning light on your dashboard when it flashes to let you know you are out of oil.

Nightmares and bad dreams, like most of your dreams, can show you what is really going on in your mind and in your heart, relatively free of the waking veils of denial and pretense. We have already discussed a number of nightmares and bad dreams in preceding chapters, because we interpret them in the same way we do other dreams. As you will see, our discussion of common dream themes will include a number of common nightmares and bad dreams. These dreams tend to recur. If they, or any other dream, recur regularly, it is an indication that the dreamer is stuck and either not recognizing the problem or not making progress toward resolving it. Once the dreamer makes progress, the dream will change to reflect her new relationship to the problem. When the dreamer resolves the issue, the theme will either disappear or transform itself to reflect that fact and move on to the next related challenge. If the dreamer has a recurrence of a dream she has not dreamed for a long time, then it is likely that she is again in a situation similar to the one she was in when she first had the dream.

COMMON DREAM THEMES

Dreams of Teeth Falling Out

In case you are still hoping that there exists a magic source that will tell you what a dream, even a common dream means, we had better consult a few sages and see what they have to tell us. In the *Vedas* we are told that a dream of teeth falling out is a bad omen.[21] The Chester Beatty papyrus tells us that in 2000 B.C. it was believed that to dream of teeth falling out meant death at the hands of one's dependents.[22] In the Talmud, teeth were interpreted as members of the dreamer's family, and death was foretold for some member of the dreamer's family after such a dream.[23] "Tooth dreams are open to many interpretations and have been handled successfully by very few of the modern dream interpreters," wrote Artemidorus in the second century. He cited Aristander of Telmessus, who was the favorite interpreter of both Philip of Macedon and his son, Alexander the Great, as the authority on tooth dreams. Thus "the upper teeth represent the more important and excellent members of the dreamer's household; the lower, those who are less important." But the ancient master of metaphor did not stop there, he went on to write, "Furthermore, the so-called incisor teeth or front teeth signify the young; the canine teeth, the middle-aged; the molars . . . old people. Therefore the type of person he is to lose is indicated by the type of tooth he loses.[24] Artemidorus also taught that teeth can represent possessions and the functions of life that will be lost if one has this dream. He provided many variations and refinements on these interpretations and then wrote:

> If all the teeth fall out together, it signifies, in the case of people who are healthy, free, and who are not merchants, that their house will be deserted by everyone alike. If they are sick, the dream indicates lingering illness and wasting away, but it clearly signifies that no death will result. For without one's teeth it is impossible to partake of substantial nourishment, but only porridge and gruel; but those who die do not lose their teeth. And the occurrence of anything that does not happen to corpses is salutary for the sick. It is better, however, for the sick to lose all their teeth. For they will recover more quickly.[25]

We are also told that if a debtor's teeth fall out, he will pay off all his debts, and if a slave dreams that he has no teeth, he will be set free. Artemidorus had more to say about this common dream, but we must move on.

Freud wrote that he had yet to find a complete interpretation of dreams of losing teeth, because he had none of these dreams himself and most of the dreams of his neurotic patients could not be interpreted to reveal the whole of their concealed meaning because of the resistance of his patients' neurotic mechanisms.[26] However, he did believe that such dreams could represent castration and agreed with a comment of Ernest Jones and a young Jung that in women this dream signified the wish to give birth.[27]

Boss suggests that one simply "ask about the immediately given meaning of our teeth."[28] He answers this inquiry by saying:

> Our teeth undoubtedly belong to the world-relationship of catching hold of, of grasping, of seizing something. It is not only our physical food that is grasped and caught hold of. We also grasp the mental content of what we encounter, in the sense of understanding and comprehending it, in order to catch hold of our world.[29]

Rather than saying that some unconscious part of the dreamer sent this dream to his consciousness, Boss notes that

> once it is clear that the teeth are nothing less than the direct physical sphere of our grasping, apprehending relation to the world, it comes as no surprise that patients are regularly visited by dreamings of tooth loss whenever the therapeutic procedure has so challenged their neurotically impaired "world-view" that it is on the point of collapsing.[30]

Thus Boss sees these dreams as reflecting the dreamer's anxiety at the loss of her old way of seeing or grasping the world, and points to the dream of one of his patients in which the dreamer, after having lost a tooth, realizes that new, stronger, and more beautiful ones will grow in its place.[31]

Other analysts have interpreted this dream as expressing a fear of aging and of death; still others as a warning to see your dentist! Well, what is your choice? My own preference is, of course, to interview the dreamer. When all the dreamer's teeth fall out in the dream, try asking, "What is it like for humans to have all their teeth fall out?" What most interpreters have neglected to take fully into account is how the dreamer feels about losing her teeth. When I ask dreamers how they feel in the dream, they often say they felt surprised, anxious, and distressed. When asked why humans would care one way or the other if their teeth were to fall out, they often say, "Well, you would look awful." Frequently, the dreamers bridge to waking feelings of looking bad or of losing face (or the fear of losing face) in the eyes of themselves or others. I have yet to hear a dreamer say that either in the dream, or in reflecting on it, that she feared death or starvation, although many have mentioned the fear of aging.

Victoria had an unusual version of this dream, in that she went beyond the first shock of the loss and reflected on it in two dreams:

> **Four teeth suddenly fell out.** Upper teeth. I was astounded. . . . I couldn't remember the name of my new dentist. I thought, "I will have to get a bridge now. Men won't be interested in me."
>
> **(FOUR LOST TEETH)**

In another dream:

> **All of my teeth suddenly fell out.** I was horrified! I knew it must be due to my gum disease. I would have to get false teeth right away. Didn't want to open my mouth, to let people see.
>
> **(GUM DISEASE)**

These dreams sometimes deal with the dreamer's fear of no longer being sexually attractive, young, and acceptable. They also are sometimes bridged to feelings of embarrassment after having revealed one's shortcomings to others. Of course, each tooth dream must be dealt with in its own context. If only particular teeth fall out, you must ask for descriptions of those teeth, and if the teeth are knocked or pulled out, you must ask about that action, which might alter the significance of the dream. The only sure way to understand any common dream is to interview the dreamer, asking for her descriptions of the particular dream and of the feelings and thoughts these descriptions evoke. This is true of each common dream we will discuss in this chapter, so please consider my comments not as interpretations, but as questions and ideas to prompt you to conduct a lively interview and discover the meaning in your common dream, which may be quite different from the possible meanings given here. Above all, remember that, just as in dealing with any dream, it is important to keep a lookout for the specific situation in the dreamer's current life that precipitated the dream.

Chase and Pursuit Dreams

In your dreams you meet whatever you flee from in your days. When you have dreams of being chased, ask yourself, "What am I running away from? What am I afraid of?" In your self-interview, focus on the person or things chasing you in your dream. If you can get a good description of them, you should be able to bridge them to something in your waking life that you are running from.

For example, if the pursuers are men with guns or knives, describe them. Are they aggressive? Do they want to murder or rape you? What in your life feels like that? After vividly describing them, some dreamers discover, to their surprise, that the threatening men in their dreams remind them of their fathers who threatened them in childhood with stern punishment, a kind of imprisonment, or sexual abuse. Some women relate this dream to their fear of aggression, and sometimes of sexuality. In some cases, the pursuers seem to reflect the dreamer's own denied and unconscious aggression.

A major problem in interpreting this dream arises when the dreamer cannot give a good description of the pursuer. You can get a better idea of what you are running away from if you rehearse in your mind—while awake—that whenever you have such a dream, you are going to try to stay asleep and dream long enough to find out all you can about the villain. You can do this by telling yourself that when you have this sort of dream, you will face your aggressor and ask him, her, or it what or who it is and why it is chasing you. Some dreamers learn to do this after a few tries, for others of us, it takes much longer. But even if you learn to tolerate the stress of the dream only long enough to get a good look at the villain, you will have much more to work with in your interview. You will also be teaching yourself to face up to your fears in a way that usually has some carry-over effect in your waking life. I am not suggesting that you can solve the problem by magically confronting it in your dream, but that your willingness to face it in your dream will help you to face it and understand it in your waking life.

It is during these chase dreams that many people become "lucid," or aware of the fact that they are dreaming while they are still in the dream.[32] If you find yourself in a chase scene, and saying to yourself, "Oh no, I'm having this dream again," take advantage of your lucidity to stop running and find out all you can about your pursuers. Sometimes when you do this, the tone of the dream will change drastically and you will be able to actually talk with the aggressors, be they animal, human, or inanimate. The worst that can happen is that the dream will not change, and you can decide to wake up. But this is rare. Most often you will be able to uncover important material, and sometimes even interpret the dream while you are in it. Whatever you do, don't use your conscious awareness of a bad dream to force a Pollyanna-like, happy ending to it. You will only be throwing away a chance to discover the dynamics of a waking, but re-pressed, problem. It would be a shame to do the same thing while you dream, because dreaming is your best time to undo the denial and repression that gets you into trouble in your life.

For more than two decades, Morilla had dreams of being pursued by queens and witches who tried to poison her or have her shot with arrows while she dined. Sometimes Morilla would be a princess at dinner with the queen; other times she would be in her own palace and the queen would have sent her servants to do the deed. The queen or witch would always plot covertly, and the unsuspecting Morilla would escape with her life only through luck or by happening to notice the threat at the last moment. Morilla had been in therapy for a few years but had never understood these dreams. She had read fairy tales and myths and had vaguely related the dreams to the Great Mother archetype, but the dreams kept coming, and she never understood what to do about them, because she could not see what they were pointing to.

Finally, one night she dreamt that she was just narrowly escaping from multiple covert attempts on her life when she suddenly realized that the would-be murderer was her mother! In the dream she flashed back to the many dreams she had had in the past of being nearly poisoned and shot and realized that all those attempts had been made on her life by her own mother in the guise of a witch or, more often, a queen. Morilla was furious. She had put up with this long enough. Up until now she had been willing to escape by using her wits and "stepping lively." No more—the assassin must die! Morilla went to the kitchen where her mother held court and found her there with a friend. She knew it would not look good to kill a frail, old lady who looked as if she couldn't hurt anyone, but that was just too bad. This assassin had to be stopped. Morilla awoke just as she was about to break her mother's neck. (Kill Mom)

Through the interview, Morilla realized that her often supportive and lovable, alcoholic, depressed mother was also an assassin. Her mother was extremely narcissistic and insecure. She tried in covert ways to keep Morilla for herself by criticizing her in front of other members of the family and the men in Morilla's life. Furthermore, the mother criticized Morilla's friends as inappropriate. She openly praised Morilla as a princess, but had criticized most of her independent ideas and interests since Morilla was a child. Morilla grew up with a picture of her mother as a sad, difficult, but loving mother. Morilla put up with the "bitter queen" behaviors of which she was not fully aware. By finding out the identity of her dream assassin, Morilla was able to face the destructive aspects of her mother and come to a resolution to confront them. This new awareness led her to see how a number of her "friends" who were older females fit into a similar profile. While saying they were friends, they resented Morilla for her gifts, felt insecure about her, were jealous of her, and took regular potshots at her while criticizing her in front of her husband and others. Morilla had been willing to put up with this because she told herself that they were only acting out of insecurity. This dream changed that. Morilla decided that such friends needed therapy, not a whipping girl. She would not be able to make them happy any more than she could ever make her mother happy. She needed to draw firmer boundaries between herself and her mother, and she did not need to have friends who acted like her mother, either.

Dreams of killing one's parents without guilt and dreams in which one has killed a parent and is surprised that the police have not arrived sometimes, but by no means always, highlight the dreamer's need to take her parent or parents off an undeserved pedestal and fight back against their destructive behaviors and attitudes, which the dreamer has often adopted as her own. Only a careful interview will make clear whether the dreamer is trying to liberate herself from certain parental influences or whether the dreamer is being self-destructive by killing off these parts of herself. I could imagine that a dream of killing a parent could reflect the dreamer's inappropriate waking-life interpersonal hostility to that living parent, but I have not seen this in my practice.

BREAKTHROUGH DREAMING

Dreams of Falling

Ask yourself or your dreamer, "How do you feel as you are falling?" Out of control? Helpless and in immediate danger? Explore the action that led up to the fall, then summarize up to the point of the fall. Where in her life does the dreamer feel as she does in the dream and what led up to this feeling? Falling dreams can, like any dream, mean a variety of things. For some, their dream fall was preceded by carelessness with people or in actions that remind them of their work or marriage. Others dream of joining up with unsavory characters who remind them of certain of their associates or of their own attitudes and lead them to the disastrous fall. One teenager told me that she recurrently dreamt that her car had no brakes and that she went over a cliff and awoke as she was falling. I asked her where in her life could she not put on the brakes and where that fact could lead to her downfall. She immediately knew that she was dreaming about her relatively new drug habit.

Nudity

Remember how embarrassed you were the last time you dreamt of being naked or partially undressed in a public place? What was the setting? Who else was there? Did you notice that no one particularly noticed your nudity? Ask yourself how you felt and see if that reminds you of a situation in waking life where you felt overexposed or vulnerable. If so, ask yourself if you were the only one who thought you were overexposed.

Barefoot Dreams

If you dream of being barefoot in the snow, on city streets, or in some other uncomfortable context, ask yourself, "What are shoes?" and then "What is wrong with being barefoot in this situation?" See if these feelings match some circumstance in your life. Some people relate being barefoot to the feeling of being unprotected, or more precisely, of not adequately protecting themselves in some harsh emotional or interpersonal environment.

Flying

What are your flying dreams like? Are they stressful, anxious? Are they among the most delightful experiences you have ever had, waking or sleeping? If you are flying to escape pursuers, ask yourself if you are doing more than running away from your problems. If you are showing your friends that you can fly while they cannot, ask yourself if your dream feelings of superiority are reflections of your waking behavior, acting superior to cover feelings of inferiority. If you have trouble maintaining altitude and fear crashing, ask yourself if there is some undertaking in your life, such as a relationship or a work project, that is just not making it. Are you having trouble keeping your spirits up? Do your moods have big valleys and peaks? Remember to explore the feelings and actions in the dream before you try to figure it out. Let the dream experience tell you what it is about. Some dreamers fly without any problem and practice their technique of flight. Sometimes these dreams seem to be nothing more and *nothing less* than marvelous experiences of soaring freedom and grace that fill the dreamers with great joy. It would be a shame not to savor such experiences.

Missing the Boat, Bus, or Train

You are late, running out of breath, perhaps carrying baggage, trying to get to the bus in time, but you miss it. Ask yourself, "What made me late in the dream?" "How does it feel to miss the bus?" "Is there some way I am missing the boat in life?"

Some people have this dream and relate it to a specific area of their lives; some say it is a good picture of how they feel they have missed the boat entirely in their lives, which are without enthusiasm and excitement.

Lost Purse, Wallet, Keys, or Briefcase

What do you usually keep (and would most hate to lose) in the object you have lost in the dream? In the case of a purse, most women answer, "my money, credit cards, and ID." These objects are then often described as being the power and identity that humans carry in purses. I then ask, "Is there any way you feel you have lost or risk losing your power and your identity?" To this, many dreamers answer yes. In fact this is a common dream among women who are facing an empty nest, and among men (lost wallet or briefcase) when they are facing retirement or have been fired.

Finding Money or Lost Treasure

Again, the details of the context of the dream will place this one in a specific area of your life, but generally finding money or treasure either signals the dreamer that she has unknown resources or reflects her recent achievements in developing her resources. The treasure can be modest or extravagant and can depict the dreamer's self-confidence, skills in relating to herself and others, or other skills of a sportive or intellectual nature.

Dreams of Being in Bed
with an Unexpected Partner

Haven't you been surprised once or twice to find yourself dreaming of being in bed or of having sex with your neighbor, coworker, Prince Charles, or a movie star? Because you already know whether or not you lust after the dream lover while you are awake, you don't need a dream to tell you that. These dreams usually are quite easy to understand and are very informative if you take the time to describe the personality of the dream lover. When you recapitulate that description, whom have you described? Who else or what part of you could be described with the same words? Frequently, the dreamer is dreaming about an unappreciated aspect of her spouse. Sometimes, when the dream lover is of the same sex of the dreamer, the dream lover is much like an unappreciated aspect of the dreamer. This is occasionally true in the dreams of homosexuals and lesbians, as well. If you find yourself in bed with a person you don't like, ask yourself if you are "in bed" with people or a part of yourself that you feel the same way about.

   If the lovemaking is not going well, describe the problems and see if your descriptions shed any light on one of your relationships.

Having Parents Observe Your Lovemaking

Have you ever dreamt that you were making love when one or both of your parents walk into the room and calmly sit down, perhaps shaking your partner's hand in greeting? When this happens, most dreamers find that while their parents are acting as if everything were normal, they are unable to stay in quite the right mood for sex. People who have had this dream often tell me in the interview that their parents had taught them Victorian attitudes toward sex and it is shocking even to imagine that the parents are the ones who are comfortable about sex while the dreamer is self-conscious. Most dreamers experience this as a dream that gives them a sense of parental permission to have sex. By the way, and perhaps by coincidence, every dreamer who has told me this dream has been married or in a long-term live-in relationship.

Trying to Find a Private Toilet

One usually feels rather awkward trying to find a little privacy, but finding instead that one must use a toilet that is in full or partial view of other people. As in dreams of being naked, rarely if ever do the other people seem to mind or even notice the fact that you are in their midst on a toilet. Ask yourself what humans use toilets for, and if you are trying to eliminate waste products in a public setting in waking life. This dream is common in psychotherapy groups, individual therapy, in dream study groups, and in any groups where people have to gather together their courage to reveal something they are ashamed of or embarrassed about that seems very private. The dream can alert the dreamer to anxieties of which she has been unaware and can help her see that her listeners are not put off by her revelations.

Examination Dreams

You probably remember this one. You are about to be given an exam and you suddenly realize that you have not studied at all, you studied the wrong thing, you are in the wrong room, or your mind has gone blank and you have no chance of passing the exam. After interviewing yourself (or your dreamer) about all the specific circumstances of the dream, ask yourself if there is any situation in waking life that is analogous to the exam situation in the dream. Is there some test or challenge you must face, like the one in the dream, for which you are unprepared? The waking test may have nothing to do with school. Most often it is a test you risk failing regarding someone close to you such as a child, a friend, or spouse. Sometimes the dream relates to failing to keep up with obligations at work or obligations to yourself. In my experience, people who have this dream once every week or two are living lives in the fast lane and have an unhealthy schedule of constant deadlines that they can only meet with great difficulty and sacrifice. Many of my lawyer clients have this dream, as do the especially ambitious business-people I see. I ask these dreamers what it feels like to live lives where each day feels like an exam and if this is the way they want to be living. Some don't mind the feeling; others don't believe there is any other way to survive.

Being Unable to Run or Call Out for Help

If you are running away from something in a dream, you may be avoiding facing a problem while awake. But what about times you feel paralyzed and can't get your legs to move when you want to run away? Ask yourself exactly how you feel in the dream, then see if that feeling matches a feeling you have had sometime in your life. When have you felt paralyzed with fear, unable to get out of harm's way? This dream often takes a dreamer back to childhood experiences with bad, threatening, or abusive parents. After exploring these memories, see if there is some current situation that could have triggered these feelings. Usually the dreamer will be completely surprised to see the relationship between his current sense of vulnerability and helplessness and that of his childhood.

Being unable to call out for help is a similar sort of dream, but adds the awareness of the need for help. Children and adults who have this dream usually do need outside help to deal with their current difficulties. Children need their parents' help—if the parents know how to give it—and may need the help of a family therapist. In my opinion, the adults who have this dream almost always need the helping hand (even if briefly) of a good therapist.

Dreams of Being Left Out

Have you ever had dreams in which you are left out by "the group," dreams of not being included, or dreams where there were enough chairs for everyone but you? Perhaps you've dreamt that the important people got to eat in the pretty room and you had to eat outside. These dreams are very uncomfortable and usually bring up memories of similar feelings from childhood. Explore the dream actions and feelings, see if they match feelings from childhood, and then see if they parallel feelings you may have recently pushed aside in your waking life. It is not uncommon for people who felt left out as an unwanted child or as a younger sibling whose older siblings would not include him to recreate adult relationships that lead to these familiar feelings. Recognizing that one feels left out often comes as a surprise and opens the door to doing something about it.

Seeing Childhood Friends in a Dream

One of the most fascinating dream experiences is to dream about people you haven't seen for years. Sometimes it is Mike from second grade or your high-school principal or Aunt Matilda who died when you were six. If you remember to describe your old friend's personality as you know it to be (this description may have remained unaltered since your last meeting, or might be updated by things you have since heard), you should not have much trouble bridging to someone or to some part of yourself. Aunt Matilda or Mike might well provide you with images that are perfect for evoking a particular web of feelings and associations relevant to your current life. By exploring their personalities and dream actions, you will probably discover not only one bridge, but perhaps a pattern of feeling, behavior, or relating as well.

Discovering and Exploring New Rooms
in a House

This is usually an exhilarating dream, in which the dreamer suddenly discovers that there are more rooms to her house than she had realized. Sometimes the house is an unknown one, but almost always the rooms are pretty and full of light and space. Most dreamers, if not all, have told me that this brings to mind recent feelings of enlarging their sense of themselves and of expanding their world view. These dreamers delight in experiencing the pleasure of finding that their world is less constricted than they had thought, that it is bright, open, and spacious. This dream seems to come at the time the dreamer is making changes in attitude or behavior that open up new possibilities in her life. It is a wonderful dream.

Dreams of Saying What Is on Your Chest
or in Your Heart

Have you ever dreamt of telling someone you love or hate or just can't stand in waking life exactly what you think of him? It can be a very satisfying experience. You may or may not discover formerly unappreciated nuances of feeling in these dreams, and while you may or may not find it advisable to repeat your dramatic performance in the flesh, you will probably feel a welcome relief on waking. It might be worth giving a second thought to letting the object of your emotions know at least some of how you feel. We often underestimate the importance of being honest and overestimate the importance of being "appropriate."

Dreams of Discovering That You Have Been Neglecting or Starving Little Animals

Are there faithful dogs or little kittens in your dreams that you suddenly realize you have forgotten to feed or have left out in the cold? People usually feel horribly guilty in the dream at this discovery and wonder how they could have done such a thoughtless or cruel thing. When they describe the nature of cats or dogs and their neglect, they find themselves talking about a vulnerable and very loving or gentle or talented parts of themselves that they have neglected to nurture in their mad rush for success or in a distorted sense of fear or self-sacrificial duty toward others. I would imagine that parents who abuse their children might have dreams like this, but I have never worked with such parents.

Mourning Dreams

After someone you have loved dies, you may have dreams about him, which can help you cope with the terrible loss. At first you may have dreams of being very angry with the doctors or the minister or rabbi who attended him. Or you might have dreams that in other ways elicit your natural angry sense of the injustice of your loved one's death. You may have dreams that bring up feelings of guilt of past hurts from the relationship. All these feelings are normal and will only cause you long-term trouble if you don't let them out. They will pass.

Sometimes you will dream that your loved one returns and reassures you that he is fine and that you should not worry. You may dream of acting as if he were still alive only to find that he is not there to answer the phone and that he has really died. From time to time, if you are lucky, he may be in a dream so vividly and happily that you awake feeling as if you were really together. If you can let yourself be grateful for this experience, you may not dissolve into tears on realizing it was "only a dream." If your mourning goes on for too long, say for several years, you may have dreams in which your loved one returns to scold you for not washing the car or mowing the lawn. These dreams are often bridged to the dreamer's sense that the one they loved is trying to get them out into life again.

Talking Animals

Dreams in which animals talk are very frequently interpreted by their dreamers as being of a spiritual or transpersonal nature. We will end this chapter with a dream of a fascinating gentleman I met while giving a workshop at Johns Hopkins University:

I'm at the Bentons' house. I go into a room to collect my thoughts and the old golden retriever pads in after me. He sits at my feet and I scratch his head and talk to him. I take my hand away and he seizes it with both paws, forcing it to the back of his head. "Poor old Rex," I say. "You're a tired old dog." "Yeah," he says. I am startled and go on to scratch his back observing that his head is balding. "Did you talk?" I ask. "Yeah," he says, his voice very guttural, "God talkin' t'ru me." As he talks, his countenance is transformed. He's completely bald, his face changes. He's like an old man, perhaps like a baby too, beautiful and wise. We continue this conversation, and I realize it must be a God-sent miracle. A talking dog. A talking God. I think to ask him whether God is a Unitarian or a Christian, but don't. God wouldn't have a *creed*. He wouldn't *worship*. But will anyone believe that God revealed himself to me through a talking dog? I look into the evening light coming through the gauzy curtains, expecting a host of

angels singing—well, maybe just one, beaming down
silently to confirm this experience. Rex follows my
gaze. "God is everywhere," he says, "In you. In me."
Meaning, Why look out there?   (REX)

Our dreamer noted in his commentary:

This dream isn't very mysterious and theologically it
isn't very complicated. God is immanent, not transcen-
dent, and reveals himself through the lowliest creatures.
This one is called Rex (king), of course. The day before
the dream, I visited the Bentons and in the evening a
neighbor's aged golden retriever, named Rex, dropped
by. But he didn't talk. I have always had a visceral fear
of dogs, but the real Rex would have none of it. Dog–
God is a nice pun. And my brother, a hindu monk,
points out to me today that many people are afraid of
God, too.

◘

CHAPTER

THIRTEEN

ACTING ON
YOUR INSIGHT

The most important work a dreamer does with a dream is accomplished in the weeks and perhaps months following a successful interview. A careful dream interview usually leads to several important insights, which are directly related to the dreamer's waking life. The specificity, depth, and breadth of these insights can be very impressive. But if the dreamer does not make a concerted effort to recall, review, and reflect on these insights, the insights often vanish into thin air, and the dreamer's old ways of perceiving and behaving reassert themselves. I have seen too many clients who have used therapy and growth-oriented disciplines as tools for contemplating and theorizing about themselves without making any concrete attitudinal or behavioral changes. Without these changes, they have remained prisoners to destructive and self-defeating patterns that keep them feeling inadequate, lonely, angry, or lead them into one painful relationship after another.

Making changes in the ways we think, feel, and behave is extremely difficult. It often seems that to act on a new insight, we have to abandon a familiar way of seeing or doing things that, despite being painful, has worked for us so far. Yes, it may have worked badly, but it feels like that is all we have, and how can we be sure that the new way will work? Imagine the woman who, through her dream work, realizes that all the neglectful or abusive men in her life are just like her father. In letting go of this type of man, she will have to reject a part of her father and give up her idealized image of him along with her hopes that somehow he will change. Will she ever be attracted to men who are unlike her early imprint male? She may feel that she will lose her father and must mourn the loss brought about by a more adult assessment of him. At the same time, if she gives up dating abusive types, will she be able to attract loving men? She is not even sure that such men exist. Maybe she will be alone the rest of her life. Is an abusive man better than being alone? That question is hard to answer for a woman who has been desperately longing for the love and support she never had as a child.

Change is a potential result of learning or insight. Learning takes review and practice. Once you have understood your dream through a good interview, you must review the dream and your work with it, so that your understanding deepens, along with your appreciation of the relationship of the particular insights from this dream to other areas or periods of your life. As Jung wrote, "A real recognition, a full realization, of these unconscious contents never happens all at once. It always comes in waves, wave after wave, with a pause in between before a new and more intense realization of what [something means]."[1] Insight does seem to come in waves if you review it and keep it in mind. Without purposely reviewing your insights, you will tend to "forget" them and have to rediscover them again and again through your dreams, therapy, or life experience. As one of our students said, "I guess if I forget which dreams I've worked on, I can't expect to get much in the way of results, can I?"

ACTIVE REFLECTION

It is in living with the dream images and the insights they offer that one is able to integrate newly formed perspectives and behaviors into daily life. We encourage our students to practice a form of *active reflection,* which helps them to consolidate and integrate their insights. Active reflection requires thoughtfulness and discipline to *review* dream work carefully and regularly. It requires courage and discipline to *practice* new ways of thinking and behaving.

Review

In its simplest form, review means rereading your dream two or three times in the days following your interview. Ask yourself, "What does this dream show me that I did not know or fully appreciate before working it?" Usually, the more extensive your review, the more you will get out of it. As you reread your dream, see if new bridges come to mind or if the ones you made in the interview become more evident as additional associations link the dream images to your life. You may want to draw, sculpt, or paint your dream. This is fun and often illuminating for both children and adults. If you also review notes, a tape recording, or a transcript of your interview, you will be better able to refine your understanding of the dream and adjust connections that were tenuous. You will also be able to reinforce your insights so that they become more integrated into your conscious perspective.

Reviewing your dream journal every month, every six months, and every year will further reinforce your insights and yield new ones as you reconsider old dreams with your growing interpretive skills and as you notice the patterns in your dreams that become evident as you consider them in series. Ideally, once you have really understood a dream, you will look back on it and think, "This dream is so obvious, how could I not have understood it right away?" Monthly and yearly reviews also give your morale a boost because you will notice that dreams that once seemed impenetrable are easier to work with a few months after you dreamt them. This may be because your work with other dreams has opened you up, making you more receptive to new insights, because you are getting better at interviewing yourself, or because with the passage of time, you have become less defensive about the issue dealt with in your six-month-old dream.

As you review your dream work, you may notice that your dreams function in a variety of ways. Loma Flowers has described four types of dreams according to the kinds of insight they offer. These dreams help us to emphasize, reconceptualize, confront, and discover particular issues in our waking lives.[2] To these we can add dreams that show a certain level in integration of new growth and dreams that offer practical solutions.

▣ *Emphasis dreams* serve to bring to our attention conflicts, feelings, or insights that are neither new nor unfamiliar but that we have failed to appreciate fully. For example, Aretha's dream of being strangled to death by her boss emphasized the urgency of a situation at work that she had been trying to minimize. Emphasis dreams are among the easiest to bridge to waking life because the dreamer has already admitted some degree of awareness of the situation into consciousness and is less defensive in bridging.

▣ *Reconceptualization dreams* help the dreamer to reconceptualize "a known issue in a more useful and meaningful way."[3] Paul dreamt of a teenage arsonist who set fire to homes. In describing the personality of the arsonist, Paul said that he probably did this to get attention, having no doubt grown up a severely neglected child. When asked if there were a part of him that felt he had been severely neglected, he quickly recognized it and said that perhaps his penchant for affairs with married women was like setting houses on fire. He certainly got a lot of attention from both husbands and wives through this behavior. This dream helped Paul to reconceptualize his understanding of his motivation to have affairs with married women. (Arsonist)

▣ *Confrontation dreams* bring dreamers face-to-face with realities they have been unwilling to admit. These realities may consist of thoughts, feelings, tendencies, self-images, attitudes, judgments, and behaviors that are unacceptable to the dreamer because they are unpleasant or unflattering.

On the other hand, these realities may well be highly flat-
tering to the dreamers, but unacceptable because the
dreamer judges them to be negative or out of character. The
material in these dreams may have been repressed or may
not yet have entered the dreamer's awareness. A mother
dreamt that she was dressing her daughter in her own
clothes over the daughter's vehement protests. Having
achieved her task, the mother noticed that her clothes did
not fit her daughter. In the interview, the mother had to face
the fact that her daughter's hostility toward her just might
have something to do with the mother's constant attempts
to mold her daughter into a clone of herself.

- *Discovery dreams* present dreamers with an entirely new perspective on themselves or on some aspect of their lives.
These dreams occur spontaneously and seem especially frequent among incubated dreams. Sometimes these dreams
open dreamers' eyes to problems the dreamers didn't even
know they had because they had so thoroughly denied and
repressed all awareness of the conflict and its symptoms.
Perhaps the most striking example of this type of dream is
one in which Valerie saw a little girl being raped by a man
who looked like Valerie's father. While exploring the dream,
Valerie noted that the little girl was wearing one of her
favorite childhood dresses, and then as her very vague
memories of early childhood began to come into focus, she
seemed to remember some very secret and awful feelings
about Daddy that would explain some of her adult attitudes
toward men and sex. (Little Girl Raped) More often, the
discoveries are less concrete, involving the recognition of
strong, but denied, feelings and attitudes.

Discovery dreams also present us with the chance to see,
for the first time, how, and often why, we are repeating life
patterns that may have begun in childhood and that cause us
frustration and pain in adulthood. The man who dreams

that his second wife looks like his first wife in the dream, and that the dream wife says something that his older sister used to say, may be looking at a pattern of choosing female partners who are like his older sister. This discovery can be shocking, but it can also be enlightening. If his sister is at heart the sort of woman who cannot give him what he needs, he is going to have to come to terms with that and consider getting interested in a different type of woman.

☐ *Integration dreams* show the dreamer acting in ways that suggest a greater or lesser degree of incorporation of recently gained insight. For example, Ivan, who had been brought up to believe that wives should obey their superior husbands, had some serious problems with his wife who, like him, was a lawyer. After a month of couple dream work he dreamt that he was in bed making love with a famous female lawyer named Deborah. In describing Deborah, Ivan said that she was not only an exceptional lawyer, but pretty and sexy, as well. Soon he bridged to his wife and sheepishly added that Deborah was a more accomplished lawyer than he. Ivan said that he was indeed beginning to appreciate his wife's legal skills and was pleased to see that he could have good sex with such a powerful woman. (Sexy Lawyer)

☐ *Solution dreams* present the dreamer with fairly direct solutions. These solutions are most often of a concrete, practical nature and frequently come in response to incubations requesting new ideas for work-related projects or fairly simple, but awkward, situations. Dreams that give you an idea for a new story, photograph, or painting would fall into this category as would solutions for mathematical problems and problems in creating new designs for a product or an instructional program.[4]

These categories overlap and are not presented as a strict or definitive listing. Dreams serve many purposes, but these seem

to be the most common when we look at ways dreams can enhance our awareness of what we are like, why we are the way
we are, and what we might want to change. By reviewing your
dream work, you will be able to see how your own dreams
function in your life.

PRACTICE

If you want to lose weight, it is rarely enough to understand
why you overeat. You must both work on the feelings that drive
you to eat too much and systematically change what and how
much you eat. Maintaining your weight loss is as important and
often more difficult than achieving it in the first place. Much the
same can be said of your work with dreams. It is usually not
enough to understand *why* you have a problem. Once you understand the dynamics of your difficulty, resolving the problem
usually takes multiple observations of how you repeat the pattern and concerted efforts on your part to try out new ways of
dealing with it. Your dream work reviews should help you to
clarify, correct, and confirm your insights; the following practice exercises should help you to implement them.

Invoking Images

As we mentioned in Chapter 2, step 9 in the interview is reflection, which includes reviewing the dream and implementing
new insights. We discussed the invoking of images from the
dream that one can hold in one's mind while walking down the
street or, more daringly, while confronting a difficult situation.
By holding the dream images—positive or negative—in your
mind, you can better see how their characteristics are acted out
by you and/or others in your waking life. If you carefully observe your dream dynamics in action, you will gain confidence
to try out new responses and behaviors when you feel ready.
    Alicia dreamt:

Sue and I are laughing about Milt's using a metal detector. Then we are at Lucy's. She is running around like
crazy doing something for somebody else. Sue looks at
me and says, "That's just like Lucy."

Then I am having lunch with a wise-looking cow-
boy named Cody. Sue enters the room, and Cody realizes we are sisters. I realize Sue met him earlier in the
day and likes him a lot. Joining us for lunch, Sue makes
a point of letting Cody know about my husband and
daughter.

I go into the kitchen; Cody follows and says, "I
didn't know you were sisters." I say, "Don't worry, it
won't interfere with your relationship with her." He
says, "No, it is you I am attracted to. You are special,
and your work is good." I am embarrassed and wake
up.   (CODY)

Alicia described Milt as her brother-in-law, who protected
himself and hid his insecurities behind an understated, com-
posed, but warm exterior. He would never be like those weird
people who use metal detectors on the beach, because that
would definitely not be cool. She described a metal detector as
an intrusive contraption she had seen people use on her recent
vacation in Fiji. They help you draw people's coins out of the
sand. Then Alicia bridged to how she is like Milt; while on her
vacation she appeared warm and friendly because she used her
skills as a psychiatrist to draw people out while she hid her personal feelings and history. Lucy is a wonderful friend who gives
of herself too much—to the exclusion of listening to herself and
reflecting on her life. Alicia easily bridged Lucy to the part of
herself that has the same problem. Cody, a dream creation, is
one of Alicia's ideal men—sporting, straightforward, grounded,
wise, and psychologically minded. Alicia was surprised and
flattered that Cody could tell she was Sue's sister, because Sue is
"very pretty, creative, spontaneous, witty, and outgoing, the

exact opposite of me." Sue also had the habit of putting Alicia into the "big sister" role of responsible counselor. Alicia, of course, played this role to the hilt, à la Lucy. The high point of the dream came when Cody told Alicia that it was she, not her sister, to whom he was attracted and whose work he admired.

Alicia now had several powerful images to evoke in the coming weeks. She was to look out for ways she acted like cool Milt, intrusively drawing others out while she hid behind her warm facade. She also needed to watch for the ways she acted like Lucy, always doing for others, looking very charismatic, but failing to take stock of herself. How did Alicia pigeonhole herself as a rather dull mother and wife, as her sister did in the dream? How did she immediately defer to others when the competition seemed out of her league? For the next week she was to keep reliving what it felt like to realize that a guy like Cody could like her, even prefer her to her sister. And finally, she was to watch how she tended to feel embarrassed by the compliments and admiration of others, and see if she could discover why it was so hard for her to acknowledge praise. This gave Alicia plenty of concrete things to think about and observe. As soon as she felt ready, she was to practice welcoming compliments rather than brushing them off and staying in the competition when she felt like withdrawing.

When you dream of a positive image with which you identify in the interview, try pretending you are that person. Ask yourself what he would feel, think, or do in a given situation. Get to know that part of yourself better and encourage its development by taking tiny steps toward acting like the person in your dream. In time, you will feel more and more comfortable adopting the characteristics you had once seen only in someone you admired. Growth can come through pleasurable experiences as well as through painful ones, so don't neglect the heroes in your dreams.

It is not necessary and often not advisable to act immediately on your dream insights. See if they are sound, observe them in operation, then step by tiny step take little risks and make changes. Talking and reflecting will get you only so far. If you want to learn how to swim, there comes a point when you have to take the plunge.

CONSIDERING OPTIONS FOR CHANGE

This is the last step in the dream interview, one that may not be taken for some time after the interview itself. When the dreamer is ready to make a change, it helps to talk about his options with a dream group or a dream partner. In addition to the crucial changes in attitude that come about with careful review and practice, the dreamer may want to communicate his dream or dream insights to concerned parties. For example, a woman who dreams of her father as a turtle that is being eaten as sashimi may want to tell him that she has come to a new awareness of his vulnerability underneath his protective shell. The man who, through a dream, realizes that his wife is more like a queen than a maid, might find that telling her this would lead to his being treated more like a king than a landlord. These examples are simple ones, but they illustrate the point.

For some dreamers, the most appropriate action to follow up on a dream is to widen or deepen the field of investigation by entering therapy, incubating a dream on a newly formulated aspect of the issue, or simply keeping their eyes open to newly recognized dynamics. It is important not to act rashly in response to a dream, but it is also important not to become like the explorer who knows the world only through travel brochures and has never risked a voyage or been changed by new experiences in a strange land.

□

**CHAPTER
FOURTEEN**

**DEVELOPING
DREAM SKILLS**

The most resistant, difficult dreamer you will ever work with is yourself. Because most dreams show us what we do not know, are afraid to know, or do not fully appreciate, they always seem to be a step ahead of us.[1] Interviewers who are not vested in your particular way of seeing things will find it easier to help you explore a dream without the same temptations you feel to avoid difficult parts and to take shortcuts that miss important material. By interviewing other dreamers, you will learn how to ask effective questions that you can then apply to your work on your own dreams. Working with dreams in a group or with a dream partner will greatly speed your learning. It is a fascinating experience to see how other people's dreams work for them. And because working with someone is far more engaging than working alone, you are more likely to continue practicing your dream skills long enough to gain some mastery of them than if you work only on your own.

WORKING ON YOUR OWN

We will all work on our own dreams even if we also have a dream partner or are in a dream group. Some of us are too shy to work with another person, although with time this shyness often relaxes and we can begin working with others. If you plan to work privately on your dreams, I would suggest the following program of study:

1. *Contract with yourself that you will study your dreams for at least six months, preferably one year.* The first six months are the most

difficult. A contract should help you stick with it long enough to notice that you have learned quite a bit about interviewing and about yourself. Promise yourself that you will keep a dream journal and interview yourself on one dream a week and that you will read at least one book on dreams every two months. Attend lectures and take as many classes in dream work as you can. If there are no dream classes available near you, see if your local community college or a local psychotherapist offers one. Even if the lectures or classes are of low quality or about theories and methods you do not agree with, they can help you to clarify your thinking about why you prefer other methods. And you may be pleasantly surprised to find that you can learn important things in unlikely places. The better acquainted you are with a variety of theories and approaches, the better able you will be to take advantage of good ideas, and to avoid making unnecessary mistakes and assumptions you see in certain approaches.

2. *Write out an entire self-interview at least once every month.* This takes time and discipline, but the rewards are great. When you write out an interview, you will be less likely to take shortcuts, which usually lead to confusion and frustration rather than to learning. A written interview should include a diagram as well as an outline so that you will be less likely to miss important aspects of your dream. Carefully follow each step of the interview, and remember to try to create for yourself an atmosphere of nonjudgmental curiosity, humility, courage, and humor.

3. *Conduct careful dream reviews on a regular schedule of once every two or four months.* Every one my clients and students has thoroughly enjoyed the review process. It involves a lot of work, but once you begin rereading your dream journal, which includes day notes, interviews, and commentary, you will find it fascinating and rewarding. When you complete a review, write a summary of at least one or more pages of issues your dreams have been dealing with in this period and of the progress you have made in better understanding and resolving the problems related to those issues. Then note which areas of dream interviewing have become easier for you and which ones remain most difficult. Before you close your journal, ask yourself if you are now willing to work on your dreams with a dream specialist, a dream partner, or in a dream study group.

WORKING WITH A DREAM SPECIALIST

Many people who are not willing to share their dreams with a partner or a group feel the need for some assistance in the development of their dream skills and feel comfortable consulting a professional dream analyst for private consultations. For most people, weekly sessions provide adequate momentum for good progress, but as one's skills improve, bimonthly sessions and then monthly sessions can be sufficient to augment private study. I have found that clients who tape-record our sessions and listen to the recordings are able to clarify and absorb their insights more readily. They also learn better and faster how to work with dreams, because this review allows them to listen to the general process once they have first gone over the specific content of the session. Those who actually transcribe and review the session on paper get the most out of the review. In the resource section you will find a list of centers where you can study dreams and suggestions on how to find a skilled dream specialist.

FORMING A DREAM PARTNERSHIP

This is perhaps the easiest and most practical way to study your dreams. Even if you are seeing a professional, practicing once a week with a friend will help you develop your skills much more quickly. Practice sessions of one or two hours in which you and your partner take turns working with each other's dreams can even be conducted over the telephone. You will probably find that telephone sessions are very nearly as effective as face-to-face sessions and the ease of arranging them will allow you to schedule practice sessions into the busiest of schedules. Here are a few suggestions for studying with a partner:

1. *Choose a dream partner.* Obviously, a partner should be someone you can trust to keep all your work confidential and who will not be judgmental, but accepting and supportive. Ideally, your partner should be courageous when it comes to self-exploration, not too defensive, and patient. A dash of good humor would also be beneficial. Choosing a member of your family as a regular partner is problematic. Parents and children make better occasional dream partners, because weekly sessions might impinge on each partner's privacy and the intimate nature of some dream work could be inappropriate for a parent to share with a child.

Working with a spouse can be wonderful—or it can be awful. The issues covered in some dreams may be too hot for a couple to work on together and a less involved friend would make a more impartial interviewer. For a couple's dream work to succeed, the pair must have an extraordinary degree of trust, acceptance, and confidence in themselves and each other as well as patience. If either one makes the mistake of using material discussed during an interview as a weapon in a fight, their ability to work together will be greatly diminished, because the dreamer's confidentiality and trust will have been violated.

Dream partners who are siblings sometimes do well together, if they are not too competitive with each other. Adults can sometimes work with their parents, but get into difficulty if the younger partner is dreaming about difficult parental relationships. As you can see, dream work with family members can be tricky. If, however, you manage to avoid the many pit-falls, you will find that you and your partner will establish a wonderful, trusting intimacy with each other. Remember that whenever you work with a family member you must be more careful than ever not to try to interpret her dream. Keeping in mind that the temptation may be overwhelming to guide your partner to see the truth that you think you already know about her, you must phrase your questions with special care in order not to "lead the witness" and cause your dreamer to feel pushed in a particular direction.

You may think that you don't have any friends who are inter-ested in their dreams. If you simply let your friends know that you are reading a book on the subject, you may find that many are eager to talk with you about their dreams. Just under the surface, most people are very curious about dreaming. As you discuss the topic with friends, you will probably find one or two with whom you would like to form a partnership. If not, go to lectures and classes on dreams and strike up conversations with as many people as you can. You may find a sympathetic soul among the attendees. With perseverance, you will usually find a partner within a few months.

In the meantime, practice with anyone who seems amenable, even if it is only for one time. Be careful, however, to be sure you are in a private environment. Because people's dreams often expose more than the novice dream teller would ever expect, your dreamer may suddenly feel embarrassed and even tricked. Learn how to retreat before the dreamer reveals more than she might really want to reveal. To do this you might have to say something like "The next question I would ask at this point may lead us into very personal material. Perhaps I could tell you my question, and you could ask it of yourself, then continue the interview on your own." In this way, you will forewarn the dreamer, who can then decide whether or not to continue the interview.

I dare not end this section without reminding you one more

time that as a dream interviewer, you must not tell your partner what her dream means. Your job is to ask questions and help the *dreamer* discover the meaning. Only as a last resort, after you have completed all the steps of the interview, might you sometimes ask the dreamer if she would be interested in hearing your hypotheses about what the dream might possibly mean. Your hypotheses are then based on all the information from the interview and are to be offered as an aid in the dreamer's own exploration, which is momentarily blocked. Do not push your ideas if the dreamer rejects them. As Montague Ullman and Nan Zimmerman say, the dreamer always has final authority over her own dream and an interviewer must always respect that authority.[2]

2. *Contract with your partner that you will begin with weekly practices for at least one month; after that contract for six months or a year, if you both agree.* If you can schedule your practice sessions for the same time every week, you will find that you are most likely to remain faithful to your contract. Together, you may want to schedule monthly sessions with a dream specialist, who can observe your interview techniques and coach you. Or you could each go to a specialist on your own, and compare tape recordings of your sessions for new ideas. Seeing a specialist is not necessary, but will help improve your skills and keep your enthusiasm up, especially in the early phases of your study.

3. *Tape-record and periodically transcribe your interviews, then examine them for a review of the dream and for a critique of the interviewer's technique.* In your first sessions, you and your partner may want to use the list of cue-card questions in Chapter 3, which includes the basic interview questions. This will help you get started with a manageable number of questions. If you transcribe the recorded session, you will get even more out of it, both in understanding the dream and developing your interview technique. I personally learn most about a dream of one of my dreamers and about my technique if I review a transcript of the interview. It is fascinating to go over every word we both said. Sometimes I find important points I overlooked in the session, statements from the dreamer that I should have followed up on, times when my questions were much more leading than I had realized, times when I came up with fabulous questions, and times when I was barking up the wrong tree and did not pick up on the dreamer's signals that could have let me know it sooner. Reviewing and critiquing transcripts of work as dreamer or interviewer are important parts of the training program for advanced and diploma students at our dream center. They are powerful and extremely satisfying methods of improving your dream skills.

4. *Schedule monthly and biannual reviews of your dream journals and compare notes.* Conducting your reviews at the same time will give you motivation and encouragement. It will also inform both the dreamer and her interviewer about important patterns in the dreams and about images and issues that are consistently difficult to understand.

5. *Ask your partner if there is anything she would like you to change about the way you work with her dreams.* You could do this at each dream session in your first sessions and then, once you know each other and the method better, you could ask this at each review.

6. *Consider having more than one dream partner.* Because different dreamers/interviewers have different strengths and weaknesses in technique as well as various defensive maneuvers that you will probably use yourself at various times, the more dreamers you work with, the more likely you are to become aware of a broad spectrum of dreamer and interviewer styles. We encourage all the advanced students at our dream center to practice with as great a variety of dreamers as possible. The students immediately appreciate how this sharpens their skills, as well as their awareness of their own behaviors as dreamers when they are interviewed.

STUDYING IN A DREAM GROUP

Joining a dream group or forming your own will vastly enhance your dream skills. By watching other people interview dreamers, you will quickly learn what tone of voice, which questions, and which strategies work best in different situations. If your group is led by an experienced professional who acts as a coach, you will benefit not only from your own interviews but also from observing how the coach corrects and encourages other interviewers. You will see how various dreamers deny and evade certain issues and how they struggle to get beyond their impasses. You will be heartened to see how members of the group make important strides in their lives as they review and practice the insights gained from their dreams. By working in a group, you will come to know your fellow dreamers in a rather intimate and trusting way that is very special and highly valued by group members I have known. While joining a group led by a professional dream interviewer is the most efficient way to get started, it is not necessary to employ the services of a professional, and you may prefer to start your own group.

FORMING A DREAM STUDY GROUP

Recruiting motivated dreamers who can all meet at the same time once a week is not easy. But if you spread the word among your friends and among classmates at lectures and in classes on dreaming, you may be able to find four to seven people who would make up a good group. In choosing group members, consider the same things you would in choosing a dream partner and make explicit the vital need for complete confidentiality within the group. I would discourage you from including members who are depressed or for some other reason need psychotherapy. These are instructional, not therapeutic groups, and unless you are a therapist, you will do much better working with people who do not suffer from psychological disorders.

Having led dream study groups for seventeen years, I have developed a format that seems to work well and may give you a model to use and modify to meet your needs. Here are the main steps I follow:

1. *Make a verbal contract with four to seven people regarding the nature and the minimum duration of the group.* I have found that a group will not survive if the dreamers do not commit at the time of joining to attend regularly for at least eight weeks. Most members stay in our groups for one or two years, and new members are admitted when a place becomes vacant. Each group should decide in advance if it wants to make any rules regarding attendance. The trick is to leave members free enough to miss a session when they have a good reason, but to have an attendance that is regular enough to maintain the continuity and cohesiveness of the group. Our groups allow unlimited absences for vacations and for work-related functions and travel. We also accept two "frivolous," or emergency, absences a year. You may be comfortable with a different arrangement, and experimentation will guide you in determining your group's structure.

If you are not a professional, you may not want to charge a fee for your services, because you may be acting more as a host than a teacher. However, I have received letters from people all around the country who have said that charging a nominal fee of five dollars a session has worked wonders in providing structure and motivation for members to attend regularly. This money can be used for refreshments, to buy books, or hire a lecturer or coach for one or more sessions. Some groups have used the money to join the Association for the Study of

Dreams, which publishes a newsletter and has annual conferences for amateurs and professionals.

2. *Outline the group procedures at the first session*. Our groups usually meet weekly for one and a half to two hours. At the beginning of each session, we designate the person who will present a dream the following week, as well as a back-up dreamer, who will be prepared to work with her dream if the scheduled dreamer is unable to attend. These two dreamers bring photocopies of one or two dreams for each member. The dreams can be copied right from a scribbled journal or they can be typed. If the dreamer can, she writes or types the dream on the page, leaving large margins on all sides so the interviewers can jot down her descriptions and bridges during the interview. This allows the interviewers to be more careful and accurate in their recapitulations and summaries.

Dreamers are invited to record the sessions in which they work on their dreams. In some cases the group also invites the other members to tape the sessions so they can review their interview techniques. We encourage group members to practice with each other or with another dream partner during the week over the telephone.

Beginning and ending the sessions on time is usually appreciated by the majority of the group, and members who are habitually late are usually told to plan to arrive fifteen minutes early. One late dreamer can hold up the whole group, even if it starts without her. The late member inevitably has difficulty following the proceedings and must ask to be caught up on the interview before she can become an active interviewer herself.

It is helpful for dreamers to have read this book and/or *Living Your Dreams* by the end of the first month of being in the group. This provides each member with a basic introduction to our approach and avoids the need to give introductory lectures to new members who enter an ongoing group. The group may then decide to read certain chapters from either book each week and to spend five or ten minutes in the group discussing the material. In our monthly workshops, which last two and a half hours, we focus on a particular element (settings, people, objects, etc.) or a particular strategy (corralling, schmoozing, etc.) in our discussions and interviews. If you decide to have longer meetings like this on a monthly basis, you might want to decide on relevant reading in advance.

3. *Decide on your group's format.* Here is the format I use in my practice:

◘ We open the session with a brief summary from the last week's dreamer's reflections on her dream. She tells us not only what she did with the dream, but what she avoided doing and how she felt about it. She also tells us if she has any pointers for us regarding questions we did or did not ask or regarding styles she especially liked or with which she felt uncomfortable while she was being interviewed or listening to a recording of the session.

◘ We then ask if anyone else has a comment on the last week's session or on a dream she has worked on with the group in the past.

◘ Next, the dreamer for the present session passes out copies of her dream and is invited by one of the members to tell the dream with feeling. The group may or may not diagram and outline the dream.

◘ Each member takes a turn at interviewing the dreamer for a section of the dream, while I coach the interviewer, suggesting strategies and questions when needed (we shall discuss the role of the group leader below). As the members of the group gain experience and become accustomed to each other's styles, one interviewer may share a turn with another or two or more interviewers may work in tandem with the dreamer. This dual interviewing can confuse both the dreamer and the original interviewer, however, and should be practiced with care.

☐ In the last five or ten minutes of the session, the dreamer or an interviewer summarizes the interview and the group elicits the dreamer's reaction to the summary. When working with novice dreamers and/or novice interviewers and/or long dreams, we may not get to the end of the dream. The dreamer and the group then need to decide whether to omit the summary or not. Does the dreamer understand the dream as she proceeds through the interview and will she be able to conduct her own summary or will she leave the session frustrated and confused if she does not summarize the work she has done so far? This can be difficult to determine, and the only comfort I can offer is that in time you will all be able to work through dreams more quickly as you refine your skills.

☐ At the end of the meeting, the interviewers offer their notes to the dreamer who can use them in her review. Jane Cunningham, a therapist and member of one of our groups, recently suggested this idea and it has been a big hit. While dreamers are working on their own dreams, they are too concrete in their thinking and too busy to take notes. In fact, note taking can be very disruptive to the interview process for the dreamer, who must be free to follow new thoughts and feelings as they pop up. Reviewing other members' notes is especially helpful if the dreamer has not tape-recorded the interview.

The Role of a Group Leader or Coach

For dreamers who have attained advanced skills in interviewing, the role of group leader rather than host may offer the other members of the group the most assistance. We train leaders to act as coaches who know the rules of the game and have enough experience to be able to make helpful suggestions. Coaches (as well as intermediate interviewers) can reassure novices that we all flounder and flail about when we first start interviewing, but that in time good questions come to mind without much effort. If a new interviewer suffers from performance anxiety, the leader might ask, "Is there anything I can do to help you feel more comfortable? Would you like me to suggest the first two questions?" The coach can model different aspects of interviewing including patience, humility, and the readiness to admit errors and confusion.

The leader helps the group follow the dream step-by-step and scene-by-scene while commenting, when necessary, on the dramatic structure of the plot. By reminding the group not to lose touch with the basic thrust of the dream story, the leader helps the group keep the dramatic context of each image in mind and not get lost in the details. The leader is also in a better position than the active interviewers to comment on the timing of the invitations to bridge and on the quality of the bridges made by the dreamer. The leader may be able to suggest that a given bridge may be worth exploring for a more general or more specific significance to the dreamer. The role of the leader is to comment on and demonstrate the interview process, not to give pronouncements on the meaning of a dream.

Group Strategies

Below are a few strategies we have used in groups. These strategies can be initiated by a leader or by any of the members:

1. *Signing*. To avoid unnecessary distraction, the leader or an observing interviewer can use a simple sign language to coach the active interviewer. To suggest that the interviewer follow up on a description by asking for a fuller one, use your hand as you do to motion someone or a pet to "come here." To suggest a bridge, make an arch with your forefinger. To suggest corralling the dreamer, point to the text of the dream or to your palm. To suggest that the interviewer encourage more unpacking of a bridge, pretend you are opening a rotary combination lock with one hand. To suggest ending the interview, make a circular "wind it up" motion with your forefinger.

2. *Humming.* At various points in an interview, group members may want to put their heads together and discuss their ideas and difficulties, and devise strategies. There may also be times when the coach would like to suggest specific questions and strategies or help an interviewer formulate less-intrusive questions that aim at proving or disproving her hypothesis. What the group needs at times like these is a time-out. Asking the dreamer to leave the room would be inconvenient and disruptive, so we ask the dreamer if she is willing to close her eyes, hold her ears, and hum a tune while we discuss how the interview is going. By having the dreamer hum during this period, our conceptual discussions do not distract the dreamer from her more concrete focus on the dream experience. The dreamer is not burdened by hearing the interviewers' hypotheses, and has a moment to rest and reflect. In fact, when we tap the dreamer to bring her back into the group, we make it a practice to ask the dreamer if she has had any ideas or associations while humming. Frequently, the dreamer has benefited by the repose and come up with helpful connections. Now and then, the tune the dreamer hummed has a title or lyrics that make a trenchant comment on the dream.

Obviously, the dreamer should hum only if she is comfortable doing so. We tell her that we need this time-out only to discuss strategy without distracting her, not to keep secrets from her. We will tell her everything we have said if she finds she is uncomfortable, as soon as she stops humming or at the end of the interview. If the dreamer is taping the session, we point out that she will hear it all on the tape. Because new dreamers take their turn sharing their dreams only after having heard a dream from each member of the group, by the time a new dreamer is asked to hum she usually agrees, because she has seen how well the process works and has sufficient confidence that we will not be "talking behind her back."

3. *Discussion observed by the dreamer.* When all of the group members are new and might hesitate to hum or when the material to be discussed would not be too distracting, strategy discussions among the interviewers while the dreamer listens in can be surprisingly fruitful. For example, as the dreamer listens to her interviewers ask each other how to help her give more specific or more feeling-full responses, the dreamer, now off the hot seat, may relax and be able and willing to help her interviewers by being more forthcoming. If the interviewers summarize their work so far and discuss possible directions for the next part of the interview, the dreamer may be able to recognize a direction that she feels would be most promising. You will probably find that this strategy is quite useful, and without making direct demands on the dreamer, it often encourages and inspires her to help her interviewers.

WHEN TO END AN INTERVIEW

A common problem for new dream workers is knowing when to stop. Overworking a dream kills its life and sometimes confuses, threatens, or alienates the dreamer. If your dreamer seems bored with the interview, she may be resisting exploration and her feelings may have gone underground. Or your style may be too ponderous. Are you bored? If your efforts to liven up the interview by injecting humor or challenge yield no greater interest, you could ask the dreamer if she feels bored and if she would like to continue the interview or end it for now.

The dreamer may be satisfied with the progress she has made with the dream before you finish the interview. She may say this in so many words, but more likely, she will communicate it by showing greater and greater resistance in the form of distracting and tangential comments. Ask your dreamer if she is satisfied and would like to stop here.

Sometimes dreamers can suffer from feeling or insight overload before you finish the dream. Check with a dreamer who seems to be dealing with material that is painful or difficult as you go along, and let her know that you can stop whenever she feels she has done enough work.

Groups can be unwittingly cruel when, at the end of an interview, each member wants to get her two cents in either by suggesting new areas of exploration or by hinting at alternative interpretations. This thinly veiled interpretive bombardment is often overwhelming as well as disorienting to the dreamer. After a good interview, a dreamer is often pleased with her work, but also fatigued by it. There comes a point when the dreamer simply cannot respond to new input. If an interviewer has ideas about the dream that she has not been able to explore via the interview, it is often best to save them for the next meeting, after the dreamer has had a chance to consider the work she has already completed.

GROUP DREAM REVIEWS

Regularly scheduled sessions for the discussion of journal reviews not only help members consolidate and appreciate their gains in dream-generated insights and in their dream skills but may also highlight important patterns. For example, dreamers notice their own and other members' repetitive dream images and motifs. New layers of meaning surface that relate to the developmental roots of problems presented in dreams. Dreamers find that reviews enrich their appreciation of the broader ramifications of a given problem or insight when they see how another member's dream has come to shed light on several areas of her life not originally recognized as related to the dream.

The group also uses reviews to see if, as a group or as individuals, they have been avoiding discussing certain types of dreams with each other and if they want to alter such patterns. Most groups simply note such omissions and leave it to the individual dreamers to bring in awkward dreams if and when they choose. Some groups discover that they freely discuss all sorts of dreams except ones the dreamers judge as ordinary or dull. In these cases, they often set aside one session to bring in such dreams and explore them briefly to see if they are as ordinary as they seem. Jung's statement that "one learns more from ordinary dreams"[3] is sometimes hard to believe, especially if one was introduced to dreams through a system that emphasized the exotic or the "spiritual." Recognizing the tremendous value in ordinary dreams can be an important liberation for dreamers who think their dreams are inadequate in comparison to the flashy dreams described in books and lectures.

During reviews, dreamers notice whether their dreams seem stuck and repetitive or if they are developing basic themes and introducing new ones. These changes—or lack of them—always parallel the dreamer's waking progress in dealing with the issues raised by the dreams. If a dreamer seems caught in a pattern that repeats itself with little or no change, this might be an indication that she needs help incorporating her insights, and may benefit from some psychotherapy. If the dreamer is able to integrate her discoveries and make necessary and desirable changes in her life, this will be reflected clearly in her dreams. The time it takes to see changes in waking and dream life varies enormously with each dreamer, but it almost always takes longer than the dreamer would like. Nevertheless, most dreamers will be able to see encouraging changes in their dreams and in their lives by the time of the first six month review, and this usually leads to a round of congratulations and well-deserved celebration.

NOTES

Introduction

1. J. DeKoninck, G. Lorrain, G. Christ, G. Proulx, D. Couloumbe, "Intensive Language Learning and Increases in Rapid Eye Movement Sleep," *International Journal of Psychophysiology* 8 (1989): 43–47.
2. A. Baillet, *La Vie de Monsieur Descartes* (Paris: Table Ronde, 1946).
3. John Milton, *Paradise Lost,* Book IX, Lines 20–47, and Book VII, Lines 27–39.
4. Leroy Loemaker, *Leibniz: Philosophical Papers and Letters,* Vol. II, (Chicago: University of Chicago Press, 1956), 1041.
5. Marsha Kinder, "The Adaptation of Cinematic Dreams," *Dreamworks,* (Vol. I, No. 1 (Spring 1980), pp. 57–58.
6. Having misplaced the source for this quote, I invite any reader who can help me locate it to write me c/o Bantam Books.
7. Friedrich August Kekulé, "Address to the German Chemical Society in Berlin, 1890," in G. Schultz, *Berichte der deutscher chemischer Gesellschaft* 23 (1890): 1265, 1306–1307. Translated by Jurgen Weber.
8. B. M. Kedrov, "On the Question of Scientific Creativity," *Voprosy Psikhologie* 3 (1957): 105–106.
9. W. B. Cannon, *The Way of an Investigator: A Scientist's Expe-*

riences in Medical Research, (New York: W. W. Norton, 1945), 61.

10. Ingmar Bergman, interview with Lewis Freedman on WNDT-TV, New York City, quoted in Lois Hendricks, *Discovering My Biblical Dream Heritage,* (San Jose, Calif.: Resource Publications, 1989), p. 120.

CHAPTER 1: Getting Ready

1. For a detailed discussion of various methods for improving dream recall in difficult cases, see Gayle Delaney, *Living Your Dreams,* rev. ed. (San Francisco: Harper & Row, 1988), 213–231.

2. Joseph Heller, *Something Happened* (New York: Alfred A. Knopf, 1974), quoted in *The Oxford Book of Dreams,* ed. Stephen Brook (Oxford: Oxford University Press, 1983), 172.

3. A. D. Sertillanges, *The Intellectual Life,* trans. Mary Ryan (Cork, Ireland: Mercier Press, 1962), 82–83.

4. W. B. Cannon, *The Way of an Investigator: A Scientist's Experiences in Medical Research* (New York: W. W. Norton, 1945), 58.

5. Gayle Delaney, "Putting Your Dreams to Work," *New Realities* 1 (1977): 22–26; G. Delaney, "A Proposed Dream Experiment: Phrase-Focusing Dream Incubation," *Sundance Community Dream Journal,* Vol. 1, No. 1 (1977): 71–83.

6. This method of incubation is the principle subject of the book by Gayle Delaney, *Living Your Dreams,* rev. ed. (San Francisco: Harper & Row, 1988).

CHAPTER 2: Unlocking the Secrets of Your Dreams

1. Ilona Marshall, a San Francisco Bay Area dream worker and former student, has drawn on her language-teaching skills to

devise an elaborate diagraming system, which indicates descriptive phrases, warnings, unpleasant images, significant concepts, positive messages, and brilliant ideas. You might like to develop your own system of markings.

2. Paul J. Stern, *In Praise of Madness* (New York: W. W. Norton, 1972), 43.

3. Thomas French and Erika Fromm, *Dream Interpretation: A New Approach* (New York: Basic Books, 1964), 28–36.

4. Louis Breger, Ian Hunter, and Ron Lane, *The Effect of Stress on Dreams* (New York: International Universities Press, Inc., 1971), 191.

5. For a discussion of this point, see John Beebe, *Contemporary Methods of Dream Interpretation* ed. Gayle Delaney, in press; C. G. Jung, *Dream Analysis,* (Princeton, N.J.: Princeton University Press, 1984); and C. G. Jung, *Modern Man in Search of a Soul* (New York: Harcourt, Brace & World, 1933).

6. See C. G. Jung, "General Aspects of Dream Psychology," in *Dreams* (Princeton, N.J.: Princeton University Press, 1974), 25–30, for his discussion of the necessity of interpretation from a twofold point of view, causality, and finality. Jung proposes that while one must try to understand the cause of a dream, one must also try to understand the sense of purpose inherent in the dream as in all psychological phenomena. He distinguishes finality from the concept of teleology by defining finality as "the immanent psychological striving for a goal" which might be as simple as the emotional reaction of anger over an insult that has the purpose of revenge.

7. Medard Boss, *"I Dreamt Last Night . . ."* (New York: Gardner Press, 1977), 171.

8. Erik H. Erikson, quoted in Richard Jones, *The New Psychology of Dreaming* (New York: Viking Press, 1974), 102.

9. Boss, *"I Dreamt Last Night . . ."* 168.

CHAPTER 3: Knowing What to Ask and When to Ask It

1. Earlier versions of the dream interviewer's cue card were published in the 1979, 1981, and 1988 editions of my book *Living Your Dreams* (San Francisco: Harper & Row) and in *Contemporary Methods of Dream Interpretation* (unpublished).

CHAPTER 4: Exploring the Dream Setting

1. C. G. Jung, *Dream Analysis* (Princeton, N.J.: Princeton University Press, 1984), 38.
2. Jung, *Dream Analysis,* 39.

CHAPTER 6: Animals in Dreams

1. C. G. Jung, *Dreams* (Princeton, N.J.: Princeton University Press, 1974), 264. This interpretation was made as part of Jung's interpretation of a series of dreams dreamt by a patient under the care of one of Jung's students. Jung admits to being in no position to "take up the context" (to gather the dreamer's associations) in these dreams. He says that this was not necessary because he was not working with an isolated dream but with a coherent series, which allowed his analysis to uncover the meaning thanks to his specialized knowledge, and to the opportunity to view the dreamer through many dreams from many angles. In my opinion, his failure to take up the context in these dreams and his reliance on his knowledge of symbolism as it had been used in various traditions led him to read into the dreams his own theories, much as Freud's reliance on symbol substitution led him to read into his patients' dreams the proof of his theories.
2. Jung's treatment of a student's dream of a bull is similar:

Jung does not ask the dreamer to establish the context, but does so himself before he interprets the dream. C. G. Jung, *Dream Analysis* (Princeton, N.J.: Princeton University Press, 1984), 35–38.

3. To insist that the dreamer wished to be caught by the threatening dangerous snake is to disregard the dramatic structure of the dream and to read into it an arbitrary interpretation. The dreamer clearly wants to escape this threat to her well-being. Her wish is to get either the snake or herself into Silas's bedroom.

4. We did not discuss this in the interview, but I wonder if getting the snake, instead of herself, into the bedroom would not suggest Rosalind's trying to slam the door on her fears related to her problems with her father. In the dream, she is paralyzed and unsure which she should do; in waking life, she resisted taking a close look at her relationship to her father and suffered paralyzing depressions.

5. Bertrand Russell, "Letter to Lady Ottoline Morrell, dictated on March 20, 1921," in Ronald Clark, *The Life of Bertrand Russell,* (New York: Alfred A. Knopf, 1976), 393.

CHAPTER 7: Objects in Dreams

1. For a discussion by Jung on the symbolism of the cross, see C. G. Jung, *Dream Analysis* (Princeton, N.J.: Princeton University Press, 1984), 340–366.

CHAPTER 8: Feelings in Dreams

1. That is, with the exception of dreams of inventions and concrete inventive ideas discussed in the introduction.

2. I disagree here with Jung, who believed that thinking types should not be encouraged to explore, identify, and bridge

to feelings in dreams. For example, in discussing one of his male patients, Jung states that he "always kept [this patient] away from emotion to let him see the facts." This is because Jung felt that such a "correct, so sincerely right," thinking type of male patient "must first do away with emotions and look at the images [in a dream] in a very calm objective way." C. G. Jung, *Dream Analysis* (Princeton, N.J.: Princeton University Press, 1984), 14.

3. Gayle Delaney, "Dreaming of Mr. Wrong," *New Realities* (Nov./Dec. 1988), 8–9.

CHAPTER 9: Action in Dreams

1. P. R. Nayak and J. M. Kettringham, "The Fine Art of Managing Creativity," the *New York Times,* Nov. 2, 1986, quoted in Richard Saul Wurman, *Information Anxiety* (New York: Doubleday Press, 1989), 191.

2. Personal communication, July 1987.

3. Robert Litman, "The Dream in the Suicidal Situations," in *The Dream in Clinical Practice,* ed. Joseph Natterson (New York: Jason Aronson, 1980), 283–299.

4. See Paul J. Stern *In Praise of Madness,* (New York: W. W. Norton, 1972); Medard Boss, *"I Dreamt Last Night . . ."* (New York: Gardner Press, 1977); and M. Boss, *Psychoanalysis and Daseinsanalysis* (New York: DaCapo Press, 1982).

5. See J. Allan Hobson and R. W. McCarley, "The Brain As a Dream State Generator: An Activation-Synthesis Hypothesis of the Dream Process," *American Journal of Psychiatry* 134 (1977): 1335–1348; and Frances Crick and Graeme Mitchison, "The Function of Dream Sleep," *Nature* 34 (1983): 111–114.

6. C. G. Jung, *Dream Analysis* (Princeton, N.J.: Princeton University Press, 1984), 21.

7. Jung, *Dream Analysis,* 46.

CHAPTER 10: Intermediate Strategies to
Improve Your
Interviewing Technique

1. C. G. Jung, *Dream Analysis* (Princeton, N.J.: Princeton University Press, 1984), 595.

2. S. Freud, *The Interpretation of Dreams* (New York: Avon Books, 1966), 377.

3. Freud, *Interpretation of Dreams*, 388.

4. Jung's habitual method of taking up the context usually consisted of inviting associations to the image and sometimes a few facts about the dreamer's waking situation. He felt that when the context offered by the dreamer was inadequate or disappointing, it was necessary for him to fill in the gaps with his specialized knowledge. See C. G. Jung, "The Structure and Dynamics of the Psyche," in *Dreams* (Princeton, N.J.: Princeton University Press, 1974), 76–79; and Jung, *Dream Analysis*, 216.

5. Boss compares Jung's approach to a dream of a serpent with his own phenomenological approach in Medard Boss, *"I Dreamt Last Night . . ."* (New York: Gardner Press, 1977), 162–174.

6. Thomas French and Erika Fromm, *Dream Interpretation: A New Approach* (New York: Basic Books, 1964), 119.

7. Compare Jung's treatment of the daughter in such a dream in Jung, *Dream Analysis*, 7–10.

8. Freud, *Interpretation of Dreams*, 486.

9. Jung, *Dream Analysis*, 48, 451. Jung writes that one must know what the dream is trying to compensate in order to make a good interpretation. I believe that the assumption that the dream is trying to compensate a waking attitude (which the analyst may or may not be able to perceive accurately) is likely to bias and perhaps distort the interpretation.

CHAPTER 11: Advanced Methods for Experienced Interviewers

1. C. G. Jung, "On the Nature of Dreams," in *Dreams* (Princeton, N.J.: Princeton University Press, 1974), 69.
2. Jung, "On the Nature of Dreams," 69.
3. C. G. Jung, "The Practical Use of Dream-Analysis," in *Dreams* (Princeton, N.J.: Princeton University Press, 1974), 93.
4. This comment was made by Bonime at a workshop he conducted for the Fifth Annual Conference of the Association for the Study of Dreams held at the University of California, Santa Cruz, June 1988. For a rich and insightful discussion of resistance in dreams in the context of a psychotherapeutic relationship, specifically in psychoanalysis, see Walter Bonime with Florence Bonime, *The Clinical Use of Dreams* (New York: Basic Books, 1962), 182–228.
5. C. G. Jung, *Dream Analysis* (Princeton, N.J.: Princeton University Press, 1984), 575.
6. S. Freud, *The Interpretation of Dreams* (New York: Avon Books, 1966), 583.
7. Jung, "On the Nature of Dreams," 80–81.
8. Thomas French and Erika Fromm, *Dream Interpretation: A New Approach* (New York: Basic Books, 1964), 22–23.
9. French and Fromm, *Dream Interpretation*, 23.
10. French and Fromm, *Dream Interpretation*, 23.
11. Milton Kramer and Thomas Roth, "Dream Translation," *Israel Annals of Psychiatry* 15 (1977): 336–351.
12. Kramer and Roth, "Dream Translation."

CHAPTER 12: Nightmares, Recurring Dreams, and Common Dream Themes

1. For fascinating discussions of nightmares, bad dreams, and night terrors, see Ernest Jones, *On the Nightmare* (New

York: Liveright Publishing, 1971); John E. Mack, *Night-mares and Human Conflict* (Boston: Houghton Mifflin Co., 1974); and Ernest Hartmann, *The Nightmare* (New York: Basic Books, 1984).

2. For a full description of the stages of sleep see J. Allan Hobson, *Sleep* (New York: W. H. Freeman, 1989).

3. John Taub, Milton Kramer, Dona Arand, and Gerard A. Jacobs, "Nightmare Dreams and Nightmare Confabulations," *Comprehensive Psychiatry* 19 (May/June 1978): 285–291.

4. Taub et al., "Nightmare Dreams," 285.

5. Hartmann, *The Nightmare,* 232.

6. Taub et al., "Nightmare Dreams," 286. The reference is to studies conducted by C. Fisher, J. Byrne, A. Edwards, et al.: "A Psychophysiological Study of Nightmares," *Journal of the American Psychoanalytic Association* 18 (1970): 747–782; and C. Fisher, E. Kahn, A. Edwards, et al.: "A Psychophysiological Study of Nightmares and Night Terrors: III. Mental Content of Stage 4 Night Terrors," *Journal of Nervous Mental Disorders* 158 (1974): 174–188.

7. Hartmann, *The Nightmare,* 233.

8. Hartmann, *The Nightmare,* 233.

9. Hartmann, *The Nightmare,* 233–234.

10. Milton Kramer, "The Psychobiology of Mental Illness: Changes in the Physiological and Psychological Aspects of Sleep," in *Dream Images: A Call to Mental Arms,* eds. Jayne Gackenbach and Anees Sheikh, in press. See also M. Kramer, L. Schoen, L. Kinney, "The Dream Experience in Dream-Disturbed Vietnam Veterans," in *Post Traumatic Stress Disorders: Psychological and Biological Sequelae* (Washington, D.C.: American Psychiatric Press, 1984), 81–95; M. Kramer, L. Schoen, and L. Kinney, "Nightmares in Vietnam Veterans," *Journal of the American Academy of Psychoanalysis* 15 (1987): 67–81; M. Kramer and L. Kinney, "Sleep Patterns in Trauma Victims with Disturbed Dreaming, *Psy-*

chiatric Journal of the University of Ottawa 13 (1988): 12–16; and M. Kramer, L. Kinney, and M. Scharf, "Sleep in Delayed Stress Victims," *Sleep Research* 11 (1982): 113.

11. Kramer, "The Psychobiology of Mental Illness," 4.

12. Hartmann, *The Nightmare,* 187.

13. For a discussion of the use of supportive therapy and of tricyclic antidepressant medication in treating individuals with this disorder, see James K. Boehnlein, J. David Kinzie, Rath Ben, and Jenelle Fleck, "One-Year Follow-Up Study of Posttraumatic Stress Disorder among Survivors of Cambodian Concentration Camps," *American Journal of Psychiatry* 142 (1985): 956–959.

14. Hartmann, *The Nightmare,* 243–244.

15. Lawrence Schoen, Milton Kramer, and Lois Kinney, "Arousal Patterns in NREM Dream-Disturbed Veterans," in *Sleep Research,* Vol. 12, ed. M. Chase, W. Webb, and R. Wilder-Jones (Los Angeles: University of California, 1983), 315. Also cited in Hartmann, *The Nightmare,* 187.

16. Ernest Hartmann, Diane Russ, Molly Oldfield, Ilana Sivan, and Steven Cooper, "Who Has Nightmares?" *Archives of General Psychiatry* 44 (1987): 49–56.

17. In a study of less frequent nightmare sufferers (having at least twelve nightmares per year), who, unlike Hartmann's subjects also suffered from other sleep disorders, Kales et al. found the same chronic schizoid pattern of adjustment, but described the subjects as distrustful, whereas Hartmann found his subjects trusting almost to a fault. See Anthony Kales, Constantin R. Soldatos, Alex B. Caldwell, Dennis S. Charney, Joyce D. Kales, David Markel, and Roger Cadieux, "Nightmares: Clinical Characteristics and Personality Patterns," *American Journal of Psychiatry* 137 (1980): 1197–1201.

18. Hartmann, *The Nightmare,* 168.

19. Hartmann et al., "Who Has Nightmares?" 56.

20. Hartmann, *The Nightmare*, 222.

21. Raymond de Becker, *The Understanding of Dreams* (New York: Bell Publishing Co., 1978), 184.

22. Norman MacKenzie, *Dreams and Dreaming* (New York: Vanguard Press, 1965), 28.

23. S. Lorand, "Dream Interpretation in the Talmud," *The International Journal of Psycho-Analysis* 38 (1957): 95.

24. Artemidorus, *Oneirocritica* (Park Ridge, N.J.: Noyes Press, 1975), 1.31.

25. Artemidorus, *Oneirocritica*, 1.32.

26. Freud, *Interpretation of Dreams*, 307.

27. Freud, *Interpretation of Dreams*, 423.

28. Medard Boss, *Psychoanalysis and Daseinsanalysis* (New York: Da Capo Press, 1982), 267.

29. Boss, *Psychoanalysis*, 267.

30. Medard Boss, *"I Dreamt Last Night . . ."* (New York: Gardner Press, 1977), 131.

31. Boss, *Psychoanalysis*, 267.

32. For more information on lucid dreaming, see G. Delaney, *Living Your Dreams* (San Francisco: Harper & Row, 1988), 166–181.

CHAPTER 13: Acting on Your Insight

1. C. G. Jung, *Dream Analysis* (Princeton, N.J.: Princeton University Press, 1984), 651.

2. Loma Flowers, "The Morning After: A Pragmatist's Approach to Dreams," *Psychiatry Journal of the University of Ottawa* 13 (1988): 66–71.

3. Flowers, "The Morning After," 68.

4. Compare Jung's description of dreams as compensatory, complementary, and parallel in C. G. Jung, "On the Nature of Dreams," in *Dreams* (Princeton, N.J.: Princeton Univer-

sity Press, 1974), 73–76; and C. G. Jung "Individual Dream Symbolism in Relation to Alchemy," in *Dreams* (Princeton, N.J.: Princeton University Press, 1974), 118.

CHAPTER 14: Developing Dream Skills

1. Jung discusses the issue of dreams being "always just ahead of ourselves" in the context of his typology and self-analysis of dreams in C. G. Jung, *Dream Analysis* (Princeton, N.J.: Princeton University Press, 1984), 252–253.
2. Montague Ullman and Nan Zimmerman, *Working with Dreams,* (New York: Delacorte Press, 1979).
3. Jung, *Dream Analysis,* 4.

RESOURCES

Associations

THE ASSOCIATION FOR THE STUDY OF DREAMS/ (ASD). The first international organization of its kind, ASD provides a forum for the interdisciplinary study of sleep and dreams. Membership is open to all and includes a subscription to a quarterly newsletter, and soon, a journal; access to a growing network of people in the field; and discount membership fees to yearly five-day conferences. Dr. Loma K. Flowers was the first chairman of the board, and Dr. Gayle Delaney is the founding president of the association. For more information, write ASD, P.O. Box 3121, Falls Church, VA 22043, or call (703) 242-8888.

Centers for Dream Study and Training

THE DELANEY & FLOWERS CENTER FOR THE STUDY OF DREAMS. Dedicated to teaching people to become self-sufficient in a straightforward approach to understanding dreams and to using them for practical problem solving. The center offers workshops for beginners, classes for intermediate-level students, and a diploma program for advanced students and professionals. Intensive study programs are available for

out-of-state and foreign students. Directed by Dr. Gayle Delaney, and Dr. Loma K. Flowers, the center also offers individual
and group psychotherapy as well as consultations and training
programs for organizations. For more information write the
center at 337 Spruce Street, San Francisco, CA 94118, or call
(415) 587-3424.

THE CENTER FOR EXISTENTIAL STUDIES. Director Dr. Erik
Craig, president of the Association for the Study of Dreams,
offers psychotherapy and dream work of the highest quality in
his Worcester and Cambridge offices. For more information
write Dr. Craig at 57 Cedar Street, Worcester, MA 01609, or
call (508) 791-0755.

THE SANTA FE CENTER FOR THE STUDY OF DREAMS. Top
quality seminars on dream work for amateurs and professionals
led by Dr. Erik Craig. Lecture series with guest speakers are also
offered. Write 1442 D St. Francis Drive, Santa Fe, NM 87505,
or call (505) 982-1211.

THE C. G. JUNG INSTITUTES. Located in several major cities
in the United States and Europe, these organizations teach the
Jungian approach to dreams to professionals and offer lectures
for the general public.

THE PSYCHOANALYTIC INSTITUTES. These institutes, located in several major cities in the United States and Europe,
train professionals in Freudian dream work and therapy. They
occasionally offer lectures for the public.

CLUB DU SOMMEIL ET DU RÊVE. Pierre Fluchaire, the
founder of this club, was originally an engineer trained at the
prestigious Ecole Centrale in Paris. When he discovered how
much one could learn from dreams, he began to explore their
practical applications. Fluchaire has organized conferences,
used the media, and offered classes to teach others about dreaming. He consults organizations on efficient uses of sleep and

dreams. For more information write 3 Rue Anatole de la Forge, 75011 Paris, France, or call (1) 380-11-68.

TATA MANAGEMENT TRAINING CENTRE. Francis Menezes is a management consultant in India who teaches managers in government and business how to include dream work as a practical tool for achieving results. For information on this residential center write 1 Mangaldas Road, Pune—411 011, India.

THE CALIFORNIA INSTITUTE OF INTEGRAL STUDIES (CIIS). An accredited graduate school offering degrees in psychology, organizational development, and Asian studies, CIIS emphasizes an integration of Eastern and Western perspectives in its programs. Students can elect to do a good deal of serious dream work with various professors, including Dr. Delaney. For more information write 765 Ashbury Street, San Francisco, CA 94117.

THE SAYBROOK INSTITUTE. Founded and directed by Dr. Stanley Krippner, a master dream researcher and author, Saybrook is an accredited graduate school that offers students many opportunities to study dreams. For more information write 1772 Vallejo Street, San Francisco, CA 94123.

THE PACIFIC NORTHWEST CENTER FOR DREAM STUDIES. Directed by Ken Kimmel, the center offers dream work classes and psychotherapy using Jungian, Gestalt, and Delaney methods as well as ceremonial art forms. For more information write 219 First Avenue S, Suite 405, Seattle, WA 98104, or call (206) 447-1895.

Various schools and universities teach courses on dreaming from time to time. Call the schools near you for information, and if such courses are not offered, request that they offer one or at least a series of lectures on the subject. A growing number of people are offering dream workshops around the country. I have listed only those I know well enough to have confidence in their quality.

Choosing a Dream Analyst

In judging the competence, expertise, and style of dream spe-
cialists in your area, I would suggest you ask them the following questions:

1. What education and training in dream work have
   you had?
2. What methods do you use?
3. What is your theoretical background in dream
   work?
4. How long have you been teaching dream work, and
   how many people have you worked with in group
   and individual settings?
5. Over what span of time do you work with the same
   client on average?

The answers to these queries should give enough information to identify serious practitioners. For example, a person
who only reads, writes, and gives lectures on dreams is not
likely to have the opportunity to see how well a given theory or
method works out in practice. A person who only sees dreamers for brief periods of time will have no way to know how well
his methods work over time or if they are effective in the long
run. You may well prefer to study with a novice, but at least this
way you will know what you are getting. A novice who is open
about his experience can be a good teacher, but a novice who
pretends to be an expert never is.

Sleep Disorders Centers

If you suffer from severe insomnia, night terrors, or other sleeping problems, you might consult a sleep clinic. For the location

of a clinic near you, contact the American Sleep Disorders Association, 604 Second Street SW, Rochester, MN 55902, or call (507) 287-6606.

Videotapes and Audiotapes

BRING ME A DREAM. A sixty-minute videotape produced at The Christian Broadcast Network in which Dr. Gayle Delaney and Dr. Loma Flowers discuss and demonstrate the interpretation and targeting of dreams for specific problem solving. For information about this and other audiotapes, write the Delaney & Flowers Center for the Study of Dreams at the address given on page 424.

BEAUTIFUL DREAMERS. A thirty-minute WGBH-TV (PBS), Boston, videotape of show aired in 1987 and 1988 on "Body Watch," which surveys the field of dreams. It includes appearances by Dr. Gayle Delaney and Dr. Loma Flowers, Ramon Greenberg, Ernest Hartmann, Stephen La Berge, and others. For more information write WGBH-TV, 125 Western Avenue, Boston, MA 02134.

CONTROLLING YOUR DREAMS. In this audiotape, Dr. Stephen La Berge describes his work with and method for inducing lucid dreams. For more information write Audio Renaissance Tapes, 9110 Sunset Boulevard, Suite 240, Los Angeles, CA 90069.

Periodicals

THE NEWSLETTER OF THE ASSOCIATION FOR THE STUDY OF DREAMS. An informative quarterly gathering of essays and news related to the field of dreams and to the activities of the association. For information write ASD at the address given on page 423.

THE LUCIDITY LETTER. Edited by Dr. Jayne Gackenbach, the letter focuses exclusively on research and developments in lucid dreaming. For information, write *The Lucidity Letter,* 8703 109th Street, Edmonton, Al., Canada T6G 2L5.

THE DREAM NETWORK BULLETIN. Edited by Linda Magallon, this grass-roots bulletin publishes dream accounts from subscribers along with essays by amateur and professional dream workers. For more information write Linda Magallon, Harvest Meadow Court, San Jose, CA 95136.

"EXPLORING YOUR DREAMS." A regular column on various dream-related issues written by Dr. Gayle Delaney, published in *New Realities* magazine. Back issues and subscriptions available from: Heldref Publications, 4000 Albemarle Street NW, Washington, D.C. 20016.

Books

Following are a few of my favorite books on dreams. I don't agree with the theory and method described in some, but I have learned useful things from each one. Because I wanted this to be a favorites list—and not too long a one at that—I have not included a number of fine books. But I trust that as you begin reading from this list, you will find your way to other books that address your interests.

AEPPLI, ERNEST. *Les rêves et leur interprétation.* Paris: Petite Bibliothèque Payot, 1978. An unusual and interesting Jungian treatment of the subject, with attention to common dream images.

ARKIN, A., J. ANTROBUS AND S. ELLMAN, EDS. *The Mind in Sleep: Psychology and Psychophysiology.* Hillsdale, N.J.: Lawrence Erlboum Associates, 1978. A fascinating compilation of laboratory research on such subjects as dream recall, REM deprivation, talking in sleep, and night terrors.

ARTEMIDORUS. *The Interpretation of Dreams. Oneirocritica.* Translation and commentary by Robert J. White. Park Ridge, N.J.: Noyes Press, 1975. Available from Ballantrae Reprint, 10 George Street N, Brampton, Ont., Canada L6X 1R2. The only dream book to survive from antiquity, this is a precious document summarizing Greco-Roman dream theory and practice from the late fifth century B.C. to about A.D. 200. Underneath the surface level of the writings, you will find surprisingly sophisticated material on the metaphorical language of dreams.

BONIME, WALTER, WITH FLORENCE BONIME. *The Clinical Use of Dreams.* New York: Da Capo Press, 1982. A sensitive, highly experienced psychoanalyst, Bonime includes important chapters on feeling, resistance, and anxiety in dreams.

BOSS, MEDARD. *"I Dreamt Last Night . . ."* Translated by S. Conway. New York: Gardner Press, 1977. A basic book on the existential-phenomenological approach to dreams. Quite different from the Jungian, Freudian, or Adlerian approaches in that Boss shows the reader how to concentrate on the dreamer's experience of the dream with little reference to a particular theoretical map of the human psyche.

BOSS, MEDARD. *Psychoanalysis and Daseinsanalysis.* Translated by Ludwig B. Lefebre. New York: Da Capo Press, 1982. Dr. Boss, a psychiatrist who studied with Freud and Jung and who left both to found his own phenomenological school, describes his work and compares it to that of his former teachers. Difficult reading, but well worth the effort.

BREGER, LOUIS, IAN HUNTER, AND RON W. LANE. *The Ef-*

fect of Stress on Dreams. New York: International University Press, 1971. Working on an information-processing model of dreaming, the authors describe two elegant studies that explore how dreams are affected by and how they affect our experience of stress.

BRO, HARMON. *Edgar Cayce on Dreams*. New York: Paperback Library, 1968. A good introduction to Cayce's surprisingly sophisticated and varied responses to his clients' dreams.

BROOK, STEPHEN. *The Oxford Book of Dreams*. Oxford, UK: Oxford University Press, 1983. A collection of comments made by well-known people on the subject of dreams.

BROSSARD, ROBERT. *Psychologie du rêve*. Paris: Bibliothèque Payot, 1972. An interesting, traditional Jungian treatment.

CAILLOIS, ROGERS, ED. *The Dream Adventure*. New York: The Orion Press, 1963. A fascinating anthology of dreams in literature including fifteen selections from ancient China.

CARTWRIGHT, ROSALIND. *Night Life*. Englewood Cliffs, N.J.: Prentice-Hall Press, 1977.

CARTWRIGHT, ROSALIND. *A Primer on Sleep and Dreaming*. Reading, Mass.: Addison-Wesley Publishing, 1978.

CARTWRIGHT, ROSALIND. "Affect and Dream Work from an Information Processing Point of View." *The Journal of Mind and Behavior* 7 (1986): 281–298, 411–428.

CRAIG, P. ERIK. "Dreaming, Reality, and Allusion: An Existential-Phenomenological Inquiry." In *Advances in Qualitative Psychology: Themes and Variations,* edited by F. J. van Zuren. Berwin, Pa.: Swets North America, 1987. A thought-provoking piece and a good introduction to this way of seeing things.

CRAIG, P. ERIK. "The Realness of Dreams." In *Dreams Are*

Wiser Than Men, edited by Richard Russ. Berkeley: North Atlantic Books, 1987. A crucial reminder not to forget the realness and the power of the dream in one's rush to interpret it.

CRAIG, P. ERIK, ED. *Psychotherapy for Freedom. The Humanistic Psychologist* Vol. 16, No. 1 (Spring 1988). This special double issue of unusual and informative anthology on Daseinsanalysis is one of Craig's major efforts to make the important contributions of existential-phenomenological psychotherapy more available to an American audience. The book includes interviews with Boss, Condrau, and Kastrinidis among others, as well as valuable commentary on the interviews and on Heidegger by Craig.

DE BECKER, RAYMOND. *The Understanding of Dreams and Their Influence on the History of Man.* New York: Bell Publishing Co., 1978. A great pleasure to read and a fine overview of the subject.

DELANEY, GAYLE. *Living Your Dreams* (rev. ed.). San Francisco: Harper & Row, 1988. A detailed presentation of dream incubation and its applications for problem solving in various personal and professional life situations.

DELANEY, GAYLE, AND LOMA K. FLOWERS. *The Delaney and Flowers Dream Workbook.* In preparation. A workbook for interactive study and practice of the methods of incubation, interpretation, application, and teaching developed at the Delaney and Flowers Dream Center.

DE SAINT-DENYS, HERVEY. *Dreams and How to Guide Them.* Edited by Morton Schatzman. London: Duckworth, 1982. Originally published in 1876, this is the first written account of a Western individual's experiments in lucid dreaming.

DESCAMPS, M. A. *La maîtrise des rêves.* Paris: Ed. Universitaires, 1983.

DEVEREUX, GEORGE. *Reality and Dream. Psychotherapy of a Plains Indian.* New York: University Press, 1969. A complex psychoanalytic and anthropological study that also employs psychological testing.

DOMHOFF, WILLIAM. *The Mystique of Dreams: A Search for Utopia Through Senoi Dream Theory.* Berkeley: University of California Press, 1985. At last someone (Domhoff) has carefully researched and published an exposé on the so-called Senoi dream work described by Kilton Stewart and many later writers, who failed to check their sources. Domhoff's discussion of just why so many were ready to believe this myth, whose anthropological and psychological assertions are so naive, is applicable to several schools of psychological and religious beliefs as well.

DUNLOP, CHARLES E. M. *Philosophical Essays on Dreaming.* Ithaca, N.Y.: Cornell University Press, 1977. An interesting exploration of the connections between dreams and issues in epistemology, the philosophy of language, and the philosophy of science.

ELLENBERGER, HENRI. *The Discovery of the Unconscious.* New York, Basic Books, Inc., 1970. An absolutely fascinating history of how we came to psychodynamic understanding of human beings. This story is well placed in the context of the cultural and scientific developments between 1775 and the twentieth century. Lavishly written and generously documented.

ÉTÉVENON, PIERRE. *Du rêve à l'éveil.* Paris: Albin Michel, 1987. A fine description of the physiology of sleep, including sections on sleepwalking, narcolepsy, and night terrors.

ÉTÉVENON, PIERRE. *Les aveugles éblouis.* Paris: Albin Michel, 1984. A specialist in the physiology of sleep, Étévenon discusses altered states of consciousness in sleep and dreams with sections on Indian yogi methods of modifying consciousness.

EVANS, CHRISTOPHER. *Landscapes of the Night: How and Why We Dream*. New York: Viking Press, 1983. Evans compares the dreaming brain to a computer that is off-line while processing the data of the preceding day.

FARADAY, ANN. *The Dream Game*. New York: Harper & Row, 1974. A nondogmatic, eclectic, and useful book with helpful descriptions of certain Gestalt techniques and some very welcome common sense.

FLUCHAIRE, PIERRE. *Bien dormir pour mieux vivre*. Paris: Éditions Dangles, 1980. A helpful book on the physiology and the psychology of getting a good night's sleep.

FLUCHAIRE, PIERRE. *La révolution du rêve*. Paris: Éditions Dangles, 1985. An engineer turned pioneer in the practical applications of dreams, Fluchaire's exuberant and straightforward treatment of the subject deals with a great variety of important questions. The book inspires readers to put their dreams to work.

FOSSHAGE, JAMES, AND CLEMENS LOEW. *Dream Interpretation. A Comparative Study*, (rev. ed.). New York: PMA Publishing Corp., 1987. Six different approaches to the same series of dreams are demonstrated.

FOULKES, DAVID. *Children's Dreams. Longitudinal Studies*. New York: John Wiley & Sons, 1982. The result of a five-year study of children aged three to fifteen years. This book describes dreaming as a cognitive activity that develops in direct relation to the development of waking cognitive skills.

FRENCH, THOMAS, AND ERIKA FROMM. *Dream Interpretation: A New Approach*. New York: Basic Books, 1964. A classic. The authors break psychoanalytic doctrine and emphasize method over theory.

FREUD, SIGMUND. *The Interpretation of Dreams*. Translated by J. Strachey. New York: Avon Books, 1966. Almost everyone who writes about dreams refers to this book with admiration or criticism. Written in 1900, it has influenced all dream work since. Freud wrote, "It contains the most valuable of all the discoveries it has been my good fortune to make."

FREUD, SIGMUND. *Three Case Histories*. New York: Collier Books, 1977.

GACKENBACH, JAYNE, AND STEPHEN LA BERGE. *Conscious Mind, Sleeping Brain: Perspectives on Lucid Dreaming*. New York: Plenum, 1988.

GENDLIN, G. *Let Your Body Interpret Your Dreams*. Wilmette, Ill.: Chiron, 1986. While the title may overstate the possibilities, focusing on your body's responses to dreams can be quite helpful.

GLOBUS, GORON. *Dream Life, Wake Life: The Human Condition through Dreams*. Albany: State University of New York Press, 1987. A well-integrated philosophical treatment of dream theory combining psychoanalytic, Jungian, and especially Bossian existential perspectives, among others. Globus invites the reader to seek knowledge of the human condition through a study of dreaming.

GREEN, CELIA. *Lucid Dreams*. London: Hamilton, 1968. An interesting collection of many people's experiences of lucid dreaming.

GRINSTEIN, ALEXANDER. *Freud's Rules of Dream Interpretation*. New York: International Universities Press, 1983. A clear, traditional guide to psychoanalytic dream work.

HADFIELD, J. A. *Dreams and Nightmares*. Baltimore: Penguin

Books, 1966. A good, brief overview of dreams even though the biology section is dated.

HARTMANN, ERNEST. *The Nightmare*. New York: Basic Books, 1984. A creative psychoanalyst, sleep researcher, and past president of the Association for the Study of Dreams, Hartmann reports on his research into those who suffer frequent nightmares. His description of these people as having thin psychological boundaries and tendencies toward creativity or madness has greatly advanced the understanding of this phenomenon.

HOBSON, J. ALLAN. *The Dreaming Brain*. New York: Basic Books, 1988. The fullest explanation of Hobson's activation-synthesis hypothesis, containing a fascinating exploration of the physiology of the sleeping brain.

HOBSON, J. ALLAN. *Sleep*. New York: W. H. Freeman, 1989. A sumptuously illustrated book that describes the physiological function of sleep in humans and other mammals.

HUDSON, LIAM. *Night Life: The Interpretation of Dreams*. New York: St. Martin's Press, 1985. A thought-provoking book that tries to clarify and synthesize many of the conflicting psychological and biological theories of dreaming.

JONES, ERNEST. *On the Nightmare*. New York: Liveright Publishing, 1971. A psychoanalytic classic.

JONES, RICHARD. *The New Psychology of Dreaming*. New York: Viking Press, 1970. An important book that clarifies many confusions and introduces the reader to an eclectic approach to understanding dreams.

JUNG, CARL G. *Dreams*. Translated by R. F. C. Hull. Princeton, N.J.: Princeton University Press, 1974. A selection of Jung's papers on dreams, serving as a good introduction to Jung via Jung.

JUNG, CARL G. *The Collected Works*. Bollingen Series. Princeton, N.J.: Princeton University Press. 1957–1984. To understand Jung's work and to get a good feel for the man, plunge into *The Collected Works*. I suggest beginning with: Vol. 8, *The Structure and Dynamics of the Psyche*; Vol. 9, *Part 1, The Archetypes and the Collective Unconscious;* Vol. 9, *Part 2, Aion;* and *Dream Analysis: Notes of the Seminar Given in 1927–30* (Bollingen Series XCIX).

KRIPPNER, STANLEY, AND JOSEPH DILLARD. *Dream Working: How to Use Your Dreams for Creative Problem Solving*. Buffalo, N.Y.: Bearly, Ltd., 1988. Krippner, the guiding spirit in the Saybrook Institute and an extraordinarily generous and creative dream researcher, demonstrates his mature, practical, and interesting approach to the problem-solving function of dreaming.

MACK, JOHN E. *Nightmares and Human Conflict*. Boston: Houghton Mifflin Company, 1970. An informative treatment of the subject, including interesting historical accounts of nightmares, children's nightmares, and a fine appreciation for the person who has nightmares. Mack's work reflects the openness and sensitivity of his well-known and well-loved teacher Elvin Semrad.

MACKENZIE, NORMAN. *Dreams and Dreaming*. New York: Vanguard Press, 1965. A lively presentation of the history and theories of dreaming. Many interesting color photographs and drawings.

MATTOON, MARY ANN. *Understanding Dreams*. Dallas, Tex.: Spring Publications, 1984. The best and clearest description of what traditional Jungians actually do with dreams.

MINDELL, ARNOLD. *Working with the Dreaming Body*. Boston: Routledge & Kegan Paul, 1985. Focusing on how dreams are experienced in the body as a take-off point to explore important feelings. Mindell looks at dream work with a welcome freshness.

NATTERSON, JOSEPH M., ED. *The Dream in Clinical Practice*. New York: Jason Aronson, 1980. A largely psychoanalytic text with contributors ranging from staunch traditionalists to psychoanalysts and other therapists whose rich experience with patients' dreams has led them to important insights. You will find many outstanding chapters by Natterson ("The Dream in Group Therapy"), Greenberg and Pearlman ("The Private Language of the Dream"), Breger ("The Manifest Dream and Its Latent Meaning"), Bonime ("The Dream in the Depressive Personality"), and Litman ("The Dream in the Suicidal Situation").

PALOMBO, STANLEY. *Dreaming and Memory: A New Information Processing Manual*. New York: Basic Books, 1978. Palombo describes his theory of dream construction, drawing from traditional psychoanalytic theory and current research in dream physiology.

PERLS, FRITZ. *Gestalt Therapy Verbatim: A Book of Gestalt Therapy Sessions*. Moab, Utah: Real People Press, 1969. The best way to get a feel for how Perls worked is to read this book.

ROSSI, ERNEST. *Dreams and the Growth of Personality*. New York: Pergamon Press, 1972. Places a good emphasis on the seeds for new growth that dreams can help us recognize.

RYCROFT, CHARLES. *The Innocence of Dreams*. New York: Pantheon Books, 1979. A psychoanalyst describes dreams as an extension of the imagination and modifies classical Freudian theory.

SANFORD, JOHN. *Dreams: God's Forgotten Language*. Philadelphia: Lippincott, 1968. A good introduction to the subject of dreams from a Christian perspective.

SANFORD, JOHN. *Dreams and Healing*. New York: Paulist Press, 1978.

SHARPE, ELLA FREEMAN. *Dream Analysis*. New York: Brunner/Mazel Publishers, 1978.

SLOANE, PAUL. *The Psychoanalytic Understanding of the Dream*. New York: Jason Aronson, 1979. A very well written overview of traditional Freudian beliefs about the meaning of dreams. Includes a useful chapter on resistance.

STEKEL, WILHELM. *The Interpretation of Dreams: New Developments and Technique*. Translated by Eden and Cedar Paul. New York: Washington Square Press, 1943. An arrogant but useful book by a psychoanalyst who reevaluated and revised Freud's work by rediscovering the importance of the manifest dream.

STUKANE, EILEEN. *The Dream Worlds of Pregnancy*. New York: Quill, 1985. Patterns in the dreams of expectant parents are described.

TEDLOCK, BARBARA, ED. *Dreaming: Anthropological and Psychological Interpretations*. Cambridge, UK: Cambridge University Press, 1987. A fascinating anthology of modern anthropological perspectives on dreaming.

ULLMAN, MONTAGUE, STANLEY KRIPPNER, AND ALAN VAUGHN. *Dream Telepathy*, 2d ed. Jefferson, N.C.: McFarland Press, 1988. An excellent history of the phenomenon of psychic dreaming and a fascinating description of recent laboratory research in the field by three men of intelligence and integrity.

ULLMAN, MONTAGUE, AND NAN ZIMMERMAN. *Working with Dreams*. New York: Delacorte Press, 1979. Written by a very creative psychoanalyst and dream researcher and his apprentice, this book presents a method of working with dreams in a group setting and emphasizes the need to make dream work available to the general public. It includes two especially interesting chapters on the history of dream interpretation.

VON GRUNEBAUM, G. E. AND ROGER CAILLOIS, EDS. *The Dream and Human Societies*. Berkeley, CA: University of California Press, 1966. A fine book, containing especially interesting chapters on Islamic dream beliefs in various periods.

WOLMAN, BENJAMIN, ED. *Handbook of Dreams: Research, Theories, and Applications*. New York: Van Nostrand Reinhold, 1979. A well-rounded collection of uneven papers on a broad spectrum of dream-related issues. The chapter by Harry Fiss, "Current Dream Research: A Psychobiological Perspective," is especially good.

WOODS, R., AND H. GREENHOUSE, EDS. *The World of Dreams*. New York: Random House, 1947. An anthology of brief essays on a wide variety of dream-related issues.

WOODS, R. AND H. GREENHOUSE, EDS. *The New World of Dreams*. New York: Macmillan, 1974. A second anthology of essays of dream-related issues.

INDEX

DREAM TITLE INDEX

ABOUT THE AUTHOR

DR. GAYLE DELANEY, Founding President of the Association for the Study of Dreams, author of *Living Your Dreams* is a pioneer in the field of modern, practical dream work. She has dedicated her career exclusively to teaching healthy people how to use their sleeping minds for applicable insight and specific problem solving. With Dr. Loma Flowers, she directs the Delaney & Flowers Center for the Study of Dreams in San Francisco and trains professionals and nonprofessionals in basic and advanced dream skills.

Dr. Delaney conducts a private practice in San Francisco and Marin County which focuses on teaching her clients to become their own dream experts. She is a columnist for *New Realities* magazine, lectures on dreaming around the world in English and French, and has been the host of a three-hour daily radio show called "Dream Talk" in Seattle. Dr. Delaney appears regularly on television and radio talk shows in a life-long effort to dispel myths and misinformation about dreaming and to inform the public of the surprisingly practical and useful nature of the work our minds do at night.